PITCH PERFECT

THE QUEST FOR
COLLEGIATE A CAPPELLA GLORY

MICKEY RAPKIN

GOTHAM BOOKS

For Jane and Lenny

GOTHAM BOOKS
Published by Penguin Group (USA) Inc.
375 Hudson Street, New York, New York 10014, U.S.A.

Penguin Group (Canada), 90 Eglinton Avenue East, Suite 700, Toronto, Ontario M4P 2Y3,
Canada (a division of Pearson Penguin Canada Inc.); Penguin Books Ltd, 80 Strand, London
WC2R 0RL, England; Penguin Ireland, 25 St Stephen's Green, Dublin 2, Ireland
(a division of Penguin Books Ltd); Penguin Group (Australia), 250 Camberwell Road,
Camberwell, Victoria 3124, Australia (a division of Pearson Australia Group Pty Ltd);
Penguin Books India Pvt Ltd, 11 Community Centre, Panchsheel Park, New Delhi–110 017,
India; Penguin Group (NZ), 67 Apollo Drive, Rosedale, North Shore 0632, New Zealand
(a division of Pearson New Zealand Ltd); Penguin Books (South Africa) (Pty) Ltd,
24 Sturdee Avenue, Rosebank, Johannesburg 2196, South Africa

Penguin Books Ltd, Registered Offices: 80 Strand, London WC2R 0RL, England

Published by Gotham Books, a member of Penguin Group (USA) Inc.

Previously published as a Gotham Books hardcover edition

First trade paperback printing, April 2009

3   5   7   9   10   8   6   4   2

Gotham Books and the skyscraper logo are trademarks of Penguin Group (USA) Inc.

Copyright © 2008 by Mickey Rapkin
All rights reserved
The Library of Congress has cataloged the hardcover edition of this book as follows:
Rapkin, Mickey.
Pitch perfect: the quest for collegiate a cappella glory / Mickey Rapkin.
p.   cm.
ISBN 978-1-592-40376-9 (hardcover)   ISBN 978-1-592-40463-6 (paperback)
1. Choral societies—United States.   2. Music in universities
and colleges—United States.   I. Title.
ML25.R36 2008
782.5'06073—dc22   2007048222

Printed in the United States of America
Set in Aldus   •   Designed by Elke Sigal

Contents

What amazed me was the amount of time the Whiffen-poofs demanded from them, the way their membership in the group seemed to define their entire identity. Most of their time outside class was consumed by Whiffen-poof functions; even their vacations were given over to the Whiffenpoof tours. It was true that they got to sleep with Whiffenpoof groupies and visit great Whiffen-poof places—you couldn't brush your teeth next to one of them without hearing about their latest junket to Monaco or Bermuda—but it still didn't seem like a worthwhile trade-off to me. The way I saw it, no amount of sex or travel would compensate for the humiliation of belonging to a group with such a stupid name.

—From *Joe College: A Novel* by Tom Perrotta

For Denise Sandole, the forty-seventh annual Grammy Awards was something to celebrate. She was working for AOL Music at the time, as a senior manager in sales, and her boss had invited her to the star-studded ceremony. It was February 13, 2005, at the Staples Center in Los Angeles, and she wore a polka dot dress from BCBG. "You never know if there will be a next time you attend the Grammys," she says.

Denise was sitting upstairs in the balcony when a then-unknown singer named John Legend came out onstage to introduce his mentor, Kanye West, who was nominated for a handful of awards that night. Legend himself would be nominated for eight Grammys the following year, but for now anyway he was just that handsome, well-dressed young man standing center stage. Upstairs, meanwhile, Denise was screaming like a crazy person. The thing is, she and John Legend were best friends, and they'd been sending text messages back and forth all evening. Long before John Legend would collaborate with Snoop Dogg and Alicia Keys, he'd collaborated with Denise Sandole. Back in 1997, onstage at Carnegie Hall, Denise Sandole and John Legend competed together in the National Championship of Collegiate A Cappella.

As an undergrad at the University of Pennsylvania, Denise Sandole majored in psychology, though her mom likes to say she majored in a cappella. Denise and John met "on the a cappella audition circuit," she says, in the mid-nineties, when the two joined the Counterparts—the university's oldest coed a cappella group. The Counterparts had been primarily a jazz ensemble. (Denise was no stranger to jazz—her father, Dennis Sandole, had mentored John Coltrane.) But the group's new music director pushed for a more pop sound, and with Denise and John Legend in the stable, the Counterparts suddenly had the talent to pull it off. Prince's "One of Us," featuring John Legend (né John Stephens) on the solo, quickly became the Counterparts anthem.

This change was not without collateral damage. Two members of the Counterparts actually quit in protest, feeling as if the musical left turn away from jazz somehow betrayed the wishes of the group's founding fathers. "Aca politics," Denise says. To make matters worse, a rift soon developed between the Counterparts and UPenn's *other* coed a cappella group, Off the Beat—who'd built their reputation on pop music. But the campus embraced the new sound, showing up to Counterparts gigs in record numbers. The animosity only intensified when the Counterparts decided to compete in the National Championship of Collegiate A Cappella (the NCCAs), pitting them squarely against their heavily favored rivals, Off the Beat. To everyone's surprise, in February 1998, the Counterparts triumphed at that regional quarterfinal round—and it was more of the same at the regional semifinals. The Counterparts' set included three songs: "One of Us," "Route 66," and the Sophie B. Hawkins one-hit wonder, "Damn I Wish I Was Your Lover." Denise sang that solo—this little girl belting out the angst. "That song put me on the a cappella map," Denise says. Against all odds, the Counterparts were headed for the finals of the NCCAs on April 26, 1997, at Carnegie Hall.

How do you get to Carnegie Hall? In this case, you rent two yellow school buses and fill them with your Ivy League a cappella entourage.

The excitement was short-lived. Denise remembers the precise moment she knew the Counterparts had lost at the National Championship of Collegiate A Cappella. In their own shows on campus, the Counterparts regularly performed silly skits, told bad jokes, that sort of thing. "We always tried to be *funny*," she says, acknowledging that the group's humor was always hit or miss. When it came time to compete in the NCCA finals, she says, "We wanted to be true to ourselves." And so, onstage at Carnegie Hall, in front of two thousand eager a cappella fans, Denise's friend Sloan Alexander of the Counterparts dropped his tuxedo pants, revealing a black lace garter belt underneath. "He made some joke about running late, and how he wanted to get dressed up for Carnegie Hall," Denise says. This had been a gross miscalculation on their part. "We thought, We're a *college* group. We entertain our peers! But that was wrong. We were there to entertain the judges." There was a long, deadly silence from the audience. "We knew right then," Denise says. "We're like, oops, *wrong crowd, wrong crowd*." She acknowledges they should have played it safe, "like the group that won." That would be the Stanford Talisman. "They did, like, *world music*. They were very politically correct. We went for the bathroom humor. And we were outclassed!"

A cappella is Italian for "like the chapel," and it describes perhaps the oldest form of music, the kind made without any accompaniment at all. That a cappella began with Gregorian chant in the church shouldn't come as a surprise—what's closer to God than the unadorned voice? The music then traveled. In time, the Puritans would embrace shape-note singing and a book of vocal spirituals called *The Sacred Harp*. Call-and-response singing from

Africa, meanwhile, would mingle with these vocal traditions to become American gospel. Somewhere along the way, what began as a service to a higher power went secular. Then it went pop. This is how:

In 1931, the Mills Brothers recorded *Swing It, Sister.* The sleeve read: "No musical instruments or mechanical devices used on this recording other than one guitar." Uh, then where did that trumpet come from? Harry Mills, as legend has it, forgot to bring his kazoo to the studio one day, which is how he figured out he could do a passable trumpet solo with just his lips. Still, some critics remained skeptical.

On September 26, 1936, Norman Rockwell's "Barbershop Quartet" appeared on the cover of *The Saturday Evening Post.* Two years later, at a hotel in Kansas City, two traveling businessmen from Tulsa would form the Society for the Preservation and Encouragement of Barber Shop Quartet Singing in America, affectionately known as SPEBSQSA. (Both Bing Crosby and Groucho Marx were later members.) Despite the name, they took themselves quite seriously, calling barbershop singing "the last remaining vestige of human liberty," reports Gage Averill in his book *Four Parts, No Waiting.* In the fifties, when Disneyland Park first opened, Walt Disney himself installed a barbershop quartet, the Dapper Dans, to perform on Main Street six days a week. (When the original Dapper Dans left for a spot on *The Mickey Finn Show,* Disney kept the name and found four new Dans.)

Barbershop most certainly had its roots in Africa, in the chanting and the close harmony—though that genre of chant would come to be known as *mbube* (pronounced EEM-boo-beh) thanks to the success of Solomon Linda's 1939 song "Mbube." You may be familiar with this tune. Pete Seeger and the Weavers covered "Mbube" in the 1950s, singing *wimoweh* instead of *mbube.* And thus "The Lion Sleeps Tonight" was born.

In 1952 Sam Cooke sang with the Soul Stirrers—perhaps the

first mingling of a cappella gospel and rock 'n' roll. In 1954, the Chordettes (the first big female barbershop quartet) released "Mr. Sandman." Barbershop further crossed over in 1962 when the Buffalo Bills appeared in *The Music Man*. In 1968, Frank Zappa released the Persuasions' first album, *A Cappella*.

In the seventies a group called the Nylons first got together in, of all places, a Toronto delicatessen. In 1981, the Manhattan Transfer released *Mecca for Moderns*, concluding the album with an a cappella track, "A Nightingale Sang in Berkeley Square," which won a Grammy for Gene Puerling. In 1983, Billy Joel's "For the Longest Time" blew a cappella wide, paving the way for Bobby McFerrin's "Don't Worry, Be Happy" in 1988. Doug E. Fresh brought beatboxing to the mainstream (or closer, anyway) with the 1986 track "The Show." ("I am the original human beat-box," he sang.) That same year, Paul Simon released *Graceland*, a collaboration with South Africa's Ladysmith Black Mambazo (who, themselves, went on to tour the States, performing on *Saturday Night Live*, even recording a jingle for MTV).

A cappella continued to assault pop music. In 1990, Spike Lee produced a documentary for PBS called *Do It A Cappella*, which introduced the world to four very white guys called Rockapella, who would soon land a gig as the house band on the PBS kiddie show *Where in the World Is Carmen Sandiego?*, introducing a whole new generation to a cappella music. (The show was not entirely altruistic, for the record. Up in the control room, employees would bet on which kid would win, says Sean Altman, then the lead singer of Rockapella.) One year later, Boyz II Men had a number-one hit with "It's So Hard to Say Goodbye to Yesterday." In 2004, Toxic Audio started an open-ended run off-Broadway at the John Houseman Theater.

Which doesn't really explain how a cappella became one of the most celebrated pursuits on our nation's college campuses.

There are more than twelve hundred collegiate a cappella

groups in the United States alone. And the good ones, well, it's not what you think. A cappella has come a long way in the one hundred years since it evolved from glee clubs into a tradition that is hugely popular (some eighteen thousand active participants), considerably profitable (the Harvard Krokodiloes earn, conservatively, three hundred thousand dollars a year, which funds the group's adventures), and much publicized (a cappella groups have appeared on the *Late Show with David Letterman*). It's not what you think. Today the music is less barbershop than *Barbershop 2: Back in Business*.

The gold standard remains the original, the Yale Whiffenpoofs—the very first collegiate a cappella group, founded in 1909 after a drunken night of singing at Mory's, a New Haven supper club. Nearly one hundred years later, the Whiffs still perform there every Monday night. And their influence has been felt well outside of New Haven. The group's signature tune, "The Whiffenpoof Song" (the name comes from a mythical fish), was later covered by Frank Sinatra and Ella Fitzgerald. Senator Prescott Bush—President George W. Bush's grandfather—was a member of the Whiffenpoofs. So was Cole Porter. Over the years, the Whiffs have traveled the world, entertaining the likes of Mother Teresa and the Dalai Lama. The Whiffs have even performed on *Saturday Night Live*. (The producers ran each kid's SAT scores across the bottom of the screen in a CNN-style crawl.) A recent addition to their clip reel: In late 2002, Aaron Sorkin—a big Whiffs fan since childhood—flew the entire group out to Los Angeles to tape a Christmas episode of *The West Wing*, where members of the Whiffs report Sorkin was jumping around the set yelling, *"I can't believe the fucking Whiffenpoofs are here."*

The Whiffs aren't the only a cappella group at Yale. Actually, there are now at least fifteen on campus. One, the Baker's Dozen, is known around New Haven as "the drinking group with a singing problem." The BDs briefly eclipsed the Whiffenpoofs in name recognition when, on New Year's Eve 2007, they were assaulted outside a party in San Francisco—a story that made international news. The *San Francisco Chronicle* ran this headline: "New Year's Nightmare for Visiting Yale Singers." The *New York Post* followed with the cheeky: "Yale Songbirds Are Pummeled."

Collegiate a cappella had been strictly a guy thing until, in 1936, the first all-female collegiate group was born at Smith College. They called themselves the Smiffenpoofs—perhaps the birth of a cappella's notorious obsession with puns. (The most egregious pun in all of a cappella may be the Harvard Law School group, Scales of Justice. Their motto: "Because justice is blind, not deaf.") The first coed group was founded in 1973 at Princeton. They're called the Katzenjammers—which is German for both "a loud, discordant noise" and (perhaps more apt) a "hangover."

You'd be hard-pressed to find a thing about a cappella—the snapping, the matching khaki pants—that your typical college kid would suggest is cool. Especially not the human beatbox, that guy (or girl) imitating a snare drum and a bass with a *sh-sh-k-ts-sh-sh-k-ts*. Even in the late 1930s, the Whiffenpoofs were already· considered to be uncool. So uncool, in fact, that a rival singing group, Yale's Society of Orpheus and Bacchus (the SOBs), was started with the express purpose of mocking the Whiffs. But cool is nothing if not relative. On campus—though it's crass to say— a cappella will get you laid. "At Duke, it's not as cool as being on the basketball team," says one of the Duke University Pitchforks, the university's celebrated all-male a cappella group. "But it's close."

A cappella is the kind of frenzied subculture that over four years—just like a fraternity—might make your name on campus. But some will spend the rest of their lives denying it. "A cappella," sighs James Van Der Beek, the onetime star of *Dawson's Creek* and Drew University's 36 Madison Avenue. "I thought it might catch up with me."

Even before his TV career took off, Van Der Beek was a big man on campus. He tells a story about the time this girl heard him perform Sting's "Englishman in New York," and invited him to hand-deliver a copy of the group's CD to her dorm room. Madison Avenue frequently took road trips. Van Der Beek recalls a memorable tour of SUNY Binghamton. Due to extenuating circumstances too difficult to explain here (something about the number of cars and available seats), one member of his a cappella group needed to spend a second night at Binghamton, hitching a ride back to Drew University the next morning. That man, the group decided, should be James Van Der Beek. Why? "Because, of all the guys in the group," he says, laughing, "they felt like I'd have the best chance of finding a place to sleep that night." And he did.

Mira Sorvino, Diane Sawyer, Art Garfunkel, Jim Croce, Anne Hathaway of *The Devil Wears Prada*, *Prison Break*'s Wentworth Miller, actress Rashida Jones (Quincy Jones's daughter), *The O.C.*'s Peter Gallagher—they all got their start in collegiate a cappella.

Full disclosure: Osama bin Laden sang in an a cappella group. Lawrence Wright, in his Pulitzer Prize–winning book, *The Looming Tower*, writes of bin Laden's teenage years and the man's "desire to die anonymously in a trench in warfare"—to be just one of the guys. "It was difficult to hold on to this self-conception while being chauffeured around the kingdom in the family Mercedes," he writes. "At the same time, Osama made an effort not to be too much of a prig. Although he was opposed to the playing of musical instruments, he organized some of his friends into an a cappella singing group. They even recorded some of their tunes about *jihad*, which for them meant the internal struggle to improve themselves, not holy war. Osama would make copies and give them each a tape."

Not everyone could be so lucky. Debra Messing was rejected

by an all-girl group at Brandeis. Worse, Jessica Biel was dismissed by Tufts University's coed a cappella group, the Amalgamates. It's shocking (or maybe not) how seriously these groups take them-selves—that they'd turn down a Hollywood starlet like Biel. *How bad could she have been?* Still, it begs the question: In collegiate a cappella, where does the line fall between serious pursuit and goofy joke? It's blurrier than one would think.

After school—but before winning Grammys—John Legend went to work for the Boston Consulting Group. But it didn't take, and he quit to concentrate on his music full-time. Some a cappella alums wind up on MTV. But most never sing again—at least not professionally. In the summer of 2007, John's friend Denise San-dole sang a Gloria Gaynor song at a friend's wedding.

These days, Denise rarely listens to the old Counterparts al-bums—though they were very well received at the time. ("One of Us," which appeared on their disc *Housekeeping*, was selected for the Best of College A Cappella series in 1998, which is sort of like the *Now That's What I Call Music!* series for collegiate a cappella.) Alums from the Counterparts, the ones in New York anyway, get together now and again for a night of karaoke. Still, even they are far from a cappella apologists, winking at the very thing that brought them together. "At karaoke, no one sings old Counterparts songs," says Denise, now a thirty-year-old grad student in psychology at Yeshiva University. "That's an unspo-ken rule. Though we love to reminisce." But what is it that drives people to such great lengths to excel at something they may spend the rest of their lives mocking?

Perhaps they are smart to deny it. Because a cappella has be-come a go-to pop culture joke. In the 2006 season premiere of NBC's *The Office*, one of the characters (played by *Daily Show* vet Ed Helms) bragged about singing in an a cappella group at Cornell called Here Comes Treble. A cappella would become a long-running joke on the show, reaching fever pitch when Helms serenaded a co-worker in 2007 with ABBA's "Take a Chance on Me"—backed by his old a cappella group on speakerphone. (The group sang, *"Take a chance, take a chance, take a chance,"* beneath his solo.) A cappella popped up elsewhere on NBC on Tina Fey's *30 Rock*, and even on Broadway in 2007 in *Young Frankenstein*, with a Whiffenpoof joke. In the movie *The Break-Up*, Jennifer Aniston's brother sang in an a cappella group called the Tone Rangers, which was played for laughs. The film's co-writer, Jay Lavender, had firsthand knowledge of collegiate a cappella. As a student at Holy Cross, his sister started a coed group, 8-Track. Jay calls a cappella a "subculture," which is how outsiders generally refer to a small group of people doing something they find unintentionally hilarious. He still laughs thinking about the time his sister berated the members of 8-Track for going flat, shouting, "Quarter tones matter, people!" These stories are comedy gold, Jay says. A joke on *The Office* is one thing, but even the Ivy League brats who inherited the a cappella legacy may be turning on their own. In 1995, some Yale students led an organized revolt against the a cappella scene; on tap night, as new members were being selected, water balloons rained down, blotting out the moon. (The university has since taken steps to control tap night, in part keeping the date a secret.) More recently, in 2007, the snarky blog IvyGate sponsored a contest to find the Worst A Cappella Group in the Ivy League.

So where does the impulse to step out in front of a group of identically dressed men and hum into a microphone before a crowd of thousands come from? What is the appeal of the human beatbox to screaming fans of bestirred coeds who seem to lose their senses at the unaccompanied rendition of Hootie & the Blowfish's "Hold My Hand?" And what of the crisis some face after graduation, suffering from the hangover of so much adulation?

"Why a cappella?" or maybe more specifically, "Why not?"

Masi Oka is the breakout star of NBC's *Heroes*. He plays fan favorite Hiro Nakamura, a man who can bend time. If Masi Oka really could go back in time, he might rethink his undergraduate wardrobe. There he was in 1997, the music director of Bear Necessities, an all-male a cappella group at Brown University, onstage at Solomon Hall on the Green. Bear Necessities is not the only all-male a cappella group at Brown, but it is the only one whose members dress exclusively in suspenders. It gets worse. One year, Masi Oka arranged an a cappella version of "Flashdance" and he came out onstage wearing a purple leotard and a tutu. In his defense, the entire group was supposed to wear tutus. "They chickened out and wore leg warmers and bandannas," he says. "But I thought we had to go all-out. A cappella is all about commitment."

Being a member of Bear Necessities was a formative experience for Masi Oka. A self-described math and science geek, he'd grown up on the West Coast, and he'd noticed something about his friends—the ones who'd gone off to Harvard and MIT. "They started talking the same," he says, "thinking the same, laughing the same, smelling the same. But undergrad is an opportunity for social growth." Masi Oka (who'd been featured on the cover of *Time* magazine as a twelve-year-old for a story called "Those Asian-American Whiz Kids") was himself accepted to Harvard and MIT. He's glad he turned them down. "I would have been comfortable in my math and science world at Harvard," he says. "I wouldn't have even thought about trying out for a cappella."

Looking back on his time singing in the Bear Necessities, he describes the group as a "geeky frat." "It was a brother*ship*," he says, inventing a word that in the end perfectly captures the experience, an experience that never really left him. In 2006, after *Heroes* hit and Masi was nominated for a Golden Globe, he caught wind of a Ben Stiller movie that was about to go into production, a movie called *The Marc Pease Experience*—about the world of high-school musical theater (it was close enough). He was desperate for an audition. No dice. "My agent told me they were only seeing white people," he says.

Collegiate a cappella is, of course, much more than some alternative to the Greek scene. Though not everybody has such a rewarding experience. Ed Helms doesn't just play an a cappella singer in *The Office*. In 1993, as an undergraduate at Oberlin, he was a member of the Oberlin Obertones—for exactly one semester. The boys wore tuxedos, exclusively. "There was no fucking around with jeans and ties," Helms says. Though the Obertones were the closest thing on campus to a fraternity and were showered with the requisite female affection, "the group was so pretentious it made me nauseous," Helms says. Especially the leadership. The Obertones' music director was a fifth-year who'd stayed in school just to direct the group. Helms had to quit when this kid said, "I love singing. But what I really love is kicking other a cappella groups' asses." Helms just couldn't deal with the personalities anymore. "I decided pot was more important than extracurricular activities," he says.

In many cases a cappella is more than an extracurricular activity. Peter Bailey runs Industrial Artist Management, a talent firm in Manhattan that represents acts like Anti-Gravity (who performed with P. Diddy at the MTV VMAs one year) in the corporate space. He is also an alum of the Harvard Krokodiloes. When he heard the Kroks were still charging a couple thousand dollars for a gig, he pushed them to up their fees. Being in the business of booking nontraditional talent, he was well aware of what the Kroks could charge. "They were undervaluing themselves," he says. (Bailey briefly considered adding the Kroks to IAM's talent roster, but with exams, holidays, and turnover, they're not an ideal client.) When Bailey graduated in the nineties, leaving the group behind, they were making three hundred thousand dollars—on a slow year. Every summer the Kroks embark on a world tour, and in his day, Bailey traveled to more than fifteen countries with the Kroks, staying in European castles and Mexican resorts—mining relationships established decades ago. Some complain that groups like the Kroks and the Whiffenpoofs are born on third base—if not home. But you can't argue with the work ethic. Very few Kroks sing all four years. "The time commitment is killer," Bailey says.

A cappella groups have tremendous self-pride, playing up their differences in dress, musical style, and personality—much like a fraternity would. At the University of Virginia, the Hullabahoos perform in brightly colored robes. Their rivals, the Academical Village People, perform in gas-station-attendant shirts. That a cappella groups are similarly self-selecting and heterogeneous says as much about race relations on campus as a study of the Greek system.

But there are generalizations to be made: Collegiate a cappella groups are largely student-run, operating outside the often staid domain of university music programs. While some employ choreography, most just stand in a horseshoe—emulating guitars with a well-placed *jeer neer*. And almost every group has, at some point, featured A-Ha's "Take on Me" in their repertoire. (The eighties were seminal for collegiate a cappella.) While professional a cappella groups like the House Jacks remain small—most pro groups have just five or six members—collegiate groups are made up of between nine and fifteen students. A cappella groups are easy to spot on campus, where they are known to invade the archways, serenading comely women. There is another generalization to be made: These groups make money, and, in some cases, lots of money. For a gig at the 2004 Republican National Convention, the UVA Hullabahoos were paid thirteen thousand dollars.

Still, a cappella is the vestige of college life that dare not speak its name. There is no shame, no real social stigma, in admitting you were a Sigma Chi. You might discuss it on a first date. You might even put it on a résumé. A cappella, however, is topic non grata. It reeks of that Folgers commercial.

But collegiate a cappella includes the drama kids and the jocks; it drives young women crazy, and some young men to violence. A cappella is a choice college students make, a choice to stand up and sing, to perform, to compete, to serenade, to profit, to hide, to seek truth, to find answers, and to commemorate. The experience is more surreal—more rewarding, more visceral—than one could imagine. And, as it turns out, painfully hard to give up. For every kid who can walk away at graduation, there are others destined to live in the past, wishing they were still up onstage snapping (likely to something by Journey). You can't really blame them. After all, no one applauds you for showing up to the Monday-morning meeting at Goldman Sachs.

For answers—for some deeper understanding of this subculture (there's that word again!)—we turn to three collegiate a cappella groups in the 2006–2007 school year, each at a crossroads. Divisi, an all-female group from the University of Oregon, had been the heavy favorites to win at the International Championship of Collegiate A Cappella in 2005. But after a crippling loss in the finals, they took a year off to regroup. Now, back in competition with a near all-new roster of girls, could they return to the ICCAs and avenge their good name?

Elsewhere, the legendary Tufts Beelzebubs were founded in 1962, and they'd always been at the forefront of a cappella recording. But their 2003 album, *Code Red*, was a complete game-changer. In a cappella circles, people talk strictly in terms of before *Code Red* and after *Code Red*. Now the Bubs were back in the studio and the pressure was suffocating. Would this be just another album, or could they raise the bar again? In short: What do you do for an encore? And is forty years of history a blessing or a curse?

Finally, the University of Virginia's own Hullabahoos may be the upstart bad boys of collegiate a cappella—breaking hearts along the eastern seaboard. As they approached their twentieth anniversary, a question arose: Could they establish themselves as a top-tier group like the Beelzebubs without sacrificing their laid-back soul? And did they even want to?

The curious, inspiring, triumphant, hilarious, and heartbreaking story of the quest for collegiate a cappella glory begins onstage at Lincoln Center.

CHAPTER ONE

DIVISI

Wherein twelve ladies in red ties are snubbed at the International Championship of Collegiate A Cappella —and contemplate returning for seconds

Evynne Smith stands onstage at Manhattan's Alice Tully Hall, the stately theater that regularly plays home to the Chamber Music Society of Lincoln Center, the province of aging subscribers and PBS tote bags. Tonight, the scene is a little bit different.

It is Saturday evening, April 30, 2005, and the stage is empty save for twelve women dressed in identical black pants, buttoned-up black shirts, and red ties. Evynne describes their look as "sexy stewardess." Their red lipstick (the kind, perhaps, favored by off-duty stewardesses) goes on like paint. These twelve women— perhaps refugees from some Olive Garden training center—hail from the University of Oregon. They're called Divisi (pronounced dih-VEE-see) and they are among the nation's most celebrated collegiate a cappella groups. Laugh if you must. But tonight's concert is standing-room only. All eleven hundred tickets sold out weeks ago—at fifty dollars a pop. Still, a few people mill about outside the venue, hoping to snag a last-minute pass. Yes, it is an a cappella show, and people are trying to *scalp tickets*. One man holds up a homemade sign, scrawled in red marker, that reads: MY SON IS PERFORMING TONIGHT. GOT AN EXTRA?

He's lucky. A twentysomething girl hesitates before selling her ticket to this desperate man—for a whopping two hundred and fifty dollars. "I'm, like, an a cappella *fan*," she says, hesitating. "But my rent is due on Monday and I could totally use the cash."

It's a tough crowd, what with the a cappella-*erati* in the house—including everyone from professionals like Rockapella's Barry Carl to Bill Hare, a top-tier producer and the Dr. Dre of contemporary a cappella recording. Divisi is the final group to perform that night. And while the order was drawn entirely at random, it is also fitting. Ask anyone in the audience to pinpoint the exact moment Divisi won the hearts and minds of the crowd, and they will likely say the same thing: somewhere around minute eight and a half of the group's twelve-minute, three-song set. The girls had already performed "Walking on Broken Glass" by Annie Lennox and Joni Mitchell's "Woodstock"—two well-executed, if highly predictable, endeavors. (Only Sarah McLachlan would have been more obvious.) But what came next was anything but expected.

The girls from Divisi stand in three rows, their heads bowed to the ground. Divisi's music director, a tiny whip of a thing named Lisa Forkish, blows the starting pitch, counting off two-three-four. And then it happens. The girls sing, *"Yeah, yeah, yeah, yeah"*—a total of seven times, building in intensity each time, eventually sustaining a G minor-9 chord. A ripple of recognition rolls through the younger members of tonight's crowd, who, in near unison, sit up at attention.

The syllables go something like this: *Bee REE // bee REE // bee REE // bee REE*. Erica Barkett steps to the mic, singing, *"Up in the club with my homey // trying to get a little ..."* Onstage at Lincoln Center, a female a cappella group (all white, by the way, not that there's anything wrong with that) will make Usher's signature track, "Yeah," their own. Two minutes in, Evynne Smith

steps out, grabs the mic, and unapologetically raps: *"Watch out //
My outfit's ridiculous! // Looking so conspicuous! // These
women are on the prowl // Try to sing against us had to throw
'em the towel."* Like Usher, Evynne Smith will not stop until she
sees you in your birthday suit. She closes the rap with this bit of
improv: *"You know you want a kiss when the lips so red!"*

The crowd is on their feet. A middle-aged man in the audience
holds a cardboard sign way above his head. It reads Hot Lips!, which
would be inappropriate in any other context. Right, context.

Evynne Smith and the ladies of Divisi (they call themselves
Divisi Divas) are competing in the International Championship
of Collegiate A Cappella. The hard-core a cappella fans refer to
this event as the ICK-ahs, though the rest just spell it out, as in
the I-C-C-As. The competition—sort of like the a cappella Rose
Bowl—began in 1995 but has quickly grown to include groups
from as far as Canada, Western Europe, and, most recently, Asia.
The whole thing is produced by an organization called Varsity
Vocals, a five-person operation run out of (in part) a strip-mall
storefront in Maine. Ignore the skeleton crew: The impact of the
ICCAs is enormous. While the winning team will leave Lincoln
Center with one thousand dollars in prize money (plus recording
time), the competition is really about bragging rights. In the same
way that winning an Oscar can bump an actor to the A-list, a win
at the ICCAs can lead to bigger-paying gigs, a spike in album
sales, and (perhaps most importantly) more friend requests for
the group's MySpace page. It's no surprise that the backstage
drama at the International Championship of Collegiate A Cappella plays out like the unintentionally hilarious scrum of a children's beauty pageant.

For Evynne Smith and Divisi, the road to the ICCA finals has
been paved with blood, sweat, and runny mascara.

———

Evynne Smith grew up in Eugene, down the road from the University of Oregon—once home to legendary track star Steve Prefontaine. Not that athletics was a draw for Evynne. She chose the school because it was close to home, and because it was affordable. It didn't hurt that her high school sweetheart would enroll there too. Walking the halls of the music building one afternoon, Evynne—tall, blond, pretty—saw a flyer for a new a cappella group, Eight Ladies and a Beau Tie. She was intrigued. She went to the audition. She sang the national anthem. And while she could wail, the truth is, even if she couldn't sing a lick, they probably would have taken her. The girls had a Beau Tie (a kid named Mike Peterson, their beatbox for hire) but not yet the titular Eight Ladies. Worse: Their Beau Tie was known around campus for another of his extracurricular activities. "He was the guy on the unicycle," says Peter Hollens, founder of the University of Oregon's all-male a cappella group, On the Rocks.

It was a rough semester for the nascent a cappella group. A couple of girls had quit. Then a few more. Worse, while most a cappella groups were singing contemporary pop music, Divisi was still singing traditionals like "Catch a Falling Star." Those were the arrangements they could find—easily, and inexpensively. They also wore unfortunate-looking green-and-yellow scarves. In the spring, the ladies traveled to Stanford to watch On the Rocks compete in the regional semifinals of the ICCAs. While the Ivy League schools out east had a long tradition of a cappella, the scene at the University of Oregon was only just beginning, and the girls wanted to show their support for their brother group. Even though they weren't competing, this would be a seminal moment for Divisi.

Seated in the Dinkelspiel Auditorium at Stanford, the girls caught UC Berkeley's California Golden Overtones. Most of the all-female groups Evynne had seen before had been a complete mess. For one thing, they showed too much skin. ("If you have to ask," Evynne says, "you're showing too much.") Second, they spent much of their time on stage tucking their hair behind their ears. But the California Golden Overtones, well, they were like nothing Divisi had seen before. They had a *female* beatboxer. They wore neckties. Their hair was pulled back, swept neatly away from their faces. They sang the "Diamonds Are a Girl's Best Friend" medley from *Moulin Rouge*. It was a wake-up call.

When Divisi returned to campus, they promptly dumped their Beau. Then they picked a new name. Sitting downstairs in their rehearsal space, Room 105 in the music building, Evynne pulled out a music dictionary, flipping through the pages, calling out musical terms. The girls very nearly became the Bel Cantos. But fairly quickly they settled on Divisi, which means "divided" in Italian. They *divide* music into parts, they figured. Evynne looked the room over. Of the original eight ladies, they were down to four. They needed bodies. And they needed a leader. On cue, a few weeks later, a pocket-size girl named Lisa Forkish walked into auditions.

Lisa Forkish wasn't even in college yet. Actually, she was still finishing up her junior year at South Eugene High School. On a lark, her boyfriend (also a junior) had decided to audition for On the Rocks. He lived locally, and he figured if the guys from OTR liked him enough, maybe they'd figure out a way for a high school kid to join. Lisa had gone along for the ride. It was seren-dipitous. Divisi happened to be holding auditions down the hall. Like Evynne before her, Lisa sang the national anthem. The girls fell in love with her. Though Lisa was still technically a high school student, that fall she enrolled in a yoga class on campus and became a full-fledged member of Divisi. Her boyfriend, like-wise, joined On the Rocks.

The fall of 2002 gave way to the fall of 2003. Lisa Forkish was now a full-time student, very likely the only freshman living in an off-campus apartment with seniors. That year Divisi competed in their first ICCAs. And in short, they had their fishnets handed to them. They sang Alanis Morissette's "Uninvited" and quickly learned an unspoken ICCA rule: Don't perform someone else's signature song. Especially in competition. "We sang that Alanis song last year," one of the girls from the USC Sirens said to Lisa after the show. Divisi did win one award that night: Most Testosterone. This was meant to be a compliment. There is a generally acknowledged bias against all-female groups in the a cappella community. People complain they sound shrill. Well, that's because women are essentially missing an entire half of the keyboard. Men can sing high, floating into their falsetto (think Frankie Valli or Justin Timberlake). But a woman just can't hit a low D. Actually, if a woman can hit a C below middle C, it's notable. Two—count 'em, two—of the Divisi girls could comfortably (and consistently) hit that guttural C. Though the girls hadn't placed in the competition, suddenly everyone was talking about the Divisi sound.

Lisa Forkish relished her time with Divisi, but truth be told, she'd never really wanted to go to the University of Oregon. She always saw herself at the Berklee College of Music in Boston (alums include John Mayer, Gillian Welch, and Branford Marsalis). But when she graduated from high school she wasn't quite ready to leave Divisi behind. She'd been admitted to Berklee, but she deferred for a year. Now she deferred again. There was something about Divisi. She thought they had a good shot at taking the ICCA title and she wanted to be onstage when they did.

And so, in 2003, Divisi competed for a second time. They added choreography. They had a surprise in their back pocket—a girl-power medley Lisa arranged, which opened with the gospel strains of Madonna's "Like a Prayer" and worked through everything from the Eurythmics' "Sweet Dreams" to the Spice Girls'

"Wannabe." Divisi won their regional competition and went on to the semifinals at Stanford. They placed third, but it could have gone either way. The men of Fermata Nowhere—a young group from Mt. San Antonio College—took second place, but even they believed Divisi had been robbed. When the boys went up onstage to collect their award, they all pointed at Divisi and bowed their heads in respect.

The car ride back to Oregon was uncomfortable. The girls felt their performance had been solid. *How can we be better next year?* Someone suggested a medley of colors, featuring Coldplay's "Yellow," "Lady in Red," and "Somewhere Over the Rainbow." It was a terrible idea. Lisa once again called the Berklee admissions office, asking to defer enrollment for a third time. Instead, they revoked her admission.

Divisi continued to think about—obsess over, really—the ICCAs. That summer, listening to the radio in her parents' 1983 maroon Honda Civic, Evynne Smith had a better idea. She called a meeting. Most of the Divisi girls lived locally (with the rest in Portland) and she invited them over to her family's house. That's where she suggested the Usher song. Anna Corbett nearly spit up her soda.

The girls were resistant. But Evynne arranged the song anyway. And she took risks. (Quick music lesson: An arrangement is the song broken up by voice part. Imagine an orchestral score, but instead of a part for the clarinets and another for the bassoons, a cappella music is arranged by voice parts, writing out *dims* and *bops* for the sopranos, the altos, and so forth. Not all of Divisi reads music, so some members have to learn their parts by ear.) In the lead-up to the bridge, Evynne threw in the bass line to Tupac's "California Love." She had the girls sing this refrain over the outro: *"Divisi knows how to party // Yeah, Divisi knows how to party."* Erica Barkett (a Divisi member and a dance instructor at a local studio) added the choreography. And the girls spent much of that first semester of 2004 practicing their three-song set, which included Annie Lennox's "Walking on Broken Glass" and Joni Mitchell's "Woodstock." They went to Erica's studio, the one near the Safeway, and practiced in front of the mirrors. One of the girls, Joanne, picked up the choreography quickly. "Do it like *this*," Erica shouted, frustrated with the lot of them. "Do it *ghetto* like Joanne!" Joanne is now a dental hygienist, a career move that surprised no one. That she could do anything *ghetto* struck the girls as impossibly funny, and this became a popular cry that year.

Musically Divisi had advanced considerably since that first competition. But something else had changed: They were *hungry*.

Three hours before showtime, the girls would sit in a circle. Each would say something she loved about the person to her right. They would talk about the music. "This song, 'Walking on Broken Glass,' sounds happy," Lisa said. "But it's really about this woman who is brokenhearted and wants to be empowered. *We have to empower her. That's our job as backup.*" Deke Sharon, a Tufts University alum often referred to as the father of contemporary a capella, judged that semifinal round. On his score sheet, he described Divisi as "rough and tight." The phrase became a Divisi mantra. They considered naming their next album "Rough and Tight" but decided against it, fearing it might be mistaken for a sexual condition.

Divisi bested a tough field at the regional semifinals, including Brigham Young's polished Vocal Point. The BYU boys had won the West Coast semifinals before but had never actually made it to New York. The ICCA finals are often held on Sundays, and the Mormons wouldn't compete on the sabbath. In 2005, however, the finals were scheduled for a Saturday night. The boys had set their sights on New York. They hadn't counted on Divisi shutting them down. And how.

On the car ride back to Eugene the girls from Divisi talked excitedly about the ICCAs and what Broadway shows they wanted to see when they got to New York.

In April of 2005, Evynne Smith, Lisa Forkish, and Divisi flew to New York for the finals of the ICCAs. One of the girls, Suzie Day, made goody bags for the trip, including mouthwash, gum, tissues, and a Snickers candy bar. The night before the show, the girls hung out at their Manhattan hotel with Lisa Forkish's boyfriend, the one who'd auditioned for On the Rocks back in high school dragging Lisa along for the ride. Believe it or not, he was now a member of the Yale Duke's Men, who would be competing against Lisa and Divisi the next night at Lincoln Center. Well, maybe *competing* wasn't the word. He'd seen Divisi perform. The Duke's Men didn't have shot, he said. They were just happy to be in New York.

Four short years after dumping their Beau Tie, Divisi was huddled backstage at Lincoln Center. They were the favorites to win. There was tension in the air. There were tears. But more than anything, there was an air of confidence surrounding this group of women. They had done the work. This was supposed to be the fun part, Lisa kept reminding them. Just before they went onstage, Lisa turned to the girls with one last bit of advice. "Do it *ghetto* like Joanne," she said.

Divisi walked onto the stage at Alice Tully Hall. "Woodstock" was more emotional than it had ever been. "Yeah" brought the audience to their feet. Evynne nailed the rap. The girls ran offstage, and they were laughing. They couldn't contain themselves—it had gone that well. The judges broke to deliberate and finally the seven competing groups were called back onstage. A few cursory awards were handed out. Erica Barkett from Divisi won the award for best choreography. The girls were feeling good, especially when the impressive University of Rochester Midnight Ramblers took third place.

Then it happened.

Lisa doesn't remember much about the next minute, other

than walking out to accept the award for second place, looking back at Divisi and thinking, *This isn't how it's supposed to happen.* The Dear Abbeys from Boston University were crowned the 2005 ICCA champions. It's not often that a Lincoln Center crowd boos, but that's just what happened.

The tears didn't come until the girls were safely backstage. "This is bullshit!" one of them yelled. It got worse. Barry Carl from Rockapella pulled Lisa aside and explained that two of the three judges had placed Divisi first. The final judge—Judith Clurman of Juilliard, the lone woman on the panel—had placed the girls at a distant fourth. It was an intentional snub. There was no other way to interpret it. If Clurman had ranked Divisi even third, the girls from Oregon would have taken the title. But she didn't, and the message was clear: This woman from Juilliard had blackballed them. Divisi turned to her score sheet for some insight into the woman's thinking. But her comments were impossibly vague. For Divisi, the hurt turned to rage. *This isn't how it's supposed to happen.*

But nothing could be done. Divisi collected their belongings and left Alice Tully Hall. There was an officially sanctioned after-party for the ICCAs, though the line stretched out the door. The girls had an entourage of seventy-five with them, including most of their families and the men of On the Rocks, who had surprised them by flying out to New York. The girls decided to skip the after-party altogether, cramming into a Chinese restaurant around the corner instead. The kitchen was about to close, but the owner agreed to keep the restaurant open if the girls promised to spend enough money. And so they piled in, ordered plates of food, and before long, there were calls for an encore. Standing on chairs with tears streaming down their faces, the girls sang the Divisi medley, the one that begins with "Like a Prayer." There would be more tears that night as the twelve ladies of Divisi, still in their bright red lipstick and red ties, huddled together on the subway platform. They stood in a circle, locked arms, and launched into the familiar strains of "Woodstock": *"I don't know who I am // But you know life is for learning // And we've got to get ourselves // Back to the garden."*

A few weeks later, the a cappella message boards at rarb.org (RARB is the Recorded A Cappella Review Board, a digital outpost for a cappella fans far and wide) lit up with a curious thread. The ICCA organizers had announced a surprise change to the competition rules going forward—a direct response to the Divisi ouster. Even the owner of the ICCAs, Don Gooding, admitted, "The girls were robbed." The new rules were as follows: There would be five judges at the finals, not three. And much like the Olympic games, the high and low scores would be thrown out. No single judge would ever again have the power to blackball a group.

This was little consolation to Lisa Forkish and Divisi. Back in Oregon, the girls in the red ties decided to take the 2005–2006 school year off from competition. The dream was not dead, just tucked away. Instead they'd focus on recording an album, *Undivided*. The inside jacket photo showed the girls, arm-in-arm, onstage at Lincoln Center. Nothing could divide them. The album, featuring "Yeah," was released to wide acclaim, snagging the Contemporary A Cappella Recording Award for Best Female Collegiate Album. "Yeah" was selected for inclusion in Varsity Vocals' Best of College A Cappella compilation (BOCA). The group even traveled to California to perform at Disneyland. But there were tough days too. Like when one of the Divisi members was busted for embezzling money from the group's bank account. Or when they traveled to New York again for a gig at Columbia University—and got in a disagreement with the host group, an all-male group from Columbia who'd promoted their concert with an image of Terri Schiavo, which upset the women of Divisi. But Divisi had established itself as a powerhouse.

Where to go from there proved problematic. Lisa Forkish

sang for one more year, even though she'd dropped out of school. (She'd reapplied to Berklee, didn't need the Oregon credits, and decided to get a teaching job in Eugene.) She's not the only one who stuck around campus for a victory lap. Several of the original Divisi girls were still singing with the group even though they'd graduated. They couldn't shake this thing they'd built.

This would nearly cripple Divisi. Most a cappella groups, on average, lose four members in the spring and replace them in the fall. It helps maintain continuity. But in June of 2006, Divisi graduated eight girls. Two others, though still students at Oregon, decided the time commitment was just too much, and so they retired. Divisi had committed to competing in the 2006–2007 ICCAs, but they'd need a whole new roster to get there. Not to mention soloists. One of their best singers, Katie Hopkins, had graduated. "She sang like Mariah Carey," says Keeley McCowan, one of the last members still around in the fall of 2006. "We need a new Mariah."

There's an a cappella tradition at the University of Oregon. Every Friday at four-thirty P.M., On the Rocks and Divisi invade the campus student center, the EMU, to put on a free a cappella concert. And no matter what is happening in class or in their personal lives, these singers can count on getting a boost every Friday afternoon as three hundred students crowd into the EMU to watch them perform. (This self-same student center famously played home to the food fight scene in *Animal House*. That it's since been hijacked by girls singing Annie Lennox covers would no doubt kill John Belushi—if he weren't already dead.)

On this late September afternoon in 2006, Evynne Smith (now a performer on the Royal Caribbean cruise line) pulls into port in San Francisco. Her cell phone goes off. She looks down. It's a text message from Lisa Forkish, who is now (finally) a student at Berklee. Four years after leaving high school, Lisa has begun her undergraduate degree again. From scratch.

Evynne looks at her watch. It's four-thirty P.M. on Friday. The text message from Lisa reads: "Hello, Divisi ladies, I love you." Her phone buzzes again. It is Erica Barkett, who has written more or less the same thing. This will repeat itself every Friday for much of the next year. At Berklee, Lisa starts an all-female a cappella group, but even she acknowledges it's not the same thing.

Back in Eugene, meanwhile, Keeley McCowan and Sarah Klein, the only two girls who remain from Divisi's first incarnation, stand in the rehearsal room looking at the twelve girls gathered before them. Keeley (pale, stern, with twenty pounds she's been meaning to lose for years) and Sarah (like a Jewish Marlee Matalin) will lead the group through the first Friday-afternoon performance of the year. They look around the room at this group of mostly strangers. They are the only two who remember firsthand the work it took to get to Lincoln Center; the only two who remember the ache, the disappointment. They are the last of the proud "rough and tight." Though more than a year has gone by since that night in New York, the wound is still raw. Sarah, who arranged "Woodstock," whose MySpace page reads *Will Sing for Food*, will be Divisi's new music director. She tells the new girls about the eight-week plan, the one Lisa Forkish devised to whip the group into shape for competition.

Peter Hollens, the founder of On the Rocks, still lives in town. Actually, he's engaged to Evynne Smith, and while she's sailing with the *Monarch of the Seas*, he's opened his own recording studio catering to a cappella. He goes to the first EMU performance to watch the new Divisi perform. The girls are shaky. He calls Evynne. "I don't think Divisi should compete this year," he says. He's worried that they will ruin the reputation Evynne and Lisa and the rest of the girls worked so hard to build. "They need more time," Peter said.

But Keeley and Sarah don't have more time. They want one last shot at the ICCA title before they graduate. They want to right the wrong. For Evynne. For Lisa. For themselves. But after that first Friday-afternoon performance—mediocre, at best—Keeley isn't sure that's possible. She goes home and calls Lisa. "It's not the same," Keeley says, her eyes tearing up. "What am I doing?"

CHAPTER TWO

THE BEELZEBUBS

Wherein the legendary Tufts Beelzebubs
face a crisis in leadership

Long View Farm Recording Studios sits on a hundred acres of western Massachusetts farm country, some two hours outside of Boston. The place is something of a commune—part bed-and-breakfast, part horse farm, part spiritual retreat, part top-tier recording studio. In the winter of 1976, Cat Stevens booked time at Long View. However, before he'd confirm the reservation, he insisted the owners install a sauna. (It's still there.) In 1981, when the Rolling Stones needed somewhere to rehearse for their *Tattoo You* tour, Long View management converted the hayloft into a makeshift stage. The Stones—joined by a thirty-person entourage—stayed in residence for six weeks. In that time, Keith Richards left the property exactly once, for a surprise performance the Stones played at Sir Morgan's Cove, a cramped rock club in Worcester; it was the first live gig the Stones had played in three years. With the parade of music legends passing through the studio, it's no surprise that (with all due respect to Cleveland) some would come to refer to Long View as the rock 'n' roll capital of the world. The allure of the place hasn't faded in these intervening years. When indie rock gods Death Cab for Cutie signed with

Atlantic Records in 2005, they checked into Long View for a month. Even Matisyahu, the Orthodox Jewish rapper, has heard the call. Before the Tufts Beelzebubs came to Long View, exactly one a cappella group had recorded there: the world-famous Ladysmith Black Mambazo.

Bonnie Milner, Long View's owner, came to the barn in the seventies to do some recording of her own and was captivated by her new surroundings. "I asked the owners"—Geoff Myers and John Farrell—"for a job," she said. "They told me to come back in ten years." They were convinced she'd run off with the first band that came to record. In 1989, Bonnie *did* come back—with her three-year-old son in tow—and got a job cleaning the horse stables. Five years later she bought the place. Today Bonnie employs a fifteen-member staff of studio engineers and groundskeepers. While the advent of professional home recording (Pro Tools, Auto-Tune, and the like) has slowly killed off residential studios, places like Bearsville—a once famous spot in Woodstock, New York—Long View has weathered the changing tides. If anything, Milner says, home recording has helped Long View firm up its identity as an escape for artists. "Home recording has really made people start thinking about their environment," she says. Long View is like recording at home, but you don't have to make your bed.

It's with that spirit in mind that, in January 2001, the Tufts Beelzebubs—the university's oldest a cappella group—came to Long View to record *Next*. Not that Bonnie Milner wasn't skeptical of the Beelzebubs. Understandably she was concerned about turning the historic studio over to a bunch of college kids. "But the Bubs had too much charisma," she says. Two years later the Bubs went back to record a new album, *Code Red*, checking into Long View for nine nights. And as advertised, the Bubs were inspired. For "Disarm"—originally a Smashing Pumpkins song—the Bubs wanted an intimate sound. And so inside the studio the Bubs dimmed the lights and lit candles while the engineer set up fifteen sets of headphones so they could record the track as close to live as possible. "It's probably my fondest memory," says Chris Kidd '05, who sang the solo on "Disarm." Still, there were drawbacks to Long View. "We were burning through money," says Ed Boyer, Beelzebubs class of 2004, the group's music director for much of that year. To cut costs the Bubs slept three and four guys to a suite. But, at the end of the week, they got a bill for somewhere in the neighborhood of fifteen thousand dollars. They would go on to spend *another* fifteen thousand dollars to mix the CD, have art designed, and print the thing. (Mixing an album means, among many other things, deciding what elements belong in the foreground of each track and what should be in the background.)

Which begs the question: How can a collegiate a cappella group afford to spend thirty thousand dollars producing an album? Especially when—despite their forty-year history and active alumni base—they don't receive a dime from the old guys? The short answer: gigs. The Bubs, because of their legacy and professionalism, can charge upward of three thousand dollars for one thirty-minute concert at a prep school. (The year the Bubs produced *Next* they earned a group record of nearly fifty-five thousand dollars.)

That so many iconoclasts recorded at Long View seems fitting. Because *Code Red* may be the most controversial album in the history of collegiate a cappella. When the album was released in 2003, the Bubs actually received hate mail. "It blows my mind that people would waste time writing *letters*," says Ed Boyer, the music director. "But they did." What did those letters say? "That the Bubs were ruining a cappella."

Despite its proximity to Harvard, the Tufts University Beelzebubs—founded in 1963—may be Boston's premier collegiate a cappella group. And the proof is in the gigs. The Bubs regularly sing with the famous Boston Pops. They've performed at Carnegie Hall. In October of 2004, they were hired to sing at John Kerry's final stump speech in Boston, just weeks before the presidential election. There have been other high-profile Beltway gigs over the years too. In 2000, Tufts president Larry Bacow hosted an event at his home, honoring an even more esteemed POTUS, Bill Clinton. The Bubs were asked to sing "Don't Stop (Thinking About Tomorrow)," President Clinton's campaign theme song, which they did. A few years later, when Hillary Clinton came through town on her own tour, again the Bubs got the call. Matt Michelson, then the group's business manager, e-mailed the Bubs repertoire over to a contact at President Bacow's office. She replied quickly, nixing nearly every song on the list—even the Simon and Garfunkel tune "Cecilia," a Bubs staple. "They wouldn't let us sing 'Cecilia' because it had the words *up in my bedroom*," Michelson says. Bacow's team, perhaps still sensitive to the Monica Lewinsky fallout, did not want to offend the First Lady and thus specified "nothing sexual." Michelson jokingly replied to the e-mail suggesting the Bubs sing the Tears for Fears track "Everybody Wants to Rule the World" instead. Bacow's assistant didn't get the joke. Left with little choice, the Bubs went back to the well and sang "Tuftonia's Day," the school fight song.

In the seventies, Peter Gallagher of Fox's *The O.C.* was a member of the Beelzebubs, and he looks back on his college days fondly. "The Bubs would have these beer-soaked road trips to Williams College," he says. "And they'd always start full of expectations. But invariably it would end up with you sitting on the curb with your fifth beer thinking, *Maybe we should go to bed.* And there'd be ten of us sleeping in some dorm room." Why weren't the Bubs more successful with the ladies? "All of the women wanted to be with Harvard men," Gallagher says, "from the Krokodiloes." Or maybe it was because the Bubs just weren't that good back then. Gallagher was a member of what the Bubs refer to as "the shitty Bubs," or "the Dark Years." Gallagher is defensive: It was a politically active era, he says, and students had more to think about than a cappella music. Still, the Bubs rebounded nicely. And they've since become perhaps the most famous collegiate a cappella group after the Yale Whiffenpoofs. The Bubs also have the distinction of being the only collegiate a cappella group whose music has been played in outer space. A Tufts alum, Rick Hauck, piloted NASA's STS-7 mission—the seventh flight of the space shuttle—and on June 20, 1983, the Bubs recording of "Tuftonia's Day" was used as the astronauts' wake-up call. There was another first on that mission; her name was Sally Ride.

The Bubs pride themselves on setting the pace of collegiate a cappella. But it wasn't always expensive recording studios and the like for the men from Tufts. Tracks for the very first Bubs record, *Brothers in Song*, were laid down in the dining room of the Delta Tau Delta fraternity house in 1964. The Bubs recorded standards like Grieg's "Brothers, Sing On!" "Ride the Chariot," and "Daddy, Get Your Baby Out of Jail"—most in one take, and the entire album was finished in an afternoon or two. But even then the Bubs were innovators. Dr. Dwight W. Batteau, a professor from the engineering department, recorded *Brothers in Song* free of charge because he had some new equipment to test out. He'd been working on advancing an experimental method known as binaural recording, which involves, improbably, singing into an actual dummy head with microphones stuck into its ears. The science (hopelessly simplified here) says that the outer and inner ears encode music in three dimensions. A binaural recording is immersive—if played back correctly, it will sound as if, in this case, the Bubs were serenading you. Unfortunately, that effect can't be reproduced without headphones. And for that reason (and others more complex) binaural recording is rare these days, though there is an underground community of audiophiles who still worship the method. In 2000, Pearl Jam even released an album called *Binaural*.

The Bubs have released twenty-three studio albums since their founding (not including live albums) and have sold more than forty thousand copies. (The 2006–2007 Bubs are charged with recording the twenty-fourth.) Their reach is pervasive. Proof: The 1991 Bubs album *Foster Street*, featuring "Rio" and "Pinball Wizard," is credited with introducing vocal percussion—the beatbox—to collegiate a cappella. For the record, Long View Farms was not the first high-profile studio they'd recorded in. *Foster Street* was laid down at RCA Studios in Manhattan in January 1991, where, just down the hall, Zubin Mehta and the New York Philharmonic were recording Stravinsky's "The Rite of Spring."

There have been times, however, when the Bubs have fallen behind the curve. In 2001, the Bubs released *Next*. "It was fashionable to be perfect," Ed Boyer '04 says. "And *Next* was not." There were tuning problems. There were issues with rhythm. The funny thing is, *Next* is still one of Ed's favorite Bubs albums. "It has character that the other albums don't," he says. But when the Bubs checked into Long View in 2003 to record what would become *Code Red*—the album some say ruined collegiate a cappella—they had a very specific goal in mind: to record a disc so perfect, so produced, that the a cappella tracks were nearly indistinguishable from the original tunes.

Bill Hare, a legendary a cappella producer based in the Bay Area (who works with groups as far away as Sweden) likes to say that a cappella has, of late, diverged into two separate and distinct arts. "Recording an album is an expression of what's in your head," he says. "Singing live is a demonstration of your real skill." Both are viable. "I've never been a believer that a group should sound live the way they do on the recording," he says. "If that were the case, we wouldn't have had everything from the

Beatles album *Sgt. Pepper's* on up." It's an apt comparison, believe it or not. Like *Sgt. Pepper's*, *Code Red* was a tour de force of production.

The Bubs ended up reverse-engineering a lot of *Code Red*. On Bush's "Machine Head," the Bubs wanted to match the distortion of Gavin Rossdale's guitar on the original, so Bill Hare brought out an actual electric guitar. He played the guitar through different Pro Tools amp simulators on his computer until he found the one Bush and Gavin Rossdale used to get that distortion. Then Bill unplugged the electric guitar and strummed. Without the amplifier, the strings sounded like *plink plink plink*. The Bubs would sing "Machine Head" one way onstage, but in the studio Bill asked them to emulate that tinny *plink plink plink* with their voices. Bill Hare ran the track through the selfsame amplifier Bush had used. And bam. "The Bubs sounded *exactly* like the original," Bill says.

Code Red, co-produced by Deke Sharon, was released in April 2004 and it received enviable notices. Dave Trendler reviewed the album for rarb.org, the a cappella equivalent of the tastemaking Web site pitchforkmedia.com, writing: "Who are these superhumans? Whether by machine, superhero, or mortal man, the Beelzebubs have blended the simple human voice with excellent studio work to create an unconventional album."

Still, the Bubs did receive hate mail. Some called the album computerized. "People said it was overproduced," Ed Boyer says. *Code Red* opened with the Styx song "Mr. Roboto." Here one might point out the inherent irony of the song's lyrics: *The problem's plain to see // Too much technology // Machines to save our lives // Machines dehumanize.* (Perhaps anticipating these complaints, the Bubs included a statement in the album's liner notes, saying, "Every sound on this recording was created solely by our fifteen mouths," much as the Mills Brothers had done in 1931 for their record *Swing It, Sister*.) It wasn't just the public that questioned the merits of *Code Red*. Some of those complaints came from the Bub alums themselves. "Perfection is an aesthetic and an accomplishment," says Bill Allen, Bubs class of '83. "But I prefer *spontaneity*."

The thing is, Bill Allen might be the one to blame for all of this. In 1985, he was working as an engineer at A & R Recording Studios in Manhattan, when the Bubs came to record *Clue*. Bill Allen ran those sessions and he believes he's responsible for the first-ever studio effect on a Bubs record. It was the intro to "Grazin' in the Grass," and Bill recorded the Bubs saying the word *pow* several times. "I had them linger on *pow*," he says. *Powwwwwww.* Bill took a pencil and scrubbed a mark on the quarter-inch tape, which he laid on the splicing block, and cut with a razor. When he flipped the tape and played it backward, the *powwwwww* became *wwwwwwwwwooopp.* "That's how we got the big crescendo that starts that track," Bill says. Still, *www-wopppp* was a far cry from an octavized bass, a Pro Tools amplifier, and Auto-Tune. (Backstory: Auto-Tune is a computer program that corrects a singer's pitch in recordings and in live performance. When Billy Joel sang the national anthem at Super Bowl XLI, some accused him of abusing Auto-Tune. How do you know when it's too much—be it live, or on *Code Red*? Well, the singer sounds like Cher's "Believe.")

Some angry (and likely jealous) a cappella readers wrote into the RARB forums insisting *Code Red* was a studio project, or that it was unfair to penalize a group that couldn't afford to record at a place like Long View. John Sears, an ICCA judge, had his own concerns: "The album bores me to tears. It's more of an album I can pop in for my friend just to say, Look what can be done when you take college a cappella to an extreme level." But the thing is, the Bubs didn't just sing those songs live—they killed them. "Every song was a showstopper," says Dr. Michael Miller, Bubs class of '74. He singles out Greg Binstock, Bubs class of '03, who sang "Nothing Compares 2 U," by Sinéad O'Connor, and Björk's "It's Oh So Quiet." Dr. Miller isn't exactly in the Björk demographic. "But that song would knock people out," he says. "The group had such control." Love it or hate it, *Code Red* was a game changer.

The Bubs never went back to Long View Farm Recording Studios. It was too expensive, and frankly, with advancements in computer technology, it was probably overkill for a self-financed a cappella project. Ed Boyer, Bubs '04, stepped up, negotiating a deal with the group. If the Bubs bought him recording equipment, he said, he'd learn how to make a Bubs album. In the spring of 2004, the group bought Ed an Apple PowerBook G4 for two thousand dollars, a Pro Tools rig for another two grand, and a preamp—later he picked up a Neumann mic from eBay. The Bubs recorded 2005's album *Shedding* in Ed Boyer's bedroom closet. It was an entirely different operation. The Bubs gave up the personal chef and camaraderie of Long View but were spoiled in other ways. Because Ed wasn't really on the clock like an engineer they'd pay at Long View, they could experiment wildly. They could do fifty takes of the same *dim dim bop* bass line. A song from a Divisi album might be made up of forty individual Pro Tools tracks layered on top of each other, but on *Shedding*, each Bubs song was made up of closer to 120 individual tracks (or more).

But something was missing. While *Code Red* had a clear mission—imitative, produced a cappella—*Shedding* was really more of the same. At least to the naked ear. Ed Boyer insists there's a difference, something about the difference between technology that's apparent and technology that's transparent. It's a valid point—if you're an engineer. The mortals didn't pick up on the subtleties. Trey Harris reviewed *Shedding* for RARB, writing: "Once you release an album like *Code Red*, it's hard to follow up. You've raised the bar for a cappella covers and production so high that it's nigh impossible to beat. After a group comes out with an album as perfectly imitative as *Code Red* was, I'd expect them to move on to different ideals." Still, it was hard to argue with perfection and *Shedding* swept the Contemporary A Cappella Recording Awards, winning Best Male Collegiate Album, Best Male Collegiate Song for "Let's Get It Started," Best Male Collegiate Solo for Andrew Savini's "Epiphany," and Best Arrangement for "Everybody Wants to Rule the World."

The pressure of the Bubs legacy mounts each year. "With *Code Red*," says Sean Zinsmeister, who graduated in '06 and shared music director duties with Ed Boyer on *Shedding*, "we really pushed it as far as we could go in terms of mimicking instruments." He talks a lot about "responding to the critics." It seems Sean graduated at just the right time. "I really wasn't sure where we could go after *Code Red*," he says. "I'm glad I don't have to be there to figure it out. I'm glad that isn't my problem."

No, that would be Ben Appel's problem.

The first thing one should know about Ben Appel is that he's young. He ran for music director in the spring of 2006, at the end of his freshman year. It wasn't so much that he felt ready for the job—he just felt he was more ready than the other prospects. "I felt it was my duty to run," he says. It seems the group agreed.

Still, Ben did not run for music director on a whim. You can't in the Beelzebubs. There is an established protocol for seeking higher office here and it involves consulting every current member of the Beelzebubs *individually*, stating your intention, presenting your platform, and opening the floor to questions. (It becomes especially awkward when one candidate for music director must approach the other candidate for the job.) Second, it's become customary for candidates to call a litany of past officers—Bub alums stretching back forty years—to get an understanding of what the job entails. In some cases, a phone call with Danny Lichtenfeld '93 or Deke Sharon '91 might turn into a three-hour conversation on the intricacies of the university administration or on navigating internal group politics. Ben Appel ran on a platform of the Bubs' motto: Fun Through Song. "He didn't want to rule with an iron fist," says Matt Michelson, the current president. "Ben didn't want to do things just because of protocol." How so? "There have been times when the Bubs ran like a machine," Michelson says. "We'd have a gig. We'd sing. We'd leave. Ben wanted to focus more on the performance." He wanted to take the machine apart.

In the fall of 2006 the Bubs returned to campus with plans to record a new studio album (as decades of Bubs have done on alternate years practically since the beginning). And this group was taking the task seriously, to be sure. Early in the year, the Bubs had a nine-hour meeting where they did nothing but debate the *title* of the new album. They have had similarly endless conversations about the direction the album should take, about the problem with verisimilitude. When your music is indistinguishable from the original tracks, what do you do next—get *more* real? That will be the essential question of this album, and the biggest hurdle for Ben Appel and the Bubs. The group will have help with the task—namely, from Ed Boyer, who shared music-director duties on *Code Red* and is now a full-time a cappella producer living in the Bronx. Boyer—paunchy, red-faced—graduated in 2004 from the dual-degree program at Tufts and the New England Conservatory. He and his business partner, John Clark (an alum of the coed Tufts Amalgamates), have made a name for themselves in a cappella circles. Boyer has agreed to produce the new Bubs album, which is scheduled for release in the spring of '07.

But the album's direction falls squarely in Ben Appel's lap. And Ben has his own ideas—ideas the Bubs are thrilled about. There is talk of going in an entirely new direction, opting for a real organic sound. Ben is even talking about making this a concept album, with tracks leading directly into each other, possibly with dialogue as connective tissue. But Ben Appel's biggest asset may be his attitude. To lead a group with such rich history, a group whose alums are often still involved in the day-to-day business of the undergraduates, one must not be awed by the legacy. And Ben isn't.

Unfortunately, though most of the Bubs don't know it yet, just a few weeks into the 2006–2007 school year, Ben Appel, their new music director, is about to drop out of school.

In late August 2006, just before the Orientation Show, Ben Appel disappeared for three days. He'd literally left rehearsal for a lunch break, said he'd be back, and got on a Greyhound bus to see his parents. It was poor timing, to say the least. The Orientation Show would be the group's first big performance of the year, and it was crucial in establishing the Bubs' alpha reputation among freshmen. Plus, it was a great place to recruit new members. The Bubs had graduated a handful of guys the previous spring and were down to ten. They needed a few good men. The Bubs had been learning Gnarls Barkley's "Smiley Faces" and hoped to debut the song at the Orientation Show. In Ben's sudden absence, Lucas Walker '08 took over, teaching the song to the Bubs. The group was curious to know where their music director was, but the officers kept his troubles a secret. "We didn't know whether he'd be coming back," Matt Michelson says. "We thought it was better to wait."

Ben Appel did return to campus a few days later. He sat down with the officers. He'd been suffering from depression and social anxiety, he said, and he was on academic probation. To make matters worse, he and his girlfriend were in the process of splitting up. But the only time he felt like himself was onstage with the

Beelzebubs, he'd said; that's when his other problems—the obsessive-compulsive disorder, the crippling inability to focus on even the simplest decisions—went away. He was seeking help, he told them—that was the important thing. Ben Appel said he wanted to resume his position as music director of the Bubs. The officers asked questions, but they didn't pry. Ben Appel had returned to campus just in time for the Orientation Show on September 4 and perhaps his issues really were under control. And so life went on. The Bubs held auditions. They picked up five new members. But Ben's problems returned. With a vengeance.

A few days before the Homecoming Show, Ben Appel called his friend Andrew Savini, a senior in the Beelzebubs. The two sat in Savini's room smoking nearly a pack of cigarettes. Together, they walked over to the Bub room (part museum, part rehearsal space, on the second floor of Curtis Hall) for a meeting with the officer corps. Ben spoke first, slowly but decisively. He was going to leave school, he said. He needed to take care of himself. He needed to get better. "I needed a drastic change," he said.

The officers were quiet. Matt Michelson, the president, said something about wanting to help Ben. He reminded Ben of what he'd told them a few weeks earlier—that the Beelzebubs had made him happy. "Wasn't that what you said?" Matt mumbled. And then tempers flared. No one involved is particularly proud of what happened next. Andrew Savini fears some of his fellow Bub leaders lost sight of the human problem—that Ben was their *friend* first and foremost, that it was about his health and not the health of the Bubs. Still, the Bubs did have the new album to think about, not to mention the Homecoming Show in a few days. The officers wanted to make sure Ben had thought this through. Earlier in the semester, Ben Appel told the officers that he'd need to see a psychiatrist and seek help from the Academic Resource Center. "Have you gone through the steps?" Matt asked. "Have you been doing what you were supposed to do?"

Matt just wanted to understand what his friend was going through. But he's not sure it read that way.

Matt had an ulterior motive. He hoped the Homecoming Show might help Ben Appel. That the crowd noise might ease whatever white noise was troubling Ben's mind. But that wasn't to be. The decision had already been made. Ben Appel wanted to tell the entire group, before they went onstage for the Homecoming Show, that he was leaving Tufts. But Matt convinced him otherwise. "I didn't want to distract from the show," Matt Michelson says. "I didn't want to ruin the night."

The Homecoming Show was held at Goddard Chapel—all dark wood and stained glass. At the right hour, the sun casts a glow inside the chapel that can only be described as divine. In the late 1800s, the entire Tufts student body would squeeze into the chapel for events. Tonight, it only feels that way. Ben Appel steps forward. He looks like he's raided Alex P. Keaton's closet, what with the khakis, navy blazer, starched white shirt, and Republican power tie. His movements are so lazy he actually appears to be moving in slow motion. Yet somehow his innate, low-energy cool makes him stand out the most. The Bubs love their group members equally, but some more equally than others. And when Ben Appel stands in front of the group, there's a perceptible change in their posture. The Bubs are not objectively as attractive as lore would have it, or as the four hundred (mostly) female members of the audience would suggest. But when the Bubs get onstage, when they stand behind a soloist like this, they look like different people. It's that way with performers.

The song is "19-2000" by the Brit band Gorillaz. The background starts in simply enough, with the Bubs later repeating in a near monotone, distorting their voices: *"It's the music that we choose // It's the music that we choose // It's the music that we choose."* Ben comes in on the solo, singing: *"You get the cool! // You get the cool shoeshine!"*

There is a tension here that was missing in earlier songs. At the bridge, the Bubs suddenly grow quiet, pulling in tight around Ben, affecting a don't-mess-with-us attitude. Ben sings, all serious and mysterious: *"They do the bop."* On *bop*, the Bubs, in unison, raise their left hands defiantly and snap twice.

"They do the bump!" (*snap snap*) *"They do the bump!"* (*snap snap*)

And just as suddenly, Ben Appel stands bolt upright and shouts, *"You get the cool!"*

It had been a rough couple of years for the Bubs leadership. Until 2003, it had been almost unheard of for an officer of the Beelzebubs to quit midterm—especially a music director. But then, in January of 2006, Ben Kelsey '08 stepped down. He wasn't a bad guy. He just realized he wasn't qualified for the job and did the only thing he could: He fled the country, taking a semester abroad in Spain. Sean Zinsmeister '06 took over, which came with its own set of problems. Sean was a divisive personality and some say he encouraged politics within the group, which resulted in a mammoth rift. Andrew Savini, now a senior, had actually contemplated quitting the Bubs. "It was like no one could lead the fun except Sean," Savini says. "People wouldn't laugh at jokes if Sean didn't laugh first."

The truth is, Sean and Matt Michelson had a complex friendship, loud disagreements punctuated by good times, and Matt was particularly looking forward to this new school year. With him as president and Ben Appel as music director, he thought they could restore some lost Bubs spirit. The Bubs would face other obstacles for which Ben was uniquely qualified. In the spring of 2006, the Bubs graduated six guys—six of fifteen. As president, it would be Matt Michelson's job to turn the new guys (including several pasty-white freshmen with oversize Afros) into Bubs, and Matt was feeling the pressure. A cappella is big at Tufts, he explains: "No one is here for Division One athletics." (It doesn't help that the school's mascot is an elephant called Jumbo.) Worse, there was a time in the late nineties when the Bubs got by on their name alone—and were embarrassed to find that their on-campus rival, the coed Tufts Amalgamates, had surpassed them in musicality. Never again, they said. Matt was looking forward to Ben Appel helping him set the agenda. But that wasn't to be.

Secretly, quietly, in the days leading up to the Homecoming Show on September 29, the officers talked about who might replace Ben as music director. They called Lucas Walker. They called Alexander Koutzoukis. They called Chris Van Lenten (who wasn't interested). They wanted someone to take the job for the entire year. Lucas balked. He knew the work it would take, and he was honest about his shortcomings. For one thing, arranging music didn't come easily to him. Second, he was majoring in physics and philosophy. Plus, Lucas had a girlfriend. She barely saw him as it was. Lucas remembers the night he got into the Beelzebubs, how he sat outside a party talking to a Bub alum's girlfriend. "She was trying to reassure me that joining the Bubs was totally worth it and that I could absolutely handle the time commitment," Lucas says. "She was completely right about the former and completely lying through her teeth about the latter. This is the great paradox of being in the Bubs: My life is simultaneously perfectly fulfilling and completely ruined, both due to the same group of fourteen other dudes."

Alexander Koutzoukis, a skinny sophomore, might have been the strongest musician, but the officers questioned his ability to command the group—he was soft-spoken, shy even. And more than anything the Bubs needed a leader, and so a decision was made: If Lucas would only commit to one semester, then so be it. "I still didn't really want to be music director," Lucas says. But he took the job. Now they just had to tell the rest of the Bubs.

After the homecoming concert, Ben Appel sat the group down in the Bub room and came clean about what what had been going on. He would be leaving school, he said. It was quiet in the room, the proceedings very matter-of-fact. Lucas Walker gave a short speech about what he'd like to do that semester, the music he'd arrange, the alumni he'd call for help. He talked about the album, which would, of course, still come out in the spring—answering the call of *Code Red* and the legacy of the Bubs. The Beelzebubs have released a studio album (more or less) every other year since the beginning. This year would be no different. This class would not be the ones to ruin tradition.

CHAPTER THREE

THE HULLABAHOOS

Wherein we meet the upstart bad boys of
collegiate a cappella

The University of Virginia, home of the Wahoos, was founded in 1819, and not much has changed since—the only color on campus comes courtesy of Ralph Lauren. Just ask Dane Blackburn. "People stop me on campus and they're like, hey, aren't you the…" Pause. "What?" Dane says. "The *black guy* in the Hullabahoos?" It's eased up a bit since they took a second black guy, Brendon Mason. He's loud and hard to miss. Plus, he was a former child star, having appeared on Nickelodeon's *Bug Juice*. "There are clips on YouTube," Brendon says apologetically.

The Hullabahoos were born in 1988 as an alternative to the Virginia Gentlemen, the staid offshoot of the campus glee club. Unlike most men of collegiate a cappella, the B'hoos (for short) don't often wear khakis or blue blazers. The first thing one notices about the Hullabahoos is the Technicolored robes draped over their street clothes. The robes are their trademark look, and it's inspired a series of cheeky fan T-shirts, like this one: ROBED FOR YOUR PLEASURE. Believe it or not, the robes are bespoke, handmade by a seamstress at Mr. Hanks discount fabrics in downtown Charlottesville. "I've still got the original pattern in the back," says Mr. Hanks—which, incidentally, isn't his name. (It's Tom.)

While the Hullabahoos may be UVA's most popular all-male a cappella group, they are not beloved everywhere. The a cappella community simmers with rivalries—sort of an East Coast/West Coast rap shakedown in sequined vests. The University of North Carolina Clef Hangers have had beef with the Hullabahoos dating back almost a decade. On that group's 2001 recording of "Nuthin' But a 'G' Thang," the Clef Hangers called out the B'hoos, rapping: "Dropping the funky tracks and making the Hullabahoos mumble." The Hullabahoos don't know why the Clef Hangers hate them—the incident long forgotten as students graduated. But Carolina-based producer Dave Sperandio—the Timbaland of a cappella recording and a former member of the Clef Hangers—remembers exactly how the feud started. "The Hullabahoos used to come to UNC and hook up with our girl-friends," he says. They still do, by the way. Even the lone, endear-ingly awkward Hullabahoo (the kind of guy prone to non sequiturs) managed to get some on a recent road trip to UNC, hooking up with a member of the all-female a cappella group the Loreleis—a girl whose grandfather just happens to be the cantan-kerous owner of a major league baseball franchise.

It's not just the Clef Hangers who've had problems with the Hullabahoos. A couple of years ago, there was an incident with a Cornell University a cappella group, Last Call. Both groups were performing at NYU one night. Keith Bachmann, a Hulla-bahoos alum, tells the story. "After the show, the Callboys—that's seriously what they're called—were like, *Hey, do you guys wanna trade CDs!*" Bachmann says. No, the Hullabahoos did not want to trade CDs. And their refusal apparently offended the bevested Callboys. The confrontation came to a head later that night when the Hullabahoos saw the Callboys coming toward them on East Ninth Street. "They were doing the *West Side*

Story snap!" Bachmann says. "We just did not know how to respond to that."

A lot of it is just plain jealousy. Because being a Hullabahoo has its privileges. Like that time they went to Asia and sold out the Hard Rock.

Ron Puno graduated from UVA in '99 and as that year came to a close, his father, a diplomat living in the Philippines, sent a handful of Hullabahoos CDs to some local radio stations. Somehow, the music started to get major airplay on the island nation, and a production company offered to fly the Hullabahoos to Manila to perform at the Hard Rock Cafe. When the plane landed in Manila, however improbably, a throng of screaming reporters and photographers met the B'hoos at the airport. Because Puno's father was a big deal, the Hullabahoos were assigned a security detail of six motorcycles. The Hullabahoos concert, by the way, sold out—some twelve hundred tickets. Or roughly five hundred more than the Hard Rock's previous headliners: Nick Lachey and 98 Degrees.

The seventeen Hullabahoos—an all-star team of members past and present—took advantage of their sudden international fame, appearing on the Filipino answer to David Letterman. They signed autographs at the mall. "There were fans screaming for us by our *individual names*," Puno says. For some, however, this attention proved problematic. "You have to understand," Puno says, "in that part of the world, there are a lot of effeminate-looking men that dress up like females. You're in a dark corner hooking up, and then you're like, *Wait, what is that!* It was like *The Crying Game*." Puno managed to avoid that particular Shanghai surprise, but some Hullabahoos (who shall remain nameless) were not so lucky.

As the fourteen-day international tour came to a close, the group's popularity only grew. And their brief appearance seems to have kicked off a wave of pop-appella in the Philippines, Puno says. (Shortly after their departure, a *Making the Band*–style TV show for a cappella swept the nation.) As unlikely as it sounds, the Hullabahoos still have a following in South Asia. Ron Puno, now thirty and a senior manager in the IT department at Enterprise Rent-A-Car, went to visit his dad in Manila in 2005. As he was standing at a bar, a man approached him sheepishly. "Are you Ron from the Hullabahoos?" the man said.

"It was shocking," Ron says.

It's not surprising that the Hullabalumni (that's what they call themselves), nearly a hundred strong, have such fond memories of their collegiate days. Though most never sang again—a few are trying to make it in Nashville, some on the indie circuit—they can take comfort in the fact that (much like Hasselhoff in Germany) the B'hoos are big in the Philippines.

Though the Hullabahoos would hate to admit it, they're more of a fraternity than most a cappella groups. (They're also a bit like the United States Marines. Before each concert they circle up, put their hands in the center, and shout, "Unit. Corps. God. Country. Hullabahoos.") For one thing, the Hullabahoos have their own de facto frat house, aka the Hullaba-house—a four-bedroom, off-campus apartment on Wertland Street, across from a local landmark, Georgia O'Keeffe's old place. Seven of the Hullabahoos live in the house, which, like most college residences, contains a glut of inherited furniture—food caked into the cushions like amber fossils of years past. The attic alone holds an efficiency kitchen, a full bath, a Ping-Pong table, two oversize papasan chairs, a futon, a magnetic darts game, and some scattered folding chairs. There is a thirty-two-inch television, an Xbox, and several predictable DVDs—*Fight Club, Reservoir Dogs*, the unrated edition of *The Girl Next Door*. One of the B'hoos also lives in the attic, having sectioned off a corner with a bedsheet and some rope MacGyver-style. The Hullabahoos have been renting the place for three years and it's home to their postconcert parties.

It's like that with the Hullabahoos—most don't fit the a cappella archetype (such as there is one). Morgan Sword—last year's president, now the soul of the Hullabahoos—is a six-foot-four prep-school kid, the kind confident enough to wear Birkenstock clogs with white socks. As a freshman he expected to play club baseball at UVA before some girls in his dorm convinced him to audition for the Hullabahoos. When he got into the group he called his high school sweetheart, Lindsay Friedman (then a student at Williams College). She was indignant. "You can *sing*?" she said. Morgan's friends back home in Princeton, New Jersey, still make fun of him for being in an a cappella group. But Morgan is recognized on campus at UVA almost daily, and stardom—albeit the kind relegated (mostly) to a five-mile radius—is a nice comeback to any ribbing his buddies might dish out. "Girls I don't know will come up to me and say, Hi, Morgan! I'm like, Hey, *friend*! I never thought I'd get social respect for a cappella." Pete Seibert is the music director of the group and his friends on campus make fun of him too. When they see him at a party, they like to run up to him and shout, "Oh, my God, are you a *Hullabahoo*!"

If there is one thing the Hullabahoos are most proud of—more than selling out their campus concerts, more than their reputation overseas—it is their intramural flag football team. They're called Hullabahoos B. What's with the name? Well, Hullabahoos B implies that there is also an A team. The Sigma Chi frat house might have a Sigma Chi A team and a Sigma Chi B team—such is the demand for flag football among their brothers. "When we beat a frat," says Patrick Lundquist, a brickhouse of a Hullabahoo, "we like them to think they just lost to the *scrubs* from an a cappella group." Patrick's can't-miss plan for on-field domination in the 2006–2007 season: "A Peyton Manning–style hurry-up offense." Before they called themselves Hullabahoos B, the team was known by a different name, the equally ironic Jazz Hands. They've placed as high as third in the UVA intramural league. Brendon "Bug Juice" Mason, a onetime high school football star who was recruited by William and

Mary, is a second-year in the Hullabahoos, and he's been a boon. How heated are the games? Last season, during the intramural play-offs, Morgan Sword felt so sick that he had his girlfriend drive him to the emergency room. With an IV in one arm and a raging fever, Morgan told the doctor that he absolutely *had* to get out of the hospital that afternoon.

"I've got a game," Morgan said.

"Do you play for UVA?" the doctor asked.

Morgan replied the only way he knew how: "Sort of?"

When Morgan was a first year, he was actually accepted to all three all-male a cappella groups. UVA is not known for its music program, and as such, competition for fresh meat is fierce among the a cappella groups. He told the buttoned-up men of the Virginia Gentlemen that he wasn't interested, that he was deciding between the Academical Village People and the Hullabahoos. Still, one of the Virginia Gentlemen called, offering to take Morgan to dinner. "Morgan, you're making the biggest mistake of your life," the kid said. That's called dirty rush, Morgan explains. The Hullabahoos consider themselves above all that. "We'd rather take the high road," Morgan says. "We don't have a single guy in the group who wanted to be somewhere else." The Hullabahoos are not, however, above shamelessly padding a kid's ego.

When the Hullabahoos came back to campus in August 2006, they began planning for auditions. The Hullabahoos were looking to pick up a bass or two. "But more than that," Morgan says, "we just need good Hullabahoos." He's not talking about good singers. "We spend so much time together," he says, "the first requirement is that we're gonna get along. We've certainly turned down kids before who sang way better than any of us. But if you take them, you're compromising the integrity of what you're doing." People can contribute in other ways, he says, like looks. You can always teach a cool kid to beatbox.

Turnout was solid for the first round of auditions this year—and fairly standard, save for one curveball: An openly gay member of the Hullabahoos watched his ex-boyfriend audition for the group. Now, the Hullabahoos are very welcoming—especially considering their relation to the Mason-Dixon Line. But most everyone was relieved that the kid's sound wasn't right for the Hullabahoos. Even if it had been, they admit, they probably wouldn't have taken him. "Hullabahoos hooking up with other Hullabahoos?" one member says. "We just can't have that."

To get to know the potential new members better before the callbacks, Morgan and the B'hoos resurrected an old tradition, the Hullabahoos-versus-Auditionees football game. The Hullabahoos have a strategy. "We dominate early," says Joe Cassara, the current president of the B'hoos, "but we let the kids win so we don't look like assholes." The Hullabahoos even throw interceptions to kids who are on the fence—kids who are auditioning for other a cappella groups. The game isn't about athletics. (Which explains why Pete, the music director, runs the field with a can of beer in his hand.) "It's about seeing who is a leader," Morgan says.

In the past four years, the Hullabahoos have lost just one kid—an honest-to-God cousin of President George W. Bush, a kid named Sam Bush. Perhaps *lost* is the wrong word. At the auditions, the Hullabahoos ask each kid to fill out a form, which lists their hometown, major, voice part, that sort of thing. There are a few personality-based questions too. Example: Fill in the blank. I have the most extraordinary _____. Sam Bush wrote *cock*. He would go on to join—and quit—the Virginia Gentlemen.

Not much was memorable about the callbacks this fall—save for Joe Whitney, a six-foot-something stringbean with blue eyes and a goofy grin, a guy whose friends regularly describe him as the whitest guy they know. For callbacks, each kid is asked to prepare five minutes of entertainment. For his talent, Joe Whitney showed up pushing a microwave on a handcart. "What's that for?" Morgan asked, though he was pretty sure Joe was about to blow something up.

"Oh," Joe said. "I'm going to cook!"

With that, Joe Whitney opened up his backpack and pulled out some peanut butter, graham crackers, Marshmallow Fluff, and chocolate bars. He used to make this snack when he was a kid, he told the Hullabahoos. He proceeded to nuke the fluff, which he then spread over the graham crackers. He handed the s'mores out to the Hullabahoos one by one. But he was not done. Just as the B'hoos were finishing up their snack, Joe Whitney removed his sweater to reveal a white T-shirt underneath. In black marker on the T-shirt he'd scrawled the words SECRET INGREDIENT, with a giant arrow pointing down to his crotch. Needless to say he was accepted.

When the audition week was up, the Hullabahoos took five new guys. Very quickly, four accepted the invitations. Joe Whitney (and his microwave) was the final holdout. He'd been leaning toward the more classic Virginia Gentlemen. What changed his mind? First, the Hullabahoos' "wall of sound," he says. Two? "Every girl I asked told me the Hullabahoos were better than the Virginia Gentlemen." What did the girls say, exactly? "AVP is the group you want to show to your little brother. The Virginia Gentlemen are the group you want to show to your mom. And the Hullabahoos are the group you *don't* want to show to your girlfriend."

The Hullabahoos are, in many ways, the anti-Beelzebubs. For one thing, they don't have that kind of discipline—and they wear their laziness as a badge of honor. Their music director, Pete Seibert (a genial kid from West Virginia who recently lost ten pounds by spending money on alcohol rather than food), often ends disagreements in rehearsal by saying, "It's just a cappella!" Also: They'd sooner disband than do choreography. About the only thing the Bubs and the Hullabahoos would agree on is the foolishness of competing in something like the ICCAs. Which is easy to say when you've already got a national reputation.

The Beelzebubs have nearly five decades of alumni experience to draw on—with alums regularly arranging new music for the group. The Beelzebubs may have an off year now and again (see the mid-seventies, or the early aughts) but what they lack in standout soloists they make up for in energy, sheer force, and dedication. The Hullabahoos, not so much. Their founder, Halsted Sullivan, remembers coming to the Hullabahoos' fifteenth anniversary show in 2003. "The group was pretty terrible," he says. It doesn't help that most of the Hullabahoos don't read music. In fact, several never sang before college.

The lax Hullabahoos attitude can come back to bite them. A few years ago, the Hullabahoos were four thousand dollars in the red. They'd recorded an album, *Jacked*, and were borrowing money from their families to pay the printing costs. "Poor planning," says Keith Bachmann, who was music director at the time.

The B'hoos have frequently flirted with insolvency, spending twenty-five thousand dollars on their 2006 album *Off the Dock*. The album has since sold more than a thousand copies at fifteen dollars apiece—which still leaves them in the red. Worse, the sales are likely illegal. Collegiate groups have only just begun paying royalties for the rights to these songs, figuring the U.S. government won't crack down on a bunch of college kids. Of late, some production warehouses—the people who actually print these CDs—have started to ask the groups to provide verification that they've secured all clearances. (The Harry Fox Agency in New York has carved out a niche securing what's called mechanical rights for bands—including a cappella groups—so that U2 actually gets a couple of pennies every time someone sells a cover of "With or Without You.") Not that the Hullabahoos worry much about the IRS, the RIAA, or anyone else. Actually, the only thing they're worried about is cannibalizing their own sales. They've laid down tracks for a new disc, including songs by Justin Timberlake and Rascal Flatts, but don't want to put the album out too soon. "*Off the Dock* is still selling well," says their music director. Though not as well as it should be. Like the major music labels, the Hullabahoos have to deal with piracy. "Our shit is all over LimeWire," Morgan says.

Salvation for their financial woes came from an unlikely source: the Republican Party. A company called Ashley Entertainment (who'd worked with the Hullabahoos on and off since the mid-nineties) hired the boys to perform for a series of events at the 2004 Republican National Convention in Manhattan, including a Union Pacific Railroad pep rally. The boys learned a bunch of songs about trains, including Marc Cohn's "Ghost Train" and Curtis Mayfield's "People Get Ready." Later, at an RNC event at Sotheby's, Trent Lott actually joined the B'hoos on "God Bless America." (Footnote: Lott was part of his own a cappella group, the Singing Senators, a barbershop quartet that also included Larry "Wide Stance" Craig.) The Hullabahoos earned thirteen thousand dollars for three days' work. Suddenly they were flush with cash. Yet, in typical Hullabahoos style, the group quickly lost touch with their contact, the owner of Ashley Entertainment and the man who had hired them for their most lucrative gig in years.

But in the fall of 2006—not long after Joe Whitney and his microwave show up—Morgan Sword gets back in touch with Howard Spector at Ashley Entertainment. Morgan is now planning the group's winter-break trip, which is set for January 2007, and he's set his sights on booking one major gig: singing the national anthem at a Los Angeles Lakers game. Morgan has been chasing the booker at the Staples Center for months, sending press kits and following up with phone calls, and he reaches out to Howard Spector for a letter of recommendation. Then there is the talk of a possible B'hoos trip to Hong Kong for the summer of 2007. If the Hullabahoos have a goal for this 2006–2007 school year, it's to compete on the level of a group like the Tufts Beelzebubs without sacrificing their laid-back soul. But can a group pull off a tour of Hong Kong when its music director still says, "It's just a cappella!" Or when its treasurer regularly forgets to cash checks—and compounds the problem by siphoning cash from the Hullabahoos' account to pay for beer?

"The Hullabahoos are nipping at the heels of the Beelzebubs in terms of success," says Lib Curlee, the business manager of the all-female UNC Loreleis. "But there's an aura around the Bubs' name." In a few weeks, the two all-male groups will collide at UNC, courtesy of an invitation from Lib, who invited both to North Carolina for the Loreleis' 2006 Fall Jam, setting the stage for an a cappella showdown.

On campus, meanwhile, the Hullabahoos have gotten a reputation for being cocky. But they may just have the goods to back it up. Not only is Hullabahoos B looking solid—they've got a new recruit, a freshman named Bobby Grasberger—but musically, as the group approaches their twentieth anniversary (with arguably its strongest lineup), this may be their best year yet. Which could be their downfall. Most a cappella groups are lucky to have one standout soloist. This year, the Hullabahoos have three—and another two who would be starters on any other team. But the proliferation of talent has actually led to a divide in the group. The biggest fear? "That we'll become Patrick Lundquist and the Hullabahoos," one of the B'hoos says.

Patrick Lundquist is the blond Hullabahoo, and he's hard to miss. He's six foot three, a natural athlete with an easy smile and cartoonish dimples, a man so good-looking your dad might sleep with him. It's almost an accident that Patrick finds himself in the Hullabahoos. When he was a kid, an older brother told him singing was "gay." But when the school's chorus teacher heard Patrick sing, she wouldn't let the boy quit. And so Patrick went on to play baseball and sing in the choir. As a senior in high school, he even starred in a local production of *Les Misérables*. No one made fun of him.

Patrick actually wanted to take this school year off. "I wanted to go to Los Angeles to act," he says. His parents—lovely, private-school types—begged him to stay in Charlottesville. Los Angeles wasn't going anywhere, they said. There was more to it. His parents weren't worried their boy would wind up waiting tables. "I think my mom was worried I'd succeed," Patrick says, "that it would be too easy for me." One gets the sense that Patrick awoke every morning to a standing ovation.

The thing is, Patrick's not even the biggest diva among the Hullabahoos. Brendon Mason is not just difficult but proud of it. Then there's Dane Blackburn, who is generally known to do exactly one selfless act a year for the Hullabahoos. "I make chicken wings for the auditions," he says.

The Hullabahoos don't really talk about any of these personality conflicts; rather it simmers under the surface, the hidden truth behind every offhand comment. And there's some healing to be done. Last year was rough, personalitywise, with the Hullabahoos essentially split in two. "There was the cool, former high school athlete house," says Joe Cassara. That's where Morgan and Patrick lived, along with another Hullabahoo. Then there was the Hullaba-house on Wertland Street—which was "the former-drama-kid" group. The Hullabahoos may just be their own worst enemy.

"Patrick probably sells more tickets than any other member of the group," Morgan says. "He's probably the most recognizable. But the one thing we do not tolerate in the B'hoos is people getting big egos." This will all come to a head. But on the most beautiful night of the school year, why ruin it?

It is close to ten o'clock on a warm September evening in Charlottesville, Virginia, and four thousand coeds crowd Thomas Jefferson's fabled Lawn. UVA was, in many ways, the first true college campus. But it's unlikely that Jefferson could have imagined this scene. Tonight, boys recline on bedsheets, passing cups of beer from some unseen keg. Pretty blond girls in strapless linen dresses greet each other with a kiss—sometimes a double kiss. The stadium lights crack on in the distance.

These four thousand students—more than twenty-five percent of the campus population—have gathered before the rotunda, an imposing bit of architecture modeled on the Roman pantheon. They've come for Rotunda Sing, an a cappella blowout that's easily the most popular orientation week event at UVA, despite its ass-numbing length. By the time the Hullabahoos take to the stage, eleven a cappella groups have already performed, including the Academical Village People—an all-male group known for humping the white columns of the Rotunda every year. A jazz group performs—something about chili con carne. There is even a Christian a cappella group, CHoosE (short for Christian 'Hoos Exalt).

The concert feels a lot like *American Idol*, a show whose effect cannot be understated in collegiate a cappella. Especially on the UVA campus. Travis Tucker, a finalist from *Idol* season three, started UVA's first R & B a cappella group, ReMix. *Idol* is the reason an otherwise good singer turns a word like *baby* into a nine-syllable vocal embarrassment along the lines of: *babe-ay-ay-ay-eh-eh-ay-ay.* (Technically, that flowery trill is called a melisma.) The Rotunda Sing organization committee likes to say the lineup of acts is drawn at random, but the Hullabahoos regularly close the show—a testament to their prominence on grounds.

For all that's been said about the Hullabahoos, they take to the steps of the rotunda casually and unassumingly, arranging themselves in a single arc. The crowd—a bit fatigued, understandably—perk up. These people have been waiting more than two hours for this moment. It's the only reason they haven't already decamped for the first fraternity parties of the year.

Pete Seibert, the music director, blows into his pitch pipe, counting off two-three-four. And the Hullabahoos come to life, singing, "*Doooooh-ooh* (pause) *doooo-ooooh.*" Perhaps it's Patrick

Lundquist stepping up to the mic. Or maybe the audience just recognizes *dooh-ooh*. There are catcalls. A guy way in the back yells, "Yes!" And a cute girl says to her friend, "I know we're Hullaba-hos, but I told Katie we'd meet her, like, twenty minutes ago."

Patrick sings: *"Turn down the lights // Turn down the bed // Turn down these voices inside my head."* He clutches the corners of his robe like a kid holding on to the last scraps of his security blanket. It may be an act. Who knows? But there is a visceral sense that he understands what he's singing—which is unnerving. That's what separates this from karaoke. He continues. *"Just hold me close // Don't patronize me."*

Last spring, Patrick suggested "I Can't Make You Love Me." He and Pete downloaded every version they could find, including one from Bonnie Raitt and another from George Michael. They even borrowed bits from a Luther Vandross version. It's been simmered down like some port wine reduction. One doesn't notice the genius of Pete's arrangement until the third chorus, where Patrick sings, *"And I will give up this fight."* The Hullaba-hoos echo, singing *"figh-igh-ight."* When they come back in, they've changed keys, modulating up a half step. The key change is a pop music cliché for a reason (see everything from "The Gambler" to the Kelly Clarkson oeuvre). It happens, famously, in Bon Jovi's "Livin' on a Prayer." If you can't hear it, just watch the video. The key change happens just as wires hoist Jon Bon Jovi into the air like Peter Pan. The key change is the reason why karaoke amateurs fall apart in the final chorus. It's why the solo is suddenly out of their vocal range. The casual listener probably doesn't know what a key change is, but they know how it makes them feel—hopeful. Tonight, Patrick throws in a Christina Aguilera–like trill. He can't help himself. Then he belts *"Ain't no use in tryin', baby."*

When a cappella is done right, it can be awe-inspiring. But when it's done badly, it can make you want to scratch your eyes out. Even if the soloist is phenomenal, it's really all about blend, not just in the notes but with the vowels. And if the background singing is off, if the chord goes flat, the whole thing is sunk. Which is what's so incredible about the Hullabahoos tonight. This is the kind of vocal acrobatics that makes one think, How the hell did they just do that? As Patrick sings, one of the B'hoos steps out from the group and quickly—with his hands in midair—pretends to draw a square box behind Patrick. The B'hoos do this often in a concert. *Box* is a slang term for the female anatomy. And this bit of sign language means that whoever is singing right then just did something so spectacular, so worthy of celebrating, that inevitably that night a stranger will offer him, well, her box.

The Hullabahoos close their two-song set with Marc Broussard's "Home." It starts with an open fifth chord—another musical cliché, this one courtesy of the Academy Award–winning composer James Horner. "He uses it all the time," Pete says. "He does it to make a classical piece sound modern. It's a jazz thing." And if it's good enough for *Titanic*, Pete reasons, it's good enough for the Hullabahoos.

After the show, the boys mingle on the side of the stage, shamelessly flirting with fans. Two freshmen girls corner Patrick. "Are you roommates?" he asks. "*Noooooo,*" one girl says, looking down at her feet awkwardly.

Morgan's girlfriend, Lindsay Friedman, who transferred to UVA as a sophomore, has a unique perspective on the so-called Hullaba-hos. "I understand the impulse," she says, "but as a woman it's hard to see other women throwing themselves at these boys."

CHAPTER FOUR

DIVISI

Wherein the ladies of Divisi struggle with more than
music while the origins of the ICCAs are explained

It seems hard to believe, considering all that has happened since. But when Adam Farb launched the National Championship of Collegiate A Cappella back in 1995 (later the ICCAs), he was worried no one would participate. "Competition just wasn't in the spirit of collegiate a cappella," he says. "A cappella was about goofing off." Farb sang with the Brown Derbies as an undergraduate in the early nineties. He talks about traveling to the Green Eggs and Jam at Washington University, or Smith College's Winter Weekend—big annual concerts where five or six a cappella groups would perform together. The show was never about one-upsmanship, at least not musically. "You were performing for the girls," Farb says. "The ones you were hoping to hook up with."

Competition was, of course, a vital part of a cappella history, notably (if a bit of a non sequitur here) among Zulu tribes in Africa. The men, mostly migrant workers far removed from their families, needed entertainment and camaraderie. And so they'd gather nightly to sing music called *isicathamiya*. In the sixties and seventies, groups like Ladysmith Black Mambazo competed regularly in Saturday-night a cappella competitions in Durban and Johannesburg. It was a mash-up of fashion show (with prizes for the best-dressed man and woman) and vocal competition, which ran through the night, often finishing up after sunrise. If the crowd didn't like the music, well, much like a college crowd at a karaoke bar, they showed their displeasure by noisily drinking through the set.

Farb graduated from Brown in 1994, but he wasn't ready to let a cappella go. He kept coming back to the idea of an a cappella competition. Competing for women was one thing. But score sheets? It felt so foreign to his drunken memories of the Green Eggs and Jam. Why would anybody want to compete? he wondered. Until he hit upon an idea: If he held the finals at Lincoln Center, the *venue* would be the draw.

"People told me I was nuts," Farb says. Which didn't stop him from writing a check for seven thousand dollars to reserve the twenty-seven-hundred-seat Avery Fisher Hall. It would cost thirty-five thousand dollars to produce the finals alone, he figured. Believe it or not, that budget included money to fly in the competing West Coast groups. He'd even include hotel rooms. Farb felt that minimizing (or even eliminating) travel costs was key to the nascent competition's success. He just didn't think a college group was going to pay to fly fifteen members out to New York to compete. How very wrong he would turn out to be.

With Lincoln Center booked, Farb hit the road to spread the word. "I remember trudging through the snow at Cornell in February," Farb says, "promoting one of the first quarterfinal rounds." The big-name a cappella groups turned him down. They didn't have anything to prove. But the younger groups greeted him with open arms. And Farb embraced the adulation. "I was twenty-three years old," Farb says. "I had long hair. I was like a rock star."

If the National Championship of Collegiate A Cappella was going to stay true to its roots, Farb felt strongly that there be very few rules. These days, each group is allotted exactly twelve minutes onstage. The clock begins, according to the guidebook, from "the first musical idea." Whatever that means. But that first year was practically anarchy by comparison. "We even let the groups do skits," Farb says. (These skits actually inspired an ill-fated album, *Wasting Our Parents' Money: The Best of College A Cappella Humor*, released in October of 1999, featuring tracks like "Taco Bell Canon," by Michigan's Amazin' Blue, and "Walk of Shame," by Connecticut College's Williams Street Mix.) The judging itself was similarly lax. Farb and his cofounder, Deke Sharon (more of an idea man in this operation), had similar philosophies on judging a cappella. "Music is so subjective," Farb says. Whatever system you use, he figured, didn't really matter as long as the results made sense. As long as the audience didn't leave thinking, How did *that* group win? And so they kept the process intentionally vague. There were no score sheets, no points for choreography, intonation, or repertoire. The judges just picked the group they liked the best. Even the name for the tournament was a joke. They called it the National Championship of Collegiate A Cappella, or the NCCAs. "It was a takeoff on the NCAAs," Deke Sharon says. "We wanted it to be like March Madness. No one cares about college basketball at any other time of the year. But they obsess over March Madness. We wanted that kind of exposure for a cappella."

The first finals were held in the spring of 1996, and it came down to the UNC Loreleis and the Yale Duke's Men. (Footnote: Ask a member of the Tufts Beelzebubs why they don't compete anymore and they'll tell you it's because they won the first-ever ICCAs in 1993, but for the record, that was a wholly separate competition.) Farb still remembers the first year of the NCCAs, how Catalina Joos from the Loreleis tore through "Fame." The Duke's Men, meanwhile, were more in the Ivy League tradition of close harmony eschewing pop music for barbershop standards.

Farb had lined up four judges for Lincoln Center, including Paul Pampinella from the pro a cappella group Vox One. Unfortunately, when it came time to vote, the judges were split down the middle. The Whiffenpoofs performed while the judges deliberated—and the Whiffs were running out of material. But the four were deadlocked. "They would not budge," Farb says. "We'd never had this problem at the earlier shows, where we had three judges." It came down to a choice between contemporary a cappella and barbershop, pop versus classic. In the end, Farb would cast the deciding vote—a fact that has remained largely a secret until now. "I never thought we'd have an all-female group win the whole thing," Farb said. Neither did the Duke's Men, who were outraged when Farb crowned the UNC Loreleis the first-ever champions of the NCCAs.

Farb sold nearly a thousand tickets that night and just about broke even. More importantly, the NCCAs had momentum. The morning after the show, Farb called Lincoln Center to book the hall for the following spring. No luck. They were booked—solid. But Carnegie Hall *was* available. More than just the venue would change that second year. Farb and the NCCAs had sponsored the first after-party. "I was buying kegs," Farb says. "But my insurance guy told me I couldn't do that anymore. There was a lot of liability. I started to realize this was a business."

By the third year Farb was selling twenty-three hundred tickets to the finals. He'd make upward of thirty thousand dollars off that show. Even the earlier rounds were coming close to selling out, in venues as varied as five hundred seats to two thousand seats. But Farb started to notice something. "The encores were almost always better than the competition sets," Farb says, "because the groups were relaxed. They got to sing with their hair down. They'd tell jokes. They'd be goofballs. It was much closer to the spirit of a cappella." Farb never imagined that a collegiate a cappella group would spend an entire semester perfecting three songs. But that's what happened. For better or worse, Farb says, "the competition had legs."

It's worth noting: No all-female group has won the competition since that first year. Which brings us back to Divisi and the fall of 2006.

That Michaela Cordova worked summers at Urban Outfitters shouldn't come as much of a surprise. When a girl grows up in Portland reading skateboarding magazines, dying her hair black, and collecting piercings, Urban Outfitters is sort of like the mothership calling its disaffected youth home. Michaela had always known she could sing. She'd gone to private school as a kid, a hippie eat-paste-if-you-got-it institution where students call their teachers by their first names. In kindergarten, Delilah (her teacher) pulled little Michaela aside. "You have the voice of an angel!" she said. Michaela, in her darkest moments (of which there have been many of late), often thinks back to this moment.

The girl was a born performer. There's a famous Cordova family photo of a three-year-old Michaela playing Snow White. She'd walked into the family room, taken a bite out of an apple, and dramatically dropped to the floor. At age twelve, Michaela cashed her first professional paycheck as an extra on the set of *The Hunted,* a Benicio Del Toro vehicle. Benicio made seven figures; Michaela made twelve fifty an hour. Still, she was hooked. Michaela later starred as Eponine in her high school's production of *Les Misérables.* (Don't use the word *amateur*—the school has a revolving set.)

When it came time to apply to college, Michaela chose a handful of music conservatories. But some personal problems— an eating disorder, depression—had over time ravaged her confidence. Her mother had long insisted on a backup plan, which is how Michaela ended up at the University of Oregon.

As fate would have it, Michaela's onetime *Les Misérables* co-star, Brenton Agena, had gone to Oregon too. While Michaela spent freshman year quietly putting herself back together, Brenton joined the all-male a cappella group On the Rocks. When Michaela finally came up for air, Brenton convinced her to audition for Divisi. And, well, you couldn't miss her that day in the fall of 2006. For one thing, she rode up to the music building on her skateboard, dressed in pencil-thin jeans and a hoodie. Then there was the copy of *Transworld Skateboarding* magazine she pulled from her bag. "The other girls were wearing skirts," Michaela says. "I felt like such a douche." Exactly one girl talked to her that day. "She was like, 'What are you reading?' It was nice of her to pretend she was interested." Michaela had a cold that day. Rather than make excuses—not her style—she auditioned with Fiona Apple's "Sullen Girl," which played to her suddenly bluesy pipes. The women of Divisi could look past the lip ring. This girl was too good to pass up.

That very same afternoon, Andrea Welsh showed up at Michaela's room to take the newest member of Divisi shopping for the group's uniform—a black tuxedo shirt, black pinstripe pants, signature red tie, and pearl earrings. Andrea talked the whole way. "Are you *excited*?" she said, pausing to take a sip of tea from her silver travel mug. "I hope you are. Because we're *really* excited to have you. You're excited, right? I knew you would be!" It wasn't an act. Andrea Welsh was excited about being a new member herself, having been accepted into Divisi just a few months earlier, in May, at the end of her own freshman year.

Some days, Andrea can't believe she's really wearing Divisi's red necktie, that she's actually one of the ladies. Women, ladies—call them anything but *girls*. "Girls," Andrea says, shaking her head. That's what's wrong with female a cappella. "That it sounds *girly*. We're women!" At the Spring Show last year, just a few days after joining Divisi herself, Andrea Welsh sat in the back row of the Trinity United Methodist Church in Eugene alongside the other new girls. The crowd was standing-room only, a testament to both Divisi's popularity and their poor planning. (The ladies had printed—and sold—more than eight hundred tickets; the church seated far fewer.) Toward the end of the show, the brand-new members of Divisi were invited to join the group on-stage for one song. Andrea's heart was pounding. "You don't understand," she says. "When they invited us new girls up, the entire audience turned around to look at us. You could feel the wind!" Together they sang John Lennon's "Imagine." Everyone but Andrea, anyway. "I mouthed the whole thing," she says. Blame nerves. She couldn't get a note out. Andrea has since found her place in the group—she's very quickly become Divisi's den mother. (She has been known to cut up crudités for short car trips, you know, in case the girls get hungry.) This is as good a time as any to reveal that Andrea Welsh has never once uttered the F-word. Not even to herself. Not even in private. "I just don't see the point of using that word," she says matter-of-factly. Andrea will, however, cop to sipping alcohol now and again—though only pink champagne.

If Michaela Cordova and Andrea Welsh seem like polar opposites, well, welcome to the new Divisi.

Though Sarah Klein, one of just two girls who remain of the original Divisi squad, has been running the show for a few months now, she hasn't yet grown into the role of disciplinarian. (It's Keeley McCowan—the other vet—who regularly plays bad cop.) Where Lisa Forkish had been definitive and exact, Sarah too often asks the girls what they think. And, so far, they're taking advantage of her easy-breezy attitude. In October, Divisi was invited to perform in a night of barbershop, a fund-raiser at the Hillsboro Armory outside Portland. It was a two-hour drive (not good), but when the organizers offered to pay Divisi five hundred dollars they consented. The ladies of Divisi were on their own in terms of scheduling. Sarah merely said: "Be at the Armory at seven P.M."

At seven-fifteen, one car was still missing. Divisi was due on-stage momentarily. Backstage in the Armory's dirty locker room the rest of Divisi applied their paint-thick lipstick.

"My throat's dry," one girl said.

"Try biting the back of your tongue," Sarah Klein said. "It's an old choir trick." A cell phone goes off to the tune of Justin Timberlake's "Sexy Back."

"Someone's bringing sexy back," one of the girls says. Sarah seethes, pulling her own cell phone from her bag and dialing. She is passive-aggressive by nature. She doesn't so much confront the girl as sigh with intention. Sarah: "Are you close? [*sigh*]"

The final car showed up two minutes before showtime. And while the rift was imperceptible to the audience, the ladies of Divisi weren't really themselves that night. They'd staked their reputation on their sound, but they were limp. For the first time since the group's founding, Sarah Klein sees a deep divide. And the mishap at the armory, she says, was proof that the group was not on the same page. "That never would have happened when Lisa was in charge," she says. It wasn't just that one car was late. It was the fact that the rest of Divisi didn't seem to care. *Sigh.*

Keeley McCowan was less polite. Keeley, who is in her fifth year, works the early shift at one of Eugene's finer restaurants. She'd been awake since four that morning. Worse, she was diet-ing. If she could show up—not just show up but *perform*—why couldn't these new girls?

If Divisi was going to compete in the ICCAs again (and they were, that had already been decided by Keeley and Sarah last spring before most of these girls were even in the group), they'd need to be a cohesive squad. And so Keeley and Sarah were particularly excited when, in October, Divisi was invited to perform at the University of Anchorage's annual A Cappella Festivella. While members of a sorority might bond at charity events or toga parties, a cappella groups have the luxury of getting acquainted on elaborate trips. And this one would be a five-day, four-night affair—all expenses paid. In Alaska, the girls conducted a beatboxing workshop. They sang five songs at the festival—the only five songs they knew. "We were so new," says Rachelle Wofford, an intense sophomore. "We didn't even have choreography." But the music wasn't really the point. Keeley and Sarah hoped the group would find some common ground.

There was the bonfire down at the beach. There were late nights at the hotel. Invariably the conversations turned personal. And that's when Michaela Cordova pulled back—when her old fears and doubts surfaced. It was a particularly difficult, tense moment. Michaela (by her own admission) never got along well with women. But this was different. "We were being so silly," she says. "We were sitting around with high ponytails on top of our heads, just acting ridiculous. It was so liberating to be goofy with this group of girls I'd just met." But on her last night in Alaska she quietly left the hotel room. "I was respectful," she says. "It's just hard for me to talk about my feelings. I don't want to say my life's been harder than everyone else's. But I had to remove myself." Which she did. Quietly the other girls wondered what had spooked Michaela.

There were highlights. Sometime that week, Divisi's new catchphrase was born. At the hotel, messing around on the Internet, the girls stumbled across a YouTube video in which a transvestite goes shopping for shoes. The whole thing plays out over a techno beat, with the tranny uttering (again and again, in various inflections) the word *shoes*. The women of Divisi adopted the phrase and made it their own. And defying logic, *Shoes* became their battle cry.

Alaska had been a step in the right direction (well, maybe not for Michaela), but despite *shoes*, the girls remained fractured, cliquey even, during the fall of 2006. As a countermeasure, Sarah introduced Thursday-night bonding sessions, but even Keeley admits you can't force these things. "Just because you're wearing the tie and the red lipstick doesn't make you Divisi," she says. She pauses. "I almost hope we lose at the ICCAs so the new girls will learn what it takes to be competitive."

Divisi worked on refining their competition set that fall, which included Stevie Wonder's "Don't You Worry 'Bout a Thing," "Hide and Seek" by Imogen Heap, and a Joss Stone power anthem, "You Had Me." Divisi worked on little else. Still, the disparate personalities, the relaxed leadership—Lisa Forkish would have been embarrassed.

At the final Friday-afternoon performance before winter break, Divisi got a glimpse of just how much work was left to be done before the ICCAs in January. "Hide and Seek" was consistently flat. "Don't You Worry 'Bout a Thing" sounded like noise—a bunch of unrelated notes that never really locked. The applause was tepid.

"What key were we in?" Keeley asked after the show.

"G," Sarah said.

It was a rhetorical question. "I meant we weren't singing together," Keeley said. Worse: On the Rocks, the all-male group on campus and Divisi's brother group—who would be their primary competition for the first round of the ICCAs—burned the house down. OTR's music director, wearing a satin On the Rocks jacket, stepped forward to make a joke. "We have On the Rocks T-shirts for sale after the show," he said to the crowd. "But these jackets…they're Members Only."

After watching the On the Rocks set, Keeley turned to the ladies of Divisi. Two groups from that first round of the ICCA competition would advance to the regional semifinals. "I guess we'll be second," she said. The ICCAs were starting to look like just another gig on Divisi's calendar. Or maybe not.

A few days before leaving for winter break, the girls threw a very Divisi Christmas party at Emmalee Almroth's house. (Emmalee, one of the new girls, has been listening to Divisi and On the Rocks since she was in high school, and some nights, when the girls are hanging out with the boys of OTR, she still can't believe she's actually there.) Divisi organized Secret Santa—ten dollars or less—and each girl quietly placed her gift beneath the Christmas tree. But Keeley had her own game planned for that night. In a last-ditch effort to light a fire under the new girls, she'd brought the competition video with her, the one with Lisa Forkish and Divisi performing Usher's "Yeah." She popped it into the computer. It was eye-opening. Andrea Welsh, sipping her pink champagne, kept getting close to the screen and then stepping away again. "I'm so nervous," she said. She didn't use the F-word, but she was probably thinking it.

Keeley saw the look in their eyes. And it wasn't hunger—it was fear. Unfortunately, the one girl who might have inspired Divisi to rise to the challenge felt too out of place that night to say much of anything.

Marissa Neitling, a fifth-year, is petite, with big bangs and bigger eyes. She's a modern-day Mary Tyler Moore. Wacky things just sort of happen to her. Like freshman year, when she accidentally wound up living in the university's lone designated twenty-four-hour-quiet dorm. "I was this little bubbly girl who likes to stay up late," she says, "and I was living with these superquiet kids." She joined Divisi in the victory lap year—the year after the ICCAs—and she loved it. Lisa Forkish was still running things. Even though Divisi wasn't competing, "the hard work came first," Marissa says. "Then the friendships."

There was so much Marissa wanted to say that night at the Christmas party—about unity, about the old Divisi, about what the new Divisi could be. "My mom always says to me, I've been your age but you haven't been mine," Marissa says. "And that's how I felt." But because Marissa is too polite, because she felt some of the new girls might misinterpret what she had to say, she kept quiet. Besides, having missed so much rehearsal herself that semester—she'd landed a featured role in the campus production of Sondheim's *Company*—she wasn't sure she'd earned the right to say anything.

There was more to the story, of course, more going on behind the bangs.

Marissa had been a precocious kid, always more of a tiny adult than a child. When she was in the first grade, she was called down to the principal's office. "Your mother is here to pick you up," the receptionist said. Marissa's eyes welled up with tears. Her grandfather had been sick and now, walking out to her mom's car, she feared the worst. "What happened?" Marissa said, opening the passenger-side door. "Get in quick!" her mom replied. "We're going to miss the two-thirty showing of *Edward Scissorhands*."

Which sort of explains how Marissa ended up double-majoring in math and theater. Growing up, Marissa always loved to perform. She's had many music teachers over the years, and they've all said the same thing: *Don't think, just sing.* But quieting that analytical part of her brain, giving herself over to the performance entirely—that's always been Marissa's problem.

This 2006–2007 year is Marissa's final in Eugene, and she's at work on her thesis—an autobiographical one-woman show that includes (among other things) the story of an ex-boyfriend, the first love who broke her heart in the way only that first one can, the one who just seven months after the breakup was already married. (He is Mormon.) But mostly, the play she is writing is about acceptance, about letting go.

Ten years ago, Marissa's dad, a brilliant orthopedic surgeon, had his license suspended. The official report said he'd been diverting all sorts of medication from his patients, which was another way of saying he was an addict, smart enough to get drugs any way he could. But he went into a recovery program. And, just as suddenly it seemed, life proceeded, the incident destined to be just a footnote in Marissa's childhood. Or so the family hoped. But in the summer of 2004 the dark times returned. Her father went to rehab again. It was terrible for all involved. Because the man was a highly functioning addict, he'd actually convinced his co-workers that his wife and kids were crazy. "We were the *bad people*," Marissa's mom says. He closed his practice—having lost his license, he had no other choice. And in February of 2005, without much warning, he served his wife with separation papers. Now, after rehearsals for *Company*, and her class work, and Divisi, there's that manuscript on Marissa's computer, that one-woman show about this man she no longer knows, this man she has not seen in over a year.

On the night of the Divisi Christmas party, Marissa Neitling finally breaks down. It's not what you think. "I don't know what *shoes* means!" she blurts out. Marissa had missed the trip to Alaska. Someone clicks over to YouTube and shows her the video. And the conversation returns—as it often does—to the ICCAs.

Keeley McCowan attempts to rally the troops. Forget the video. She's enlisted the help of Lisa Forkish and Erica Barkett, legendary Divisi alums who will come back to campus in January to work with the girls on their competition set. Keeley has the best of intentions. But what she doesn't know, what she can't foresee, is that this, too, will end in tears.

CHAPTER FIVE

*Wherein we pull back to explain the collegiate a cappella
explosion of the late nineties, meet the self-proclaimed
father of contemporary a cappella, and find out how
an a cappella album can possibly be overproduced*

Deke Sharon is commonly referred to as the father of contemporary a cappella, and while he may have bestowed that
title upon himself, the name rings true. In 1990, Deke started the
Contemporary A Cappella Society of America (CASA) out of his
dorm room at Tufts. The organization's mission was (in part) to
foster communication between all of the disparate a cappella
groups popping up across the country. CASA began with the
"Collegiate A Cappella Newsletter," which featured album reviews and classified ads, where groups like the Bubs would offer
their services to other schools. Like everything in a cappella, the
newsletter was better known by an acronym, the "CAN." (Letters to the editor were printed under the rubric KICK THE CAN.)
When Deke graduated, so, too, did the "CAN," which quickly expanded to include coverage of the professional a cappella scene,
where groups like Rockapella (which grew out of the Brown University High Jinks) were suddenly thriving, touring as far as Ja-
pan. "The Collegiate A Cappella Newsletter" was reborn as "The
Contemporary A Cappella Newsletter," so as to keep the acronym. "The only reason this whole movement isn't called *modern*
a cappella," Deke says, "is because I needed to use the letter C."

In 1992, Deke founded the Contemporary A Cappella Recording Awards—the CARAs. He started the ICCAs (then the NCCAs) with Adam Farb in 1995. He and Adam also created the BOCA series—the Best of College A Cappella compilation. If there's an acronym in a cappella, Deke Sharon probably had something to do with it.

In the mid-nineties, collegiate a cappella exploded from an Ivy League curiosity to a full-blown coed pursuit. "We went from two hundred and fifty groups to more than twelve hundred and fifty," Deke says. He credits the growth spurt to a number of factors, from Boyz II Men to the Internet. Deke's role is easier to quantify. While collegiate a cappella groups everywhere were singing four-part harmony reminiscent of the choral tradition, he began arranging music instead for a vocal band. In short, it was the difference between a bunch of guys singing an A chord or a bunch of guys singing the guitar part. This innovation might have remained a local phenomenon had Deke not figured out a way to get the music played on campuses across the country.

While Deke may be a critical figure in contemporary a cappella, as an undergraduate at Tufts, the kid was rejected by the Beelzebubs. Twice.

Deke grew up in the Bay Area, a kid musician who once sang with Pavarotti at the San Francisco Opera in a production of *Turandot*. On weekends he'd troll the aisles at Revolver Records in the Haight, picking up recordings by a cappella groups like the Nylons. In what would be a seminal moment in his life, the Tufts Beelzebubs performed at Deke's high school. Deke bought one of their LPs, *Score*, which he wore out playing "Ticket to Ride" and "Rainy Day Man." A few years later, he enrolled at Tufts. And he was hard to miss. As a freshman in a sea of khaki, he was the kid in the orange T-shirt and leather *man*dals. "I was from northern California!" he says.

The Bubs have a standard form they fill out for each prospective kid who auditions. At the bottom of the sheet there's a line drawing of a penis. Or, rather, two penises—one erect, one flaccid. It's Bubs shorthand. If they like a kid and want to see him again, they circle the erect penis. If the kid is rejected, he gets the flaccid penis. Neither was circled on Deke's audition sheet. The Bubs called him back, but they weren't yet ready to award him the erect penis. Why? He was too much of a fan. This was the era of the Bubs as comedians, and the guys were more interested in making people laugh than impressing them with their music. "And I came across as a total snot," Deke says. He actually stopped his own audition to correct himself. "I sang a B instead of an A," he said. "It worked in the chord, but it was wrong." Deke was rejected a second time that spring. Finally, in the fall of his sophomore year, he was accepted—only after his roommate (a Beelzebub) vouched for him. "Deke's not insane," the guy testified. "He's just *eager*." Nine months later, in the spring of 1988, Deke was elected music director of the Bubs. And the changes he made there would impact all of collegiate a cappella.

It started with a movie. Deke Sharon saw *Say Anything* on opening weekend—April 14, 1989. When John Cusack stood in the rain with the boom box above his head, blasting Peter Gabriel's "In Your Eyes," Deke knew he was seeing something big. "It was this obvious canonical moment," he says. But how, exactly, could the Bubs *do* that song? "In Your Eyes" wasn't built for the kind of four-part harmony the Bubs (and everyone else in collegiate a cappella) had been singing. But he didn't want it to sound choral. Deke had an idea. He pulled a blank piece of orchestral paper from his desk, the kind of paper with musical staffs running clear down the page. "I imagined I was arranging the song for a vocal orchestra," Deke says, breaking the song down by instrument. The first tenors would become the synthesizer, the second tenors the lead guitar. It was nothing short of a "Helen Keller at the well" moment. "Multiple standing ovations," Deke recalls of the response.

This change in arranging style—from choral to multi-textured—opened up doors (or the Doors) for the Bubs. Back then, collegiate a cappella groups performed the same music, classics like "The Lion Sleeps Tonight" and "In the Still of the Night." It was like *Name That Tune,* Deke says. "We would sit in the back row of a show at UPenn and within the first three notes we'd know what the song was." But the Bubs could suddenly do Prince. Adam Farb, who sang with the Brown Derbies in the early nineties and went on to create the ICCAs with Deke, remembers the first time he heard the new Bubs sound. "It was like the invention of rock 'n' roll," Farb says. "When the doo-wop groups first heard rock 'n' roll, they were like, We could do *this*? Why are we doing this doo-wop shit?" The innovations continued. The Bubs soon introduced vocal percussion—the beatbox. Deke arranged a song for the Derbies. The Derbies saw the vocal percussion written out on the page but didn't quite grasp what the notation meant. "The Derbies would be like, 'You want me to sing *Doof ka doof ka doof ka*?'" Farb says. "'I don't get it.'"

Deke went on to arrange "Rio" by Duran Duran that same way. He arranged Pink Floyd's "Comfortably Numb." The Bubs took their act on the road, and they were cleaning up. Now, it's important to remember that this happened pre-Internet. The revolution (and it was a revolution) might have remained close to home had it not been for the Bubs' incessant touring schedule. The Bubs were the rare collegiate group that would pile into a van, then drive overnight to schools like UNC and Duke to sing five songs. The Bubs kept a continuously updated file of contact information for some two hundred collegiate a cappella groups nationwide. (The list was later augmented with help from Rex Solomon, perhaps the collegiate genre's first superfan, who kept his own continuously updated database.) The Bubs wrote in to the CAN. "We have a solid willingness to party," one letter read. They were doing eight road trips every semester. "We were the *Animal House* of a cappella," Deke says. Not surprisingly, Deke met his wife, Katy, on a road trip. She sang with Duke's premier all-female a cappella group, Out of the Blue. Still, there were only so many road trips the Bubs could squeeze into a semester. It would take a Trojan horse to spread the love.

In early December 1989, the Bubs invited the Princeton Katzen-jammers and Penn's Pennsylvania Six-5000 (among others) to perform on campus at Goddard Chapel. They contracted Bill Allen, Bubs '83, then a sound engineer in New York, to record the show—which they'd release as a live album, *The Beelzebubs Winter Invitational MCMLXXXIX*. And it wouldn't cost the Bubs a dime. The business model was genius. The Bubs convinced each of the four guest groups to buy four hundred albums at five dollars apiece—which basically covered the cost of recording and pressing the album. More than a moneymaker, it was a way to bring Beelzebubs music into the homes of unsuspecting Princeton students. (There was precedent: RCA Records had dabbled with a similar format way back in 1964 with a record called *Campus Hootenanny*—recorded live at Brown University and featuring five or six collegiate a cappella groups. "Disciplined and dedicated—and what a sound!" according to the liner notes.)

The Best of College A Cappella (BOCA) series was inspired by the *Winter Invitational*. Each edition of BOCA, now available on iTunes, regularly sells close to five thousand copies—a not-insignificant number. In the music business, if an indie band sells ten thousand copies of an album, it's considered a success. Adam Farb and Deke Sharon never imagined the beast that BOCA would become. But suddenly, groups across the country could hear what their contemporaries were doing. Or more specifically, *how* they were doing it. There was a side effect to all of this sharing, the spawning of a new industry: the big-time (horribly expensive) a cappella producer. Deke Sharon actually likens the amping up of collegiate a cappella recording to the Soviet arms race.

In many ways, the history of collegiate a cappella recording is the Bill Hare story. Bill Hare is sort of like the Dr. Dre of a cappella recording. He charges one hundred and twenty-five dollars an hour on weekends, one hundred and five dollars during the week. And the only thing he can't do, he says, when it comes to a soundboard is make a crappy soloist outstanding. "But you can make a crappy soloist sound OK!" he says.

It's not like he set out to revolutionize a cappella recording. When the Stanford Mendicants walked into Bill Hare's studio in northern California in the late eighties, he didn't know what to make of them. "It was strange," Bill says. "A glee club singing the Police!" He described their sound as "weird and dull." Still, Bill Hare was recording a lot of hair bands back in the day, not to mention beatnik jazz groups, and the Mendicants were paying cash. And so they made an album together, *Aquapella*. The Mendicants, in turn, referred other a cappella groups to Bill Hare, but still, he didn't think much of all this. "I didn't even know there were a cappella groups outside of Stanford," he says. "I just thought it was this weird thing happening here."

One day Bill had a simple thought that would (in not so simple ways) change the way people recorded collegiate a cappella music. Deke had begun arranging music for a vocal band. Similarly, Bill Hare realized, if the baritones were singing a guitar line, why not mic them like a guitar? Previously he'd just placed the groups around one microphone and hit Record. Suddenly he was running a microphone through a guitar amp. The first Mendicants album cost seven hundred and fifty dollars to produce and was recorded in a couple of days. This second album cost three thousand dollars and took much longer. But the difference in the sound was immeasurable. One day Bill Hare got a handwritten letter from some guy out in Boston who was starting the Contemporary A Cappella Society of America. It was Deke Sharon. Deke had heard the Mendicants album and was impressed. "I couldn't believe someone in Boston had heard this album," Bill Hare says. He finally began to see the growth potential of collegiate a cappella.

Home recording—the advent of the desktop program Pro Tools and others—would drastically change the recording landscape both for indie artists and collegiate a cappella groups. Bill saw the writing on the wall. "In the seventies and eighties, you needed a hundred-thousand-dollar investment—minimum—to get a quasi-professional-sounding studio," he says. By 1996, you could get the same results with a desktop computer, adding distortion, or dropping an octave with the stroke of a key. It was all digital. He'd also stopped recording groups all together—sixteen students at a time, say—recording them instead individually. And so Bill sold his huge studio and downgraded to a smaller space. The breakthrough album, he says, was the 1999 Stanford Harmonics disc, *Insanity Laughs*. "That's when vocal percussion really started to sound more like a drum set than vocals," Bill says. The challenge was invigorating. It was also lucrative. At this point Bill was making more money in a cappella than he could have ever made recording hair bands. "I had a student who used to drive up to the studio in an Aston Martin," he says.

Bill Hare would become the most influential a cappella producer in the business, landing tracks on every BOCA album since the series launched in 1995. "When I was first starting out," says James Gammon, who records with the Hullabahoos, "I would listen to albums that Bill had mixed and I'd try to figure out how he did it."

The competition to land a track on BOCA is fierce. As such, a cottage industry has sprung up around collegiate a cappella. A handful of producers—guys like Freddie Feldman of Vocomotion in Evanston, Dave Sperandio of diovoce in Chapel Hill—now make a living solely producing collegiate a cappella music. Tat Tong, an alum of Cornell University's Last Call, actually lives and works overseas in Asia, corresponding with his groups in the States via e-mail, posting unedited tracks on an FTP site. There's Ed Boyer and John Clark of CB Productions—both Tufts alums (from the Bubs and the Amalgamates, respectively). These producers often e-mail with one another, comparing notes, discussing new talent. But it's not all, ahem, collegial, and a healthy rivalry has sprung up. Freddie Feldman, an alum of the Northwestern group Purple Haze, takes issue with Boyer and Clark. "Those two over–Auto-Tune," he says. "It's too processed for my taste." The height of this crime, he says, is the Hyannis Sound album *Route 6*. "If you're just processing cover tunes to sound like the original," Freddie says, "you might as well just listen to the original." When the BOCA 2007 set list was released, featuring some collegiate a cappella groups no one had ever heard of before, some quietly started to wonder if hiring a guy like Bill Hare wasn't just buying a spot on BOCA.

If it sounds far-fetched, think harder. A cappella recording isn't happening in a bubble. In fact, the same complaints that have plagued the legit music industry (overproduction, Auto-Tune) have spilled over into collegiate a cappella. For years, major-label producers, artists, and executives have been fighting the so-called Volume Wars. Even Bob Dylan weighed in, telling *Rolling Stone* in 2005, "You listen to these modern records, they're atrocious, they have sound all over them. There's no definition of nothing, no vocal, no nothing, just like—static." To oversimplify matters, the Volume Wars comes down to compression, one of the last steps in mastering an album. Compression eliminates a lot of the dynamics in a recording making everything even—and loud. Compression brings the song to the foreground and gives it that in-your-face feel. Back when engineers were still working with LPs, there was a limit to how far you could compress a song; if you pushed too hard, the needle would pop out of the groove. Bob Dylan's complaint (and he's right) is that the brain can't process supercompressed sounds for too long. Without dynamics—without some soft to balance the loud—the ears get fatigued. (When people say they love vinyl, this is what they mean.) Big Music is convinced louder records sell more copies. Apparently, a cappella producers agree (or at least have recalibrated their ears to match the industry standard). "I've noticed that Dio's albums are the loudest," says Bill Hare, calling out Dave Sperandio of diovoce (and an alum of the UNC Clef Hangers).

This new sound—arranging music for a vocal band, recording like a band—contributed to the explosion in collegiate a cappella. It was one thing to sing "In the Still of the Night." It was quite another to go to a professional recording studio and lay down your own version of Radiohead's "High & Dry." In the mid-nineties the number of a cappella groups on U.S. collegiate soil spiked. Today, the list is conservatively numbered at twelve hundred and fifty—up from three hundred just fifteen years ago. And they are a diverse bunch. Take Penn Masala, an early Hindi a cappella group. Or ReMix, an R & B a cappella group at UVA. There are many Jewish a cappella groups, including Pizmon at Columbia. Mayim Bialik, aka television's Blossom, started her own Jewish a cappella group at UCLA. They called themselves Shir Bruin. Yes, Shir Bruin was a pun. *Shir* (pronounced *sheer*) is the Hebrew word meaning "song"; Bruin is the UCLA mascot. The group sang mostly traditional Jewish music, but Mayim had a sense of humor about the whole thing. She arranged a medley of Madonna's "Like a Prayer," Bon Jovi's "Livin' on a Prayer," and a spiritual, "T'filah" (the word means "prayer" in Hebrew). Being observant Jews—and still trying to gig on weekends—proved challenging for the members of Shir Bruin. Jewish law prohibits the use of instruments on the Sabbath, and the pitch pipe (which all a cappella groups use to get their starting note) is considered an instrument. Shir Bruin had a crafty solution. When you open and close a metal *kippah* clip—the sort of bobby pin that keeps a yarmulka on a guy's head—it makes a noise. Or rather, a musical note. "The kippah clip opens on, like, an F-sharp or something," Mayim says, laughing. On the Sabbath, this is how they found their starting pitch.

CHAPTER SIX

THE HULLABAHOOS

*Wherein the Hullabahoos' origin story unfolds and
the 2006–2007 lineup spends a chauffeur-driven
weekend in Portland*

The Hullabahoos may be rising stars in the world of collegiate a cappella. But their founder, Halsted Sullivan, is surprised the group still exists. "The Hullabahoos almost folded after our first semester," he says.

A cappella groups frequently talk about their founders in hushed tones—as if these mystical men were endowed with some divinity. The Hullabahoos are no different. The current members of the B'hoos (even the ones who've never met Halsted) can recount stories of this man's undergraduate sexual conquests—in unfortunate, graphic detail, often without prompting. The truth is, more often than not, these founders of a cappella groups were not divine, but rather rejects from existing a cappella groups. "That's right," says Halsted Sullivan, UVA class of 1989. "I was rejected from the Virginia Gentlemen. Twice." Mark Lyons—the first music director of the Hullabahoos—was rejected from the VGs too.

Despite the dismissal, Halsted was determined to sing in an a cappella group. And if the Virginia Gentlemen (a subset of the UVA glee club) wouldn't have him, well, he'd start his own. In the fall of 1987, with the blessing of the music department, Halsted made his move. He placed an announcement in the school paper, *The Cavalier Daily*, that read, simply, CAN YOU SING IN THE SHOWER? The ad stressed the fact that, unlike the Virginia Gentlemen, this new a cappella group wouldn't require its members to join the glee club. In fact, reading music would be strictly optional. The first auditions were held at Cabell Hall in January of 1988 and interest was tepid. Halsted actually had to fill the sign-up sheet with fake names. "I wanted to *prime the pump*," he says. (Not a surprise, really, that Halsted would use a Reaganite phrase; his father had been the secretary of health and human services in President Bush I's cabinet.) Despite the low turnout, Halsted was impressed with the talent that did show up. Though he admits they accepted a few guys who blatantly couldn't sing. "We called them *bait*," Mark Lyons says. "They were the good-looking guys."

Halsted and Mark wanted the Hullabahoos to be different from the Virginia Gentlemen, they just didn't know exactly how. And so the two took a road trip—a reconnaissance mission, if you will—to the Cherry Tree Massacre, an annual a cappella festival put on by the Georgetown Chimes since 1974. There, the Hullabahoos would find their inspiration in a visiting a cappella group from Cornell University, Cayuga's Waiters, a group that wore jeans and tie-dye T-shirts. It was nothing short of revelatory. "The Waiters matched," Halsted says, "but weren't *identical*. And they had this fantastic energy." They were, he says, cool.

On the drive back to Charlottesville, Halsted and Mark debated stealing the tie-dye thing. But the Hullabahoos weren't sold on the idea. One of the new guys, Andy Erickson, suggested white tie and tails instead. That wasn't quite right either. In the end they settled on multicolored robes, inspired by an honor society at Sewanee: the University of the South. With a two-thousand-dollar grant from the student senate's appropriations committee, they promptly spent six hundred dollars on handmade robes from an upscale fabric shop on Barracks Road in downtown Charlottes-ville. Mark's robe was red and gold. Halsted's was a royal-blue plaid. It was a risk. "We looked like Color Me Badd," Halsted says.

Now they just needed a name. Not surprisingly, they considered an embarrassing number of puns. Someone suggested the Rotoondas—a takeoff on the campus's signature piece of architecture, the rotunda. What about the Poe Boys? (Edgar Allan Poe was a UVA alum.) The Harmonticellos? (Jefferson's residence, ten miles away, was Monticello.) The Jeffersongs, anybody? Halsted opened up the dictionary to the letter *H*. He was looking for some play on 'Hoos, as in the UVA Wahoos—a campus nickname dating back to the late 1800s. (Though any UVA student will proudly tell you that a *wahoo* is a fish that can drink twice its body weight, it seems the name actually originated with a Dartmouth cheer, Wah-Hoo-Wah.) Halsted came across the word *hullabaloo*—meaning "a din or uproar." And so the Hullabahoos were born.

Halsted was a conscientious founder and sent typewritten letters to a cappella groups around the country asking for advice. One group wrote back, "No Gilbert & Sullivan." Another sent the Hullabahoos an arrangement of Squeeze's "Black Coffee in Bed." At their first rehearsal, the B'hoos learned "At the Hop." Then came Billy Joel's "For the Longest Time." They were quick, easy arrangements, which was good, because the Hullabahoos had just booked their first high-profile gig. They would be the guest group for the Virginia Belles, the university's all-female a cappella group.

It would be the Hullabahoos' first legit university performance, though the show proved memorable for more than the music. "Phil Byers," Halsted says, "broke his leg onstage." It had something to do with the choreography. Halsted was too excited to care. After taking a bow, he told Phil to put himself on the bus to the UVA hospital.

The show had been a success, but the Hullabahoos were still fighting the popular perception (not entirely unfounded) that they were nothing more than Virginia Gentlemen's leftovers. Complicating matters, Mark Lyons (their music director) was graduating. Fearing the worst, three of the Hullabahoos secretly auditioned for the VGs—and got in. Halsted couldn't blame them for seeking other options. "The Hullabahoos were too much of an unknown quantity," he says. Even Halsted auditioned for the VGs again! But he withdrew his name.

When the B'hoos returned to campus in the fall of 1988, their numbers had whittled down to just five. Chris Walker, then a second-year, stepped into the role of music director. No one knew Chris could read music, let alone that he was a prodigy. Salvation was nigh. In December, at Garrett Hall, the B'hoos held their first Christmas show. They even had Yuletide robes made. "It was a *Peanuts* pattern," Halsted says. More impressively, they draped themselves in Christmas lights and extension cords. There was one problem. "Two songs in," Halstead says, "the lights started to burn through the robes."

The group's profile continued to grow, and it soon became popular for women on campus to steal the robes after bedding a Hullabahoo. Perhaps feeling the pressure of their new on-campus rival, the Virginia Gentlemen suddenly stopped requiring its members to join the glee club. But the B'hoos' reputation really took shape at the end of their second year with the arrival of Paul Snow Hudgins—aka Snowdy. The guy had till then been a brother at Beta Theta Pi, before the fraternity was kicked off campus. A lapsed frat guy? He was perfect for the Hullabahoos.

Just before Halsted graduated, the group received an invitation from the Waiters, the Cornell group that had inspired their cool ethos nearly two years before. The Waiters wanted the Hullabahoos to sing at their big show, Spring Fever—one of the largest a cappella shows in the nation, regularly filling Bailey Hall's two-thousand-seat auditorium. It's an unspoken rule in a cappella: Never invite a guest group who is better than you. The Waiters could not have been happy when a review of the concert appeared in *The Cornell Daily Sun* on March 13, 1989. Four paragraphs down, Krista Reid '91 wrote the following about the visiting Hullabahoos: "Their appearance on stage was quickly followed with whispers and giggles from the women in the crowd. It was said by many that these guys were better looking than Waiters—could it be possible?"

Since Halstead's era, the Hullabahoos have had pockets of musical brilliance punctuated by mediocre (but raucous) good times. Andrew Renshaw's version of "Wonderful Tonight" from the early nineties is legendary, even on LimeWire (where it's often mistakenly credited to Rockapella). But what has remained constant is the look: clean-cut, All-American, handsome. In off years, what they lacked in talent they made up for in charm. And luck.

Howard Spector is the president of Ashley Entertainment, a Washington, D.C.–based event-planning firm. In 1995, he happened to walk by Boston's Faneuil Hall, where the Hullabahoos (on their annual road trip, Fall Roll) were busking. Howard bought a CD, said he was interested in hiring the B'hoos, and handed a business card to John Stanzione, then the music director of the group. "Like most people we met who said they were somebody," Stanzione recalls, "we never expected to hear from him again." But Howard did call, with a gig no less: He wanted the Hullabahoos to perform at Burger King's annual corporate Christmas party in Miami. He offered airfare, accommodations, not to mention all the Burger King one could eat. Stanzione details his thought process: "You want to fly us to South Beach in the middle of finals and pay for us to eat and drink?" Stanzione pushed his luck. He told Howard they'd love to do the gig, but he'd need to fly in some "key alumni" to help out. Howard consented and the deal was done. Just out of curiosity, Stanzione said to Howard, who did the Burger King gig last year? "Bill Cosby," Howard said. Stanzione wrote letters to relevant professors asking if the Hullabahoos could schedule make-up exams.

It was likely the most lucrative gig in the short history of the Hullabahoos. But it came with its own unique demands. Howard wanted the Hullabahoos to learn the Burger King jingle. And so John Stanzione arranged "Aren't You Hungry for Burger King Now?" the one that went *"Aren't You Hungry? Aren't you hungry for Burger King now?"* An hour before showtime, the Hullabahoos ran through their set for Howard. "I meant the *other* jingle!" Howard said. *"Hold the pickles, hold the lettuce, special orders don't upset us."* So Stanzione and Nick Geisinger (who'd flown in from Chicago) threw together a Burger King medley, which the B'hoos learned on the spot. Not surprisingly, the executives loved it. "Particularly the lady in marketing," Stanzione says. "The woman who came up with the idea for the New Fries."

"The Burger King people went *nuts!*" Howard says.

Now, this is where their stories diverge.

Howard is a big-picture guy. "I told the Hullabahoos—you need to get into a studio and record that jingle right now," he says. Burger King was talking contracts, he says. The fast food chain was preparing a new campaign aimed squarely at the African American community. Howard says they were interested in signing up one of the B'hoos. "They wanted to bring back the 'Have It Your Way' jingle," Howard says, "and they wanted Kevin Fudge from the Hullabahoos to sing it."

Stanzione has his own version of events. "I remember Howard mentioning something about recording the jingle, but we all assumed he was blowing smoke up our ass," he says. "No one from Burger King ever talked to us about it, nor did Howard encourage us to talk to anyone." Kevin Fudge has no recollection of any interest from Burger King.

Periodically, Howard Spector would call the Hullabahoos

with a gig, including an event for Vice President Dick Cheney. In 2004, he hired the B'hoos for the Republican National Convention. (The client had wanted Rockapella but, alas, the Folgers boys were booked.) "Howard told us we'd get four thousand dollars," says Keith Bachmann, who was the music director at the time. This was good news. The Hullabahoos had been living hand-to-mouth for years. They were working on a new album, *Jacked,* and were several thousand dollars in the hole. Parents had kicked in money to finish the album, and morale was low. But then, suddenly, there was this luxury bus picking the Hullabahoos up on campus and delivering them to New York.

"The Hullabahoos were one of my special, magic tools," Howard says. "They're crisp. They're all-American. They're good kids. They always sound good." Howard has worked with Gloria Gaynor, Clint Black, Aaron Neville. "Some acts are really good," he says, "but they're assholes. I'd rather go with really good and professional. The Hullabahoos have a great working attitude—and that's half the battle." At the close of the 2004 RNC convention, Howard surprised the B'hoos with a check for thirteen thousand dollars. "Suddenly we were eight thousand dollars in the black," Keith says. If the Hullabahoos had been smart, they would have sent Howard periodic updates, CDs, that kind of thing. But, true to form, they forgot all about Howard, and quickly lost touch with the man from Ashley Entertainment.

But in the fall of 2006, Morgan Sword got back in touch with Howard, who was happy to provide his old friends from the Hullabahoos with a letter of recommendation for their planned trip to Los Angeles. Also: Much to Morgan's surprise, after his pursuit of Lisa Estrada from the Lakers, she agreed to book the Hullabahoos for a date in early January. The B'hoos were thrilled. That Hong Kong trip they'd been talking about, however, was quickly sidelined. For all of their talent, the B'hoos don't really have the drive to put on a tour of Asia—at least not without assistance from the Philippine government. But a Lakers game was certainly something to talk about.

From the first days of the 2006–2007 school year, it was looking to be the group's best ever. It had been luck that led the Hullabahoos to Howard Spector outside Faneuil Hall in 1995. (He could have just as easily fallen for the Beelzebubs.) Lady Luck would smile again on the Hullabahoos when, three weeks after auditions, they found themselves on a plane to Portland, Oregon—all expenses paid. The attention was almost embarrassing. A fleet of Town Cars greeted them at the airport in Portland, waiting to shuttle them to the Hilton downtown. And upon check-in, each was handed a wicker basket containing local potato chips, a Portland guidebook, and a Pendleton blanket. It was a fitting gift for a boy band, this blanket. Pendleton, based in Portland, is an internationally known manufacturer of woolens. In 1960, a music group calling themselves the Pendletones (after the wool shirts they wore) made their debut. That group would later change their name to the Beach Boys.

But there was something else in the basket—a handwritten note from Julie Neupert Stott, the woman who'd sponsored this trip. Mrs. Stott bristles at the term *benefactor.* "If I can open a door or make something happen," she says, "I will. I'm just enthusiastic about the Hullabahoos." Or *one* Hullabahoo anyway.

"Mrs. Stott wants Patrick to marry her daughter," Morgan Sword explains.

The backstory: Two years ago, when Patrick Lundquist was a freshman, he'd been flipping through the campus Facebook when he came across a picture of a girl named Preston Stott. She was gorgeous, he was lonely, and so he went online to investigate. "I pretty much stalked her," Patrick admits. Preston eventually agreed to meet her stalker. And Patrick, ever the gentleman, walked her to class. He even carried her books. When Preston's mom and dad came to campus that fall, she took them to see the

Hullabahoos perform. While Preston's romance with Patrick was short-lived, her mom still carries a torch. "I think I have the bigger crush on Patrick," Mrs. Stott says. For Preston's last birthday, her mom threw her a blowout party in Charlottesville and hired the Hullabahoos to perform. "I don't think Preston even wanted us there," one of the B'hoos says.

If there's something Julie Stott loves more than the Hullabahoos it's UVA itself. In 2006, she and her husband kick-started a local booster club for the Jefferson Scholarship program, which sends thirty-five ultracompetitive students to UVA every year, free of charge. She'd planned a fund-raiser in Portland and imported the Hullabahoos. "The Hullabahoos are the best ambassadors for the school," Mrs. Stott says. She also filled their schedule. A friend at Nike arranged for a VIP tour of the company's Beaverton headquarters, including a stop at the employees-only store, where the Hullabahoos bought a boatload of Nike gear for something like ten cents on the dollar. Mrs. Stott also booked them a lucrative gig at a prep school. That the Hullabahoos were driven around Portland in a stretch Hummer was just gravy. "When they came out of the limo at the school," Mrs. Stott says, "some of the students were like, *Is that 'N Sync?*" That week the Hullabahoos sold forty-five hundred dollars' worth of CDs.

That Facebook message Patrick sent may turn out to be the best thing he's done for the Hullabahoos. As it happens, Julie Neupert Stott sits on the board of the National Committee for the Performing Arts at the Kennedy Center in D.C. The Kennedy Center happens to be in the midst of planning a ten-day celebration of a cappella music, "A Cappella: Singing Solo," set for May 2008. The lineup is still in the works. "I'm trying to get the Hullabahoos' name in front of the committee," she says.

———

It's good to be a Hullabahoo. And the trip to Portland went a long way toward ironing out the personality conflicts Morgan had worried so much about. A subsequent trip to Princeton—in an RV—for their annual Fall Roll would only serve to foster the group's newfound unity. As for missing so much class, well, Joe Cassara (the president) offered to write each student a note. (He even wrote one for Kyle Mihalcoe's Spanish teacher *in* Spanish.) The notes are "all in the phrasing," Morgan explains. "No teacher actually knows the rules to this stuff, so we're at liberty to make them up a bit. One thing I picked up along the way is that saying something with enough conviction can make it true."

It wasn't just the traveling that brought the group together. It was, more than anything, as simple as the group having a convenient, neutral place to hang out. That place was Morgan's room. Morgan lives on the west side of the UVA Lawn—the heart of campus. It's a coveted spot, and it's easy to see why. Each room opens directly out to the Lawn, which gives the whole thing the feeling of some Ivy League Motel 6. It's sort of like living in a brochure. While the bunks may be tight, this is one instance where size really doesn't matter. To land a room on the Lawn, one must go through a rigorous application process. Thus, Morgan lives two doors down from a Rhodes scholar, the editor-in-chief of *The Cavalier Daily*, three varsity athletes, and the student-body president. Morgan never locks his door, and on any given Sunday—or Monday, or Tuesday, or any day of the week, for that matter—he might come home from class to find one or more of the Hullabahoos watching TV on his couch. The other night the Hullabahoos even had a mixer there, with one of the better-looking sororities spilling out onto the Lawn. The homemade liquor-dispenser on his dresser—loaded with Jose Cuervo and Tanqueray—was a nice conversation piece, much more so than the Jose Reyes bobblehead.

Musically, things are falling into place too. Pete Seibert is something of a prodigy, despite himself. He came to music late;

he quit saxophone early, then quit piano only to come back to it in the eighth grade. He is not an audiophile. He counts *Sister Act* among his musical inspirations. But it turns out that his inherent laziness may be an asset. Where the Bubs arrangements often try to mimic the original song—down to every last high hat and tambourine—the Hullabahoos are finding their own voice. "I'm not going to listen to a song five hundred times," Pete says, "to imitate every sound in the background." Instead, he starts with the simple chords and the solo (the foundation) and adds his own ideas from there—usually a jaw-dropping bridge. James Gammon owns a recording studio nearby and works with the B'hoos. "Pete's arrangements are pretty much all the same," he says. "But at least they have a musical idea. There's some tension. There's some drama. I mean, you could say the same thing about Coldplay. But that formula works for them."

The Hullabahoos are working on U2's "One." (Pete first heard the song when Elliott Yamin sang it on the *American Idol* finale with Mary J. Blige.) He actually sat down to arrange the song with pen and paper. "But it sucked," he says. "So I threw it away." While the Bubs arrangements are written down—practically in stone—you'd be hard-pressed to find a stash of Hullabahoos arrangements. Most of the Hullabahoos don't read music, and Pete teaches by ear, often arranging songs on the spot, with the Hullabahoos gathered around the piano. He knows it's tedious. "The guys don't like it because they feel like I'm just shooting in the dark for a good arrangement." Which he is. He remembers the night he taught "One." "That rehearsal was terrible," Pete says. But there was a turning point. "When we added the vocal rhythm part"—the song goes all hip-hop in the second verse as they sing *nomina nomina nomina nomina*—he knew they were onto something.

The Hullabahoos needed a big song like this. Because they were headed for a showdown with the Beelzebubs. They just didn't suspect it would involve fists.

CHAPTER SEVEN

THE BEELZEBUBS AND HULLABAHOOS COLLIDE

Wherein two groups clash in a very unusual Mason-Dixon throwdown in October of 2006

Sometime after midnight on Saturday, October 4, the Beelzebubs and the Hullabahoos come face-to-face in a parking lot outside a house party at the University of North Carolina. The night had started innocently enough. The Bubs and the B'hoos had both performed at Fall Jam, an annual a cappella concert hosted by the all-female UNC Loreleis. But then here we are, bathed in the yellow glow of a streetlight, tensions high, the members just inches from each other. Members of the Beelzebubs are holding back their man Andrew Savini. "We respected you!" Andrew Savini shouts at the Hullabahoos. *"And you crossed the line!"*

Riding high on liquid confidence, Patrick Lundquist and Bobby Grasberger of the Hullabahoos approach the Bubs. "Look, nobody wants a fight," Patrick says. Though if it came to that, Patrick was pretty sure he knew how it would end. "Bobby and I are both significantly bigger than most Bubs," he says. Still, Patrick attempts to diffuse the situation. "It was a rookie move," he says. "It wasn't the Hullabahoos. It was *one* Hullabahoo. Don't hate the entity."

Doug Terry of the Bubs watched this scene play out. Though Doug was openly gay, this wasn't the kind of man-on-man action he was hoping for on this road trip. Just as the situation seemed to be cooling off, from deep within the Beelzebubs camp came this cry: "You have a small dick!"

Weeks later, Andrew Savini would describe Patrick Lundquist as "that tall kid with the big voice." Patrick would refer to Savini as "incoherent" and "that kid who really wanted to fight." How did it come to this?

Being a Beelzebub means giving your life over to the hive. On top of the travel schedule—it is not uncommon for the Bubs to drive through the night to sing a five-song set at, say, the University of Michigan—there were rehearsals three nights a week. In the days leading up to a concert, Bub rehearsals had been known to last until sunrise. When you are the first a cappella group to have your music played in outer space, that comes with some expectations. Their album *Code Red* had been about perfection— imitative a cappella that was indistinguishable from the original tunes. The Bubs held themselves to the same impossible standard.

When their music director, Ben Appel, left school suddenly on medical leave, the Bubs found themselves in a precarious position: They had nothing to sing. It had been Ben Appel's job to make sure new arrangements were coming in, to make sure the Bubs had music to learn at each rehearsal. As president, Matt Michelson shoulders some of the responsibility here. "I should have seen the warning signs," he says. He would ask Ben about the arrangements but always got the same response. "We're all good," Ben would say. This arrangement was coming in on Tuesday, another on Monday, that sort of thing. "He was specific about it," Michelson remembers.

When Ben Appel left Tufts, he sent an e-mail to the Bubs'

alumni network, the Bubnet—a listserv of members dating back to the group's founding fathers, some now in their sixties. The response came in loud and clear. "The alums thought the group was falling apart," Michelson says. Lucas Walker was the newly installed music director and one of his first moves was to e-mail Danny Lichtenfeld '93, who'd previously agreed to put together a song for the Bubs. Unlike the alumni of most a cappella groups, the Beelzebub alums still frequently contribute music arrangements. Danny was surprised to hear from Lucas. He'd had no idea there was a deadline attached to the arrangement. "Do you need it *now*?" Danny said. There were other mix-ups. Marty Fernandi '85 had agreed to arrange "Love It When You Call," a catchy bit from a new British pop band, The Feeling. Lucas was eager to add the song to the Bubs' repertoire and e-mailed Marty for a status update. Marty was floored. "Lucas even offered to send me the song," Marty says. Marty didn't need the song. He'd suggested the damn thing to the Bubs in the first place. "In this game of telephone," Marty says, "that seemed to have been forgotten."

This was not the first time the Bubs had looked to the alumni for help. In the mid-seventies, the Beelzebubs nearly called it quits. Tim Vaill—the founder of the Beelzebubs—recalls brokering a peace agreement between two warring factions who showed up late one night at his house in Wellesley Hills. The situation in the fall of 2006 was not nearly as dire. But still, the Bubs' alumni network—extensive, smart, thoughtful, concerned—threw open its safety net. They had never given the undergraduates money, but they certainly wouldn't let the group fail. Membership does have its privileges. And, just as suddenly, music arrangements were on their way and the Bubs were back on track. Travis Marshall, Class of '03, arranged Keane's "A Bad Dream." And to fill a hole, Alexander Koutzoukis, a Bubs sophomore, quickly put together "Inaction," a song from an obscure Brooklyn-based indie band called We Are Scientists. If the song appeared to be an odd choice, the Bubs didn't see it that way. No, the Bubs are musically quite cocky (perhaps with good reason—their blend is legendary). Most a cappella groups have a repertoire heavy on kitsch, like eighties tunes and one-hit wonders. "But I like to think people come to hear the Bubs," Lucas Walker says, "not a cover band." The audience might smile when they hear a song they recognize, he says, but then what? "Then you've got another three minutes of 'Hey Ya!' to sit through." It should be noted that the Bubs recorded the Black Eyed Peas song "Let's Get It Started" (a kitch classic) for their 2005 album, *Shedding*, though Lucas insists the Bubs were trying to be ironic. That point was apparently lost on the Best of College A Cappella committee, who selected "Let's Get It Started" as the opener for the 2006 BOCA compilation album.

"We only perform a song when we think we can improve upon the original artist," Lucas says. Perhaps their hubris is to be expected. Even the president of Tufts, Larry Bacow, is indebted to the Bubs. It's not just the music. "Alumni who are active tend to be alumni who were deeply engaged and connected to something during their time in college," he says. To translate, *active alumni* means alumni who donate money to the school. (In February, the Bubs will perform at the grand opening of the Granoff Music Building at Tufts, home to the BEELZEBUBS TICKET OFFICE. Price tag? A two-hundred-thousand-dollar donation from The Beelzebubs Alumni Association.)

The Bubs have staked their reputation on perfection, and they treat every show as if it is a nationally televised competition that might ruin the group's good name. They even have a saying for it. "We like to *win the show*," Doug Terry says. Andrew Savini, a senior, believes they have been beaten only once in recent memory—by none other than the Lisa Forkish–era Divisi. The ladies from Oregon had been out to Boston for spring break 2006.

The Bubs were exhausted from their own travels, and they hadn't been expecting much competition, especially from an all-girls group—on their home turf, no less. By the time Divisi unleashed "Yeah" on the Tufts crowd, there wasn't much the Bubs could do. They haven't been caught off-guard since.

Ben Appel's replacement, Lucas Walker, quickly grew into the position of music director—able to quiet the group down with a simple command. He even held the electric pitch pipe with assurance. (An electric pitch pipe? "It's more professional," Lucas says later. "The old pitch pipe, depending on how hard you blow, it changes the pitch.") The new Bubs album was on track too. Several times that semester, Ed Boyer '04 had come to campus to record background tracks (the chords, the *oohs* and *aaahs* that would make up the foundation of each song). But if there was one thing still troubling the Bubs—one thing the alumni network couldn't help with—it was stage presence. In Ben Appel's absence, it had fallen to Andrew Savini to teach the new members how to perform.

There is a difference between singing well and performing well. But the Bubs are so preoccupied with their past—so awed by their own name and legacy—that they are afraid to make mistakes, even in front of one another. This may be the one thing Savini hates about the Bubs. It happens all the time—especially when a guy is auditioning for a solo. Savini will hear someone practicing in the hallway and he'll nail it. Then, when it comes time to sing in front of the group, the kid tanks. "It happened with Lucas and 'Love It When You Call,'" Savini says. (Though Lucas eventually got that solo, it could have gone either way.) Savini encourages the Bubs to take risks in their performances— but the Bubs are sick of hearing it from him. They call him "Baby Savini" when he acts up. The name-calling is understandable, however. It's a reaction to his ego. Savini has the best solo voice in the Bubs. (Just ask him.) The fact that he has also now lost a hundred pounds only complicates matters. Without Ben Appel, there is no one to put Savini in his place.

Andrew Savini had always been one of the most recognizable Bubs on campus; a rotund Hawaiian in a sea of New England white, he was literally hard to miss. More than his size, however, was that voice. Freshman year he'd walk into a party and the girls would shout, "Pony!" This wasn't a fat joke; Savini's big solo at the time was Ginuwine's "Pony." (The Bubs haven't sung the song in two years, but the catcalls persist—at shows, in the cafeteria, wherever the kid goes.) How Savini lost the weight is a matter of some speculation. More than one member of the Bubs had spotted him with a bottle of TrimSpa. Savini, however, has vehemently denied snacking from Anna Nicole Smith's candy jar. "I finished one week of TrimSpa," he says, laying rest to the rumors that have dogged his remarkable extreme makeover. "But I didn't have the discipline. You have to take those pills an hour before every meal!" He lost the weight the old-fashioned way— eating less, exercising more—inspired by an old photo of himself. "I never realized this loud personality was coming out of such an obese unattractive person," he says. "I mean, I didn't smell. But I had a mustache. I was gross." That Savini has the strongest voice—and is suddenly the best-looking too—strikes some within the organization as impossibly unfair. Savini, for his part, is enjoying his new body, and the confidence that comes with it. "Everything in college is about aesthetics," he says. "And sexual drive."

It's with that spirit in mind that the Beelzebubs find themselves backstage at UNC's Hamilton Hall in October of 2007, preparing for the showdown. It's a peculiar scene. Every a cappella group has their own set of warm-ups. The Bubs stand in a circle, slap themselves in the face repeatedly, and shout, *"Ooooh oooh EEEK*

EEEK EEEK." They beat their chests. They drag their hands behind them. This exercise, designed to get the blood flowing, is affectionately known as "gorillas." If this appears to be outside the norm, who are we to judge? Divisi has a warm-up that involves singing *"Chicken of the sea // chicken of the sea // chicken of the sea // chicken of the sea // chicken chicken chicken of the sea."*

The Hullabahoos, just down the hall at UNC tonight, have their own way of getting their heads in the game. The ritual is a song—Curtis Mayfield's "People Get Ready," which the B'hoos first learned for a performance at the 2004 Republican National Convention. Though no one remembers exactly how, it has recently become a preshow must. It's doubtful any of these students (all born in the eighties) are aware of the song's legacy—that it was written in the wake of Martin Luther King Jr.'s "I Have a Dream" speech—but the lyrics translate. Backstage tonight Patrick Lundquist sings: *"People get ready // There's a train a comin' // You don't need no baggage // You just get on board."* It wasn't just the song that got them jazzed for the show. The Hullabahoos had something else working in their favor tonight. Earlier in the day they had presented their five new members with their robes—an emotional, pride-pumping exchange. Before showtime, Joe Whitney clutched his new robe—the one with the cartoon dogs on it—smiling wide, repeating, "Feels good, feels good."

Truth be told, with the Bubs and the Hullabahoos on the card, it's as if the Backstreet Boys and 'N Sync had met in some deranged battle of the boy bands. Four hundred fans crowd into Hamilton Auditorium for Fall Jam 2006—hosted by the all-female Loreleis. Hamilton is really more of a classroom than anything else, which may explain why there's a competitive spirit in the air. It was nothing short of a clash of the a cappella titans in a Mason-Dixon throwdown: the Bubs from the North (the birthplace of collegiate a cappella) and the Hullabahoos from the upstart South.

The Hullabahoos perform first, casually dressed beneath their robes, unfazed by the hollers and whistles that greet them. Myles Glancy (who bears a passing resemblance to Harry Potter) sings a new song by The Fray, "How to Save a Life." When Myles sings, a hush falls over the largely female crowd. Which is precisely why the B'hoos chose this one. If nothing else, they know their audience. "The song is big from *Grey's Anatomy*," says Pete Seibert, their music director. "Girls like it." (Not surprisingly one member of the B'hoos steps forward and draws a *box* behind Myles.) Ballads should be used sparingly in collegiate a cappella. Without instruments, a love song can feel like an interminable four minutes of *ooohs* and *aaaaahs*. But the percussion on "How to Save a Life" keeps it alive. The beatbox holds two microphones in his hands, one against his throat, the other at his mouth. These are AKG D12 mics—honest-to-God drum mics—the kind designed to pick up the low tones in a kick drum. Tonight, they're picking up a mix of *dim dim ch ch dim dim ch ch*. It looks silly, but you can feel the bass in your stomach. Myles sells the solo, clenching his fists and waving them in the air like a crying baby on the chorus. "Yeah, Hogwarts!" someone yells. When Brian Duhon, a new guy, steps up to sing the harmony on the chorus, one can see the difference the robe makes; there's a confidence, a sudden weight, to his step.

It will be U2's "One," however, that really connects. Pete blows the starting note and the song begins: *"Ohhhhhhhh // SHA-DAAAAAA // Ooooooh // DOOO DOOO."* Patrick sings: *"Is it getting better? // Or do you feel the same?"* It's a duet. And Brendon Mason comes in, deferentially at first, echoing Patrick. But it quickly devolves into a pissing contest—an excuse for each to test his vocal range in public. Pete's arrangement (all block chords and vocal rhythms) is not subtle, but then again, neither is that U2/Mary J. Blige retread. And the Hullabahoos—not to mention the audience—is feeding off that vibe. Patrick is suddenly elongating notes that barely appear on the page; for better and often worse, he could make a rest fortissimo.

The Hullabahoos sing in unison, *"Have you come here to play"*—and then, as per the arrangement, they drop out entirely, letting Patrick and Brendon harmonize (loudly) on *Jesus*. The crowd is applauding, not even realizing why they're doing it, just reacting to the sound.

The Beelzebubs are seated up in the back row. They're set to perform after intermission, and if they're rattled by the Hullabahoos, they won't admit it. But it's easy to see why the two groups might clash. Their styles couldn't be more different.

The Bubs—dressed in coats and ties—don't so much as walk out onstage as bound. One of the guys attempts a 360-degree midair spin. The stage looks like a mosh pit at the Gap. The Bubs settle into their standard U-shape, turning their attention toward Lucas Walker, who hits a little button on the electric pitch pipe in his right hand, which buzzes with the group's starting pitch. He counts off one-two-one-two-three-four and in unison the Bubs sing: *"Buuuum ba bum // buuuum ba bum // ahhhhhhh."* Matt Thomas, a bulky sophomore with a goatee, steps out, inviting the audience to: *"Roll up, roll up to the Magical Mystery Tour! Step right this way!"* The song slows down at the bridge—John and Paul's ode to those hazed and confused days—and the Bubs break formation, stumbling around in all directions, staring into space even as they continue to sing. One kid is licking his own face. Matt Michelson wanders way left. Someone pretends to smoke a joint. And just as suddenly they're back, hitting the mark, as crisp and professional as legend has it. The tempo creeps back up on the march toward the end of the song and Chris Van Lenten (on vocal percussion) sways back and forth like a star child.

If the Bubs have a song to rival the Hullabahoos and "One"

it's "Smiley Faces," a Gnarls Barkley bit that Andrew Savini owns. He is the group's resident face guy, and he's in fine form tonight. It's not just his voice. His hips seem to be entirely disconnected from the rest of his body. The song will become the de rigueur set closer for the rest of the semester, and with good reason. The choreography—which includes three Bubs stepping out on the left for some Temptations-like intrigue—is stellar, providing much-needed humor but not distracting from the music.

There is something undeniably endearing about the Bubs. Doug Terry is the theatrical one—his eyebrows have their own choreography. (It will come as a surprise to no one that, as an eleven-year-old child, Doug played Chip in the national touring company of *Beauty and the Beast*. Or that he's thinking about waxing his chest.) Matt Kraft is a natural physical comedian. But their set list is off. The Bubs sing two ballads, "Gracie" by Ben Folds and "Ruby Falls" by Guster, which sucks energy from the room. And they don't seem to exhibit much discernible personality. If anything, they're overrehearsed. It's like the *Code Red* complaint—that in ironing out the imperfections they've lost some human quality. They are a machine with one setting: On. The head fakes, the choreography—it doesn't leave much room for spontaneity. It's not that the Hullabahoos were technically better; they weren't—by a long shot. Their arrangements weren't nearly as complex (fewer parts, easier rhythms). But sitting in the audience, it feels as if the Hullabahoos are in on the joke. One gets the sense that Ben Appel might have loved to be a Hullabahoo.

Still, no one would have guessed that three hours later the showdown would come to this. Lib Curlee of the Loreleis searches for a word to describe what happened later that night. "It was an *incident*," she says.

Andrew Savini, his face flush with alcohol, bathed in the glow of a streetlamp, comes face-to-face with the Hullabahoos. *"We respected you!"* Savini shouts. "And you crossed the line!" Outside the postshow party, the Beelzebubs are holding their man back. Patrick Lundquist approaches.

"It was a rookie move," Patrick says. "Don't hate the entity."

It *was* a rookie move, and this is what happened: Just minutes earlier, while the Bubs and the Hullabahoos were inside the party—playing beer pong, likely—Jack Stump of the B'hoos stepped out for some air. That's when he happened upon the Beelzebubs' fifteen-passenger white van parked outside. Jack looked left. Jack looked right. He sidled up to the vehicle, unzipped his pants, and painted the thing yellow. It was out of character for Jack, the endearingly awkward Hullabahoo. And precisely because it was so out of character, he was dumb enough to get caught.

Patrick and Bobby Grasberger of the Hullabahoos, meanwhile, stumbled out of the party. Patrick had other plans—he'd hoped to spend the night with Lib Curlee of the Loreleis before he got sidetracked. But one of the Hullabahoos came running by, shouting: *"Jack just pissed on the Beelzebubs' van!"*

The two sides quickly materialized. There was a lot of yelling. "This prick just pissed on our van," Andrew Savini shouted.

Jack actually shouted back, as if this were some Aaron Burr–era duel, "That's a lie!" In response, one of the Bubs yelled: "You have a small dick!"

For a second there it looked like the confrontation might end with fists—a full-on a cappella rumble. But, in a compromise that must make sense only under the influence of alcohol, one of the Bubs defused the situation by suggesting "intergroup public urination as a show of good faith." Which is what they did. While one of the Loreleis looked on, Patrick Lundquist and Matt Kraft, side by side, unzipped their pants and pissed into a garbage can.

For the Bubs, the rest of the semester seemed pretty tame in comparison. There were more road trips—to UPenn, to New York City. And the group worked tirelessly on the music. Lucas Walker more than survived his surprise and sudden tenure at the helm. In January, Alexander Koutzoukis would take over as music director, proving his mettle when, on the Monday night before the group's winter show, he came up with a Bubsian idea: arranging a medley of Justin Timberlake's "Sexy Back" and the Pussycat Dolls' "Buttons." The Bubs learned the medley on a Tuesday night. On Thursday they came up with some choreography— a PG-13 striptease. And on Friday they performed the thing, flawlessly, at their concert (thanks to an up-all-night rehearsal). Maybe the Bubs were missing some of the artistry Ben Appel might have brought to the group, but they had more than stabilized, and the alums were relieved. In January the Bubs would meet in New Hampshire to record the majority of their next album. How exactly the sound would differ from the perfection of *Code Red* was still a mystery.

The Hullabahoos, for their part, returned to campus, convinced they'd embarrassed the Bubs at UNC. And for the first time perhaps since their founding—when Halsted Sullivan had performed onstage draped in Christmas lights—the Hullabahoos put on a Yuletide show. The highlight: Blake Segal, Dane Blackburn, and Brian Tucker—the three tiniest Hullabahoos—stepping out from the group to sing the Chipmunks' Christmas carol. (Blake Segal asked, "Does Santa come for Jewish children?" to deafening cheers.) The Christmas show was so well received that the B'hoos began work on a Christmas album. The music they'd learned for the show—"Silent Night," Mariah Carey's "All I Want for

Christmas"—came in handy when, just after finals, the Hullabahoos landed a high-profile gig performing for the AOL corporate
Christmas party at the new Air and Space Museum in D.C. out
by Dulles Airport. Joe Cassara, the president of the Hullabahoos,
booked the gig—and he'd negotiated masterfully: On top of a
five-thousand-dollar fee, the Hullabahoos scored two hotel rooms
plus airfare to fly in their music director, Pete Seibert, who'd gone
home for winter break. Between sets that night the Hullabahoos
abused the open bar. Such was their enjoyment of the festivities
that the lot of them nearly missed the last shuttle bus back. Running for the jitney, Pete Seibert actually collided with Randy
Falco, the newly installed CEO of AOL. "Sorry!" Pete shouted,
both embarrassed and impressed with himself at the same time.

In a few weeks the Hullabahoos would fly to Los Angeles to
sing the national anthem at the Lakers game. And for the first
time in recent memory, the group was thinking ahead and planning for a future beyond the next gig, beyond the next free beer.
At Morgan's request, Howard Spector (head of Ashley Entertainment) had supplied the B'hoos with a letter of recommendation
for gigs in L.A. Now Patrick Lundquist picked up where Morgan
had left off, courting the man who'd booked the Hullabahoos for
so many lucrative gigs in the past. It started with an e-mail. "In
groups like this," Patrick wrote, "it often takes just a little boost
to turn fickle success into perennial success, and you've given the
group several big boosts over the past several years, so I just
wanted to say thanks." The Hullabahoos wanted to return to the
Republican National Convention in 2008, to get back in Howard's
good graces. But for now the Hullabahoos had more pressing
concerns: namely, a highly anticipated stop in Los Angeles at, yes,
the Playboy Mansion.

CHAPTER EIGHT

DIVISI

Wherein the original members of Divisi return (disastrously)
to prepare these new girls for the quarterfinals of the 2007
International Championship of Collegiate A Cappella

Keeley McCowan had always assumed that when Divisi re-turned to campus after winter break, the girls would buckle down. First semester had come with its own set of problems. Divisi was essentially a brand-new group—with personality issues and inexperienced musicians—working from a standing start to do the impossible: win at the International Championship of Collegiate A Cappella. But surely, in the face of the fast-approaching regional quarterfinals, they would prioritize, Keeley thought. Or maybe not. Maybe these girls were right to slack off. They'd inherited this vendetta, after all. And it wasn't necessarily their war to fight.

But the problems began almost immediately. Jenna Tooley (a blond freshman with braces) took a leave from the group. "I thought it was strep throat," she says. But this fatigue, this cough-ing, was something else. The doctor at the campus medical center diagnosed her with the one-two punch of tonsillitis and mono.

Keeley had her own problems. She was essentially mounting this ICCA quarterfinal concert herself. Though Varsity Vocals, the organization that sponsors the ICCAs, hires producers to run each event, the majority of the work is done in advance by the

host groups. Keeley was responsible for securing the venue, selling tickets, and even finding housing for the visiting students.
Sadly, Keeley was having trouble getting members of Divisi to
volunteer for even the simplest tasks. She might have given up
had the competition not been Divisi's biggest source of revenue.
If done correctly, the group would pocket ten thousand dollars in
one night—money they'd desperately need if they hoped to
travel to New York for the finals. (Varsity Vocals long ago stopped
subsidizing travel for competitors.) Keeley decided to up the
stakes (and potential profits) this year by holding the quarterfinal
round at the Hult Center in downtown Eugene—a twenty-five-
hundred-person venue that, to put it in perspective, had previously hosted the touring company of *Wicked*. Divisi would need
to sell seven hundred and fifty tickets just to break even. In a
stroke of marketing genius, Keeley used the posters to play up
the intrastate rivalry between the competing a cappella groups
from Oregon State and her own University of Oregon. The posters read: CIVIL WAR OF A CAPELLA. If a cappella was spelled incorrectly, so what. Keeley had other concerns.

Still, rehearsals were tense. Divisi, so used to talking about
every emotion and hurt feeling, had finally gone quiet. The elephant in the room was Betsy Yates.

Betsy Yates grew up in Wilsonville, just outside Portland, not far
from Bullwinkle's Family Fun Center and the Fry's Electronics
store. That's about all that goes on in Wilsonville. While most kids
were working at the mall, Betsy was a singing waitress—a very
pretty singing waitress at that, with thick chestnut hair that seemed
to move as if it were starring in its own Pantene commercial—
aboard a restaurant cruise ship that paddled up and down the Willamette River. As a senior in high school, Betsy won a statewide
singing competition. These days, Betsy is easy to spot on campus.
Though she is not proud of it, that's her on the Razor scooter.

Betsy was supposed to be in Costa Rica over Christmas break. But a few days before her family was to leave for the big deep-sea diving adventure trip, Betsy's dad broke his foot. With Betsy's schedule suddenly clear, she decided to have her tonsils removed—which her doctor had been advising for months now. She'd had chronic tonsillitis (stuffed nose, a sore throat) and the surgery would relieve all of that, the doctor said. Betsy was worried about her voice, though—she was the soloist on "Don't You Worry 'Bout a Thing," which would open Divisi's three-song competition set. Her doctor assured her she'd be in fine form for the ICCAs in January. If anything, he said, the surgery would help: "Without two golf balls in your throat, you'll be able to resonate." And so just before Christmas, Betsy went under the knife. For the next ten days she didn't open her mouth to speak, let alone sing. On that tenth night she grew restless. She couldn't sleep. She was worried about the quarterfinals, which were a few weeks away. Late in the night, tucked under the sheets of her childhood bedroom, she started humming quietly to herself. She couldn't sing low. She couldn't sing high. She was terrified.

Previously, Betsy sang "Don't You Worry 'Bout a Thing" in full voice—big, loud, rich. But when it mattered, a week before the competition, she was still relying on her head voice, which was breathy, bordering on inaudible. The women of Divisi had their concerns, but no one dared discuss it with Betsy—not even Sarah Klein, the group's music director. Ironically, it would be Sarah Klein's *mom* who would broach the subject when, the night before the ICCAs, Mrs. Klein sat in on Divisi's final rehearsal. "Betsy, I know that you just had surgery," Sarah's mom said. "But it's hard to hear you." The woman meant well. But coming on the heels of a difficult few weeks, the criticism threatened to upset the group's delicate emotional balance leading into the ICCAs.

Not that she was the only one.

A few weeks earlier, Lisa Forkish had flown in from Boston to refine Divisi's sound. It had been Keeley's idea to invite some of the all-star alumni back, with Divisi picking up the tab. Finally, the girls had reason for hope. In that first rehearsal, Lisa Forkish tore them apart. Where Sarah Klein had no discernible leadership style, Lisa was blunt, firm, but still warm. When girls would talk out of turn she'd say, "I'm feeling really disrespected right now." Some of the girls got off on the act. But for most of Divisi, this just did not flow with the lax vibe of the past six months. At least Lisa didn't make them cry. That was Erica Barkett's job.

Erica Barkett—who'd graduated one year earlier—had boarded a plane from New York to Eugene and for the next six hours had choreographed "Don't You Worry 'Bout a Thing." Lisa stepped aside and Erica worked the choreography in a separate rehearsal. The girls certainly couldn't sing if they were still counting numbers under their breath. "Wait, I stomp on seven, but my shoulders move on *six*?" one member of Divisi asked. It was a lot of talk like that.

The song actually opened with two couples doing the tango. "There was a lot of dancing on the beat while singing off the beat—left brain, right brain," Keeley says. It was too complex, distracting even. But Erica kept at it. "You're not even trying!" she shouted. "It's never taken me so long to teach someone choreography. I flew out here because *you* asked me to come. You wanted me to help. Why am I even here? You're never going to win." Michaela Cordova was particularly upset by what was happening. She took it personally. She felt the alumni didn't like her, perhaps put off by the piercings. Michaela left that rehearsal in tears. She was not the only one.

Inviting Lisa and Erica had been a mistake, Keeley admits. But in the end, it might turn out to be the thing to unite them. After that rehearsal, Keeley sat down and composed an e-mail to Divisi. She'd realized an essential truth about the group. She was tired of hearing these girls talk about the *old* Divisi. She'd perpetuated it herself, was possibly even the worst offender. But with the competition just days away, it was time to make a change.

"This fighting isn't getting us anywhere," Keeley wrote. "No one can make you have pride in this group. You can't love it for the reasons the alumni love it. You have to find your own way. We need to want the same thing. If we want to win, let's do it together. If we just want to have fun, learn a whole bunch of music, relax, and have the Spring Show be our big thing for the year, that's fine too. But whatever we do, let's do it together."

And just like that, something clicked.

Divisi gathered in their dressing room at the Hult Center an hour before the quarterfinals of the ICCAs was to begin. Eight collegiate groups would compete tonight, but Divisi had drawn the short straw. They would open the show, a notoriously bad position. "We'll just have to set the standard," Keeley told the girls, trying to put a positive spin on it.

The heavy-red lipstick had been painted on; the fishnet stockings pulled high. The hair was pulled back, shellacked down with Aqua Net—they looked like the women in that Robert Palmer video. The women of Divisi were once again sitting in a circle, tense. The afternoon sound check had not been encouraging. Peter Hollens, the founder of On the Rocks and the producer who had recorded Divisi's last album, offered some advice. "You can't trust your ears onstage," he said. "It can sound like you're in a shoe box. Don't worry about that." Sarah Klein had expected the alums to call with good wishes, but few did. Lisa Forkish was in school and wouldn't be there to cheer them on. Sarah would have to be the strong one.

Downstairs in the dressing room, Sarah Klein spoke. "I know we're all anxious," she said. "But there's no need to be. We've come so far. Let's have a great time. It's about giving the audience a good show. Don't forget that." Finally, six months into the job, she sounded like a leader.

Divisi broke down their set. They liked to discuss each

song—what the lyrics meant, what their motivation should be. Sarah began. "Our set is like a relationship," she said, which made the girls smile. "'Don't You Worry 'Bout a Thing'—that's our carefree song. It's about love. Be *flirtatious*. Then 'Hide and Seek' is the breakup. And 'You Had Me' is about getting our confidence back."

The girls went around the circle, many echoing what Sarah had just said. Finally it was Michaela's turn to speak. She started. She stopped abruptly, tightening up.

"I'm not sure if I should tell this story," Michaela said. She looked at Emmalee Almroth seated next to her. She looked down at the floor. She took a breath and then, encouraged by Emmalee, she spoke, slowly, deliberately, eloquently. "I have not been well," Michaela said. "I've been a wreck." She did not waste time. "Last year I had a problem with cocaine." She'd quit, she said. She'd worked very hard. She'd been dating a guy, and she thought he was supportive. "But he was still using," she says. The breakup tore a hole in her heart. She talked about "You Had Me," about the song she'd sing tonight, about what the lyrics meant to her. No one knew quite what to say. A few of the girls wiped tears from their eyes. It was Keeley who broke the silence. "We'll have to kill him," she said.

Sarah brought it all back, sounding very much like Lisa Fork-ish. "When you're singing 'You Had Me' tonight," she said, "think about Michaela. Be her support." And with that, Divisi moved the chairs aside to run through bits of their set. There were last-minute questions about choreography. Marissa Neitling reminded people where to put their hands during a bit of Stevie Wonder choreo. "Don't *cup* the ovaries," she said, "just put your hands over them."

Divisi took to the stage, confidently getting into formation for "Don't You Worry 'Bout a Thing." Andrea Welsh, up front, crouched down with attitude. And as the song began, she kicked up her heel, shouting, *"Ee ee!"*

"Don't You Worry 'Bout a Thing" opens with the girls singing: *"Don't you // don't you // don't you // don't you."* But tonight it sounded like *don't chew, don't chew.* Divisi had recently recorded the song in the studio with Peter Hollens. He'd wanted that massive diphthong—don't *chew.* "It gives the track some sauce," he'd said. But what works in the studio doesn't always work onstage. The sound was abrasive. The audience was cold, and Divisi retreated, losing their cool. They suddenly looked timid. And their fears about the choreography were confirmed— it was overkill. Distracting even. For Betsy, the slide from head voice to chest voice—as she sang *"Don't you worry 'bout a thing- eh-ing-eh-ee-ing-eh-eeing"*—was rocky. Halfway through the song, her posture seemed to fall, betraying some sense of disappointment in herself.

"Hide and Seek" was much stronger. The choreography was intricate and precise. It was a lot of hand motions, a lot of evocative head-turns. The girls sing: *"Oily marks appear on walls // where pleasure moments hung before the takeover."* The word *before* is strung out, the group building to fortissimo. The girls put their hands in front of their faces, pushing out toward the audience. They clench their fists. For some, the song's lyrics never made much sense. But the choreography somehow crystallized the message, delivering the emotional punch. The intonation was flawless. The dynamics—the swelling, the softening—were perfect. But the highlight on the set would be Michaela Cordova, who stepped to the microphone for "You Had Me" with a singular focus, as if there weren't another person in the building, let alone seventeen hundred in the crowd. The lyrics—about an abusive boyfriend and his drug abuse—well, it's as if the song were written for her.

She sang: *"Spitting in my eyes and I still see // Tried to keep me down I'm breaking free // I don't want no part in your next fix // Someone needs to tell you // This is it."* Whether it was the revelation of her drug abuse, that raw exposed wound, or merely the relief that the ladies had gotten through the most difficult elements of their set is unclear. But the song took on an entirely different feeling tonight.

"You Had Me" built to the bridge, and Michaela burned with intensity. She sang: *"Vodka and a packet of cigarettes // that's all it used to be // but now you're sniffin' on snow when you're feeling low // suffocating dreams that could have // Maybe for a minute I'll be down with that // but it didn't take long for me to see the light."*

The solo was so overpowering you almost forget the rest of Divisi was onstage—that's how consuming Michaela is as a performer. But there, just as the bridge came to an end, Divisi marched forward until they were flush behind Michaela, supporting her just like Sarah had said. This is where the choreography delivers—it *complements* the song instead of competing with it. The song ended with Divisi chanting in unison: *"Takin' it back // I'm takin' it back // Takin' back my life."*

Divisi's performance that night took on a secondary meaning whether they intended it to or not, for anyone who knew the Divisi backstory—the disappointment at the ICCA finals in '05, the near-entire group turnover—"You Had Me" read as a defiant statement of independence. They were not the old Divisi. They could never be that group. They would honor the memory of those girls, and the reputation they'd built from the ashes of a Beau Tie. But if this incarnation of Divisi was to succeed, these women would need to make it on their own terms.

But was it enough? "Don't You Worry 'Bout a Thing" had left Divisi vulnerable. In the end, it was just plain luck that brought them victory in that quarterfinal round of the ICCAs. It happened like this. First, Dulcet, a mixed group from Southern Oregon University, had the misfortune of performing "Don't

You Worry 'Bout a Thing" just ten minutes after Divisi. Though not anybody's fault, it was no less embarrassing for Dulcet. Especially since the song was a hot mess. For an audience member, it was a bit like watching figure skating on television. You know that fourteen-year-old girl is going to end up on her ass. It's just a matter of when.

But more than that, it was On the Rocks who did Divisi the biggest favor of the night. OTR's set opened with "Smile Like You Mean It," by the Killers. While the choreography was impossibly cheesy—there was a lot of air guitar followed by the Michael Jackson lean—it worked for them. "We could never get away with that choreography," Marissa Neitling says. But ultimately, it was a wardrobe malfunction that sealed the deal. Divisi's brother group, On the Rocks, wears armbands and vests for a retro barbershop look. Tonight their music director Brenton made a tactical error when, midsong, he tore off his vest in a comic striptease, tossing it to the side of the stage. When it came time for OTR to sing their final song, a medley of Stevie Wonder's "Superstition" and Alicia Keys's "Karma," Brenton looked confused. The group was staring at him, waiting for him to blow the pitch pipe. He tapped his trousers—both front and back. Doh! While the striptease had looked cool in the moment, Brenton's pitch pipe had been in his vest pocket. He quickly ran offstage to retrieve it, as the men from OTR just stood there smiling awkwardly. The damage was done. Spooked, perhaps, their final song was disastrously flat.

ICCA West Coast producer, Jen Levitz, appeared onstage, inviting the competing a cappella groups to join her onstage as she read the results. "Can I get a drumroll from the vocal percussionists," Jen said. Ha. Ha. Divisi won with a commanding lead. In sports (and a cappella is a sport) that's called an ugly win. Still, Divisi was jumping up and down wildly, some of them crying through their encore.

Later that night, Divisi retreated to Emmalee Almroth's house for the postshow festivities. The members of On the Rocks, having changed out of their barbershop gear, were visibly crushed. Divisi's Megan Schimmer was torn between celebrating with her girls and comforting her boyfriend—a tenor in On the Rocks. To make matters worse, On the Rocks had landed in third place, a mere *two points* behind the second-place finishers, Oregon State's Outspoken.

Peter Hollens was at the party. He congratulated the ladies of Divisi on the big win. What he didn't say was that the next morning, when he'd be phoning Sarah Klein to recap the show, he would have to deliver some harsh news. "You can't win at semifinals with Stevie Wonder," he will say. "You need to cut Betsy's song from the set." But tonight, well, there's drinking to be done. Andrea Welsh stands in the kitchen and pops open a bottle of her signature pink champagne.

Divisi sold more than seventeen hundred tickets to the show and will pocket fourteen thousand dollars. They won't have to fundraise a dime to get to the semifinals, which are scheduled for March 10 outside San Francisco. Divisi books their hotel rooms. They have five weeks to prepare.

What they don't know is that a big ol' Mormon torpedo is headed straight for them. Keeley comes home from class one day not long after the quarterfinals to find an e-mail from Catherine Papworth, the music director of Noteworthy, the all-female a cappella group from Brigham Young University. Like Divisi, the Mormon women had won their own regional quarterfinal. The a cappella message boards at RARB had lit up with talk of Noteworthy's impressive showing—these girls had the highest point totals in the nation.

The e-mail to Keeley went something like this: "We see that

'Don't You Worry 'Bout a Thing' is in your repertoire. We just
wanted to let you know that *we're* going to sing that song at
semifinals. Also, we know that you wear red ties and black shirts.
We wanted you to know that we'll be wearing *green ties* and
black shirts. If you feel uncomfortable with that, you might want
to wear red shirts."

Keeley is dumbstruck by what she is reading. Considering
these Noteworthy ladies are Mormon, she concedes that this e-
mail affront may have been unintentional. Still, she is incensed,
and quickly hits REPLY. "We've been wearing these outfits since
2001," Keeley writes. "Why would *we* change our outfits? If you
feel uncomfortable, feel free to change *yours*."

Marissa Neitling is particularly troubled by this note from
Brigham Young's Catherine Papworth. And it has nothing to do
with Stevie Wonder or what color ties the girls will be wearing in
competition. No, this is *personal*. Marissa Neitling's ex-boyfriend,
the one who was married just seven months after they broke
up—he's Catherine Papworth's brother.

CHAPTER NINE

THE BEELZEBUBS

*Wherein the Bubs descend on their founder's lake house
for ten days of recording in January while a true Hollywood
a cappella story unfolds*

Shortly after New Year's Day, the Beelzebubs descend upon a lake house in Moultonborough, New Hampshire, set deep back in the woods. It's easily a twenty-minute drive to get milk, farther for anything more substantial. The refrigerator is stocked with dozens of eggs. The kitchen counter is lined with loaves of white bread and jars of peanut butter. Over the next ten days the Beelzebubs will complete most of the raw tracks for their new album. And surprisingly—or maybe not—there's not a beer in sight. Alcohol would be a distraction. (By contrast, the Hullaba-hoos regularly show up at the recording studio hungover and carrying McDonald's.) This seclusion—this a cappella monastery, if you will—is an ideal place to record; the lake house affords the inspirational quiet they found at the legendary Long View Farms but doesn't cost fifteen hundred dollars a day. In fact, this house is free to use. This New Hampshire estate is owned by the sixty-something founder of the Beelzebubs, one Tim Vaill '64.

The Bubs have settled on a sound for the new album, though they have a hard time putting that aesthetic into words. "They just want to make it *organic*," says Ed Boyer, the Bub alum being paid to produce the album. *Organic* is a nebulous word. But Ed knows what they mean. It's a reaction to the too-perfect, polished (some say computerized) feel of their own most recent albums *Code Red* and *Shedding*. "We wanted to get away from mimicking instruments," says Alexander Koutzoukis, who just took over as music director of the Bubs. "We didn't want people to question whether they were hearing voices or not."

"The Bubs want an album that showcases more of the group's energy and their live performance," Ed Boyer says. "As opposed to something that says, Hey, this is what we can do in the studio." This is easier said than done.

On that second morning, Ed Boyer gathers the Bubs in the house's great room, with its cathedral ceiling and wood beams, not to mention its panoramic view of Squam Lake. Each day begins with an hour-long discussion of what's to come, followed by an elaborate set of warm-ups and exercises. Today the Bubs talk about recording Gnarls Barkley's "Smiley Faces"—that morning's project. They talk about what the song means. "Even if you're not happy," Chris Van Lenten says, "you're putting on this smiley face and pretending."

When it comes time to warm up their voices, Ed leads the exercises. After their usual warm-ups and scales, Ed asks certain Bubs to step out in front of the group and sing a song in, say, "the style of Greg Binstock." Greg Binstock, an alum, had arguably the best solo voice in the history of the Bubs, but he had a certain swishy quality to his trills. It's a round robin game of imitation. "Sing 'Smiley Faces' in the style of Jay Lifton," Ed shouts, pointing to someone else. "Sing 'Cecilia' in the style of Marty Fernandi." Marty Fernandi graduated before some of these kids were born.

This may all seem haphazard—overkill, even—but there is a method to Ed's madness. "I'm trying to get the Bubs creatively invested in the recording process," he says. "Because if they're not invested they'll stop contributing. I'm showing them how to

sing outside the box. I need them to be spontaneous and un-
afraid." The biggest problem with a cappella recording may be
capturing the combustion, the blood presence of a live performance. "I keep telling them," Ed says, "don't get hung up on
rhythm and pitch." With Pro Tools, with Auto-Tune, Ed can fix
all that. "Just worry about keeping the energy up."

The Vaill compound consists of two residences—the main
house (a cavernous maze of bedrooms) and a guest cabin some
thirty yards away. The cabin is outfitted like some Barbie Goes
Camping play-set—what with the bedroom set seemingly made
of Lincoln Logs. Ed Boyer '04 has set up his equipment in this
bedroom-cum-control room, the Pro Tools rig up on the computer screen, the soundboard to Ed's right. Across the hall is a
second bedroom—now a makeshift studio where the Bubs hang
patches of gray foam, the kind legit studios use to dampen reverb
and echo.

How exactly can the Bubs get *Code Red*–level professionalism
out of this tree house? For one thing, when recording went
digital—and portable—everything changed. The act of recording is
no longer linear; you don't have to record in a timeline. "You have
the *authority* of the computer," Ed explains. A great band might
still record live. That's ideal. "A live band finds their groove," Ed
says. "But what are the chances that fifteen guys will have that
groove together?" Instead, the Bubs record individually with Ed,
each listening to a cue track in his ear and singing directly into the
mic. (A cue track is nothing more than a note-by-note recording of
a tune—it might even be Ed playing, say, the baritone part to "In
Your Eyes" on a keyboard, or a MIDI file of the actual arrangement.) Since its introduction to collegiate a cappella in the mid-
nineties, the cue track has revolutionized recording, in that each
member can record separately—knowing that he or she will maintain the same pitch and tempo as the rest of the group. All of those
individual tracks are then edited together in a painstaking, boring

process. And what of the sound quality itself? Thankfully, this is all what's called close mic recording, and a Bub singing into even a half-decent microphone will produce usable audio.

Ed Boyer is surrounded by Matt Michelson, Andrew Savini, and a handful of Beelzebubs laid out across the bed. A freshman, Tim Conrad, sits over to the side, asleep on a rocking chair. It is four-thirty on Monday, January 8, and much of Moultonborough, New Hampshire, has iced over. The sun is starting to set when Ed asks for candles. He likes to work by candlelight when he can. It sets the mood, relaxing the gray matter and setting the stage for creativity. Someone runs down to the house and comes back with a couple of candles, which they light and set about the two-bedroom wood cabin.

Matt Michelson, the president, issues a warning. "Let's try not to burn *this* house down," he says. He is not kidding.

Why, exactly, Tim Vaill agreed to let the Bubs invade his New Hampshire residence time and again remains a mystery. Because this man, the founder of the Bubs, remembers exactly where he was when the Beelzebubs burned down another of his properties. "It was June first, 2005," he says, matter-of-factly. And Vaill, class of 1964, was on vacation deep within the lush countryside of western China, alongside John McCarthy '68 and fellow Beelzebub alum Ray Tang '72. At some point in their journey Ray's BlackBerry managed to pick up a signal—for a split second, anyway—just long enough to receive a message from Tim's assistant back in Boston. She kept it short: "Your house in Somerville burned down." It would be twelve hours before Vaill would get a Beelzebub on the phone. "I had no idea if anyone was hurt," Vaill says. "And I was worried about the guys." To make matters worse, the house at 157 College Avenue had been on the market, and just a few days earlier Vaill accepted an offer to sell the place.

Tim Vaill grew up in Bethany, Connecticut, just outside New Haven, the son of a Yale man, class of '35—a man who in his day had been the head of the Whiffenpoofs, the first-ever collegiate a cappella group. There was always music playing in the Vaill household, and more often than not it was one of his father's old Whiffenpoof records. When it came time to apply to college, the young Tim Vaill wanted to get away from New Haven and settled on Tufts (though whether he had the grades for Yale is another matter). His father's parting words were, prophetically: "If there is an a cappella group on campus, join it. If not, start one."

The thing is, there *had* been an a cappella group on campus, something called the Tuft Tones, but they were long gone. It was the fall of 1960, Tim Vaill was a freshman, and folk music was the thing—the Kingston Trio, the Weavers, that's what the kids wanted to hear. So Tim Vaill joined a five-man folk band, the Nomads V. Improbably, the group got an agent who booked them at colleges along the eastern seaboard. The boys would leave campus on a Wednesday night and return bleary-eyed on Sunday. Believe it or not, Dizzy Gillespie once opened for Tim Vaill and the Nomads V somewhere outside of Philadelphia. "No one was interested in jazz at the time," Vaill says. Success was fleeting. During Vaill's sophomore year, two of the V flunked out of school (only to sign contracts with MGM). Tim Vaill, meanwhile, a math major on an ROTC scholarship, returned to his studies.

That's when Tim remembered his father's advice. In October 1962 he convinced his buddies, Barrie Bruce '63 and Neal Robison '63, to start an a cappella group. Neal would be the music director and together they recruited six others for their first rehearsal in the basement of West Hall.

The first song the group learned was "Winter Wonderland"; their first set included "No Man Is an Island" and "Theme from Exodus." "It was ponderous stuff," Vaill says, with a smile. As for dress, the a cappella group wore madras jackets. "Everyone owned a madras jacket in those days," Vaill says.

The gigs were slow in coming. The first would be a sorority Christmas party in early December 1962 at a hotel in Lexington, Massachusetts. But the group's real coming-out party would be the Tufts annual Christmas Sing—a campus-wide talent show held at the Cousins Gym. At the time, it was very fashionable to attend. "The Christmas Sing was the thing to do," Vaill says. And confident in the group's musical progress, Vaill set about registering for the show. There was only one problem: They still didn't have a name.

Vaill retreated to Barrie Bruce's dorm room. Names were bandied about, including Jumbo's Disciples—after the Tufts mascot. Still, the men could not agree. In the midst of a spirited two-hour discussion (the first in a history of marathon sit-downs for the Bubs), John Todd mentioned Beelzebub. His roommate had been reading Milton's *Paradise Lost*, in which Beelzebub was the devil's right-hand man. Tim Vaill liked it. The name was dangerous, he says. And weren't they dangerous guys? Still, the conversation dragged on and a compromise was eventually made. The next day Vaill scrawled a name, JUMBO'S DISCIPLES: THE BEELZEBUBS, on the sign-up sheet for the big Christmas Sing.

From the very beginning the Beelzebubs (they soon dropped the cumbersome Jumbo's Disciples bit) remained independent from the university. Why they valued their independence so much is the subject of some speculation. There are current Bubs and Bub alums alike who believe it was part of some countercultural movement. Not true, Vaill says. "This was before people were antiestablishment," he says. "It's because none of us liked the chair of the music department." The feeling was mutual. The man's name was Rod MacKillop (now deceased) and he despised the Bubs. You can't blame the guy. "We were raiding from his choir," Vaill says.

Over the course of 1963, word of the Beelzebubs spread about campus. Still, the group was limited by their repertoire. "We needed *music*," Vaill says. And so he rang up his father, who wasn't just a Whiffenpoof alum but an administrator at Yale. One weekend Vaill *père* unlocked the music department archives for his son, who proceeded to "borrow" from the Yale Glee Club library. "Were there Xerox machines in 1963?" Vaill asks. He can't remember. But somehow the four-part arrangements from Yale made it back to Tufts. The Beelzebubs recorded their first album, *Brothers in Song*, in the spring of 1964 in the dining room of the Delta Tau Delta fraternity house.

Tim Vaill graduated in June of 1964 and the future of the Bubs was very much in doubt. Vaill, a navy man, was off to Vietnam. Bill Duvel had taken over as music director from Neal and would remain in charge, but Vaill had been the driving force. When the Bubs reconvened in the fall of 1964, Vaill was aboard the USS *Taluga*, floating somewhere in the South China seas. (Their mission: to supply jet fuel to fighter planes.) Despite his far-flung surroundings, not a day went by when Vaill didn't think about his beloved Beelzebubs back at Tufts. He wrote letters home but heard nothing.

Finally, one day in early October, a bruised and battered manila envelope showed up on the deck of the USS *Taluga*. Vaill still remembers that day, how he tore into the envelope. In his hands, he held a reel-to-reel tape the current Beelzebubs had recorded for him. The Bubs had survived. Vaill spent nine months in Vietnam. Later, safe at home, he sent the Bubs a typewritten letter (now preserved in the 1965 Bubs scrapbook) along with a check. The return address read: USS *Taluga* (AO-62), FPO SFRAN, CALI, Ensign T. L. Vaill. "Please find the first of what I hope will be many contributions to the cause of the Beelzebubs," Vaill wrote.

In the years since, Vaill has never been far from the Bubs. He started the Beelzebubs Alumni Association (the BAA) in the summer of 1966. In 1973—for the group's ten-year anniversary—Vaill organized a dinner at the Sheraton Commander Hotel in Cambridge. To mark the occasion, Vaill and a couple of alums—under cover of night—met to form a quartet. They called themselves Peking and the Mystics and they wore hospital whites because Ray Tang could "borrow" them from the nursing home where he worked. In the middle of the inaugural performance, the men of Peking stripped down to reveal blue Peking and the Mystics T-shirts they'd had printed up.

Years later, Vaill and his wife began inviting the undergraduates to his house in Andover, Massachusetts, twice annually for formal Bubs events: In the fall, there was the annual Vaill football game, and in the spring, Lasagna Night. "It's rare for a man in his sixties to know so many young people," Vaill says, "to be on a first-name basis with so many. But the intergenerational contact is one of the best things about the Bubs." For Tim Vaill, the whole experience was doubly sweet when, in the fall of 1998, his own son, Sam Vaill, transferred to Tufts and auditioned for the Bubs. There's no room for nepotism in a smallish singing group, and the audition could have been awkward for all parties involved. But the call came at four A.M. Sam Vaill had been accepted into the Bubs.

Over the years, the Bub alums had often talked about securing a Beelzebubs House—a home base, of sorts, that would be part rehearsal space, part museum, part dormitory. "I had no desire to be a landlord," Vaill says. But, in the spring of 2003, Tim Vaill put his money where his mouth was and launched the Beelzebubs Housing Project, signing the papers on a two-family, wood frame house with a porch on College Avenue, across the street from the Tufts football field. He made some minor home improvements—including new appliances in the kitchen. But the house was meant to run itself. He rented the ground floor to a couple of Tufts students and saved the top two floors for the Bubs. Ed Boyer was among the first to move in.

Very quickly, however, Tim Vaill's worst fears were confirmed. The kids on the ground floor called when the toilet broke. Vaill was the president of Boston Private Bank, with a thousand employees working for him. He certainly didn't need the aggravation. Vaill would rent the house to the Bubs for a second year, but in the spring of 2005 he put the place on the market. It sold quickly. On May 28, 2005—Memorial Day weekend—he received an offer. Vaill wasn't evicting the Bubs. The sale was contingent on the new owner leasing the house to the Bubs for the 2005–2006 school year. And Matt Michelson, Matt Kraft, and three others had already committed to living there in the fall. Until, that is, Sean Zinsmeister '06 decided to have a barbecue. ("I'm not talking about this," Zinsmeister says.) Details are scarce. What we do know is that sometime around two in the morning a gust of wind knocked over the barbecue, spilling hot coals and ash onto the wood deck. Kyron Rogers '06 would bang on doors, shuffling sleepy Beelzebubs out of the house. No one was hurt, though all were shaken as they watched their beloved Bubs house burn to the ground. When people on campus ask what happened to the house, Michelson likes to tell them "It was a grilling accident." Tim Vaill got the call in China. When he returned home to Boston he would sell the scorched earth to another buyer. Somehow, against reason, he still allows the fifteen members of the Beelzebubs to enjoy his lake house in New Hampshire unsupervised.

And in January 2007, after a long day of recording, the Bubs sit around the dinner table eating a pot of beef stew one of their own cooked up. There are compliments for the chef, but not much in the way of meaningful conversation. Rather, the Bubs are preoccupied with a DVD playing on screen, something called *Pirates!*—a take-off on *Pirates of the Caribbean*—which any Bub will proudly tell you is the most expensive porno ever made.

These are long days—and nights—at Squam. While some of the Bubs relax after dinner (with another screening of *Pirates!* or with bowling on the Nintendo Wii) Ed Boyer returns to the log cabin to record soloists. It's a smaller group tonight when Andrew Savini steps into the second bedroom to lay down the solo for Ozzy Osbourne's surprisingly sweet ballad "Mama, I'm Coming Home." It is ten-fifteen at night. Savini will not emerge—save for a cigarette break—for nearly four hours. (For the record, Ed gets a flat fee for the week. With his other a cappella clients he will work by the hour, but for the Bubs, he gives himself over to the project unconditionally.)

"Let's just try it once to see where we are," Ed says.

Savini sings the song clear through before joining Ed at the computer to listen to the playback. Savini is worried that the solo sounds too boy-bandish. He puts a lot of pressure on himself. His solo, "Epiphany," off of 2005's *Shedding*, won the Contemporary A Cappella Recording award for Best Soloist, and he'd like to repeat the honor. Ed has his own thoughts. "On the first verse," Ed says, "keep it simple. You don't want to empty out your bag of tricks there. The song has to build—it needs somewhere to go."

And so Savini goes back to the booth to sing again. This time, on *home*, he sings high—and dramatic. *"Mama, I'm coming HOME."* Ed interrupts. "That there," Ed says, "when you go up, that was a major chord. Let's keep it minor." There are similar problems with the chorus. It's all too big too soon. Ed sends Savini back into the booth and has him record the solo sentence by sentence. It is excruciating. When Andrew reverts back to his vocal tics, to singing *ty-hi-ime* instead of *time*, Ed abruptly cuts him off and rewinds. "That last take sounded a bit *Phantom of the Opera*," Ed says. The conversation drags on. At times Ed gives Savini advice that is long on words, yet short on practical suggestions. It's starting to feel a bit like that scene in *Lost in Translation*—where the Japanese director speaks for thirty seconds and it's translated into *More intensity!* But somehow it works, and Savini—never known for subtlety—delivers a re-strained, moving vocal for the solo.

Later in the week, Matt McCormick (a freshman) comes in to record the lead vocals on U2's "City of Blinding Lights." It is a different session entirely, with its own set of challenges. "Sometimes they don't know how to connect their voices to the emotional message of the song," Ed says. On the verses Matt McCormick was a bit too happy-go-lucky. "In concert, when you're singing live, you need to be big," Ed tells him. "But in the studio, let's bring this down. There should be a contrast with the chorus and the verse." He pushes Matt. "In the studio," Ed says, "you can go for a note you wouldn't necessarily get live. Don't cop out."

As Sean Zinsmeister '06 had said, the Bubs needed to "respond to the critics." And they would, in their own way. With Ed's help, the Bubs find their voice that week, find a way to make something organic that still sounds full. Many of the arrangements this time out featured the Bubs singing actual words, as opposed to just *jeer-neers* for guitars and random *ooh*s and *aah*s. Leading into the chorus on "Mama, I'm Coming Home," the Bubs sing *selfish love-aaaaaahhhhh*. Later the group echoes the solo, singing *have it all*. It may sound simple, Alexander Koutzoukis says. "But these are textual things. If we're singing words, like *selfish love*, it gives us a chance to emote and express the song. It's singing words versus singing *dim* and *wow*. It allows us to embed that aspect of our live performance into the album." It's brilliant. No matter how much you tweak a guitar in Pro Tools, it ain't gonna sing *selfish love*. The album would be produced, polished. But it would unmistakably be the product of the human voice. Which is, after all, what a cappella is all about.

Ed Boyer has his own bag of tricks, his own bit of artistry to add. One afternoon, Ed sends Matt Michelson into the padded room, where he directs him to pluck out the notes to "Mary Had a Little Lamb" by tapping his index finger against his teeth. Ed adjusts the speed of the recording. He adjusts the pitch. Colors flash on the screen. Lines bend. The Bubs call this noisemaking gilding.

While one can't exactly make out what's going on in the background, this much is clear: When Ed places this track behind the trippy fifteen-second bridge of "Magical Mystery Tour," for whatever reason, the song sounds better, fuller, more fleshed out. This is just one tool in Ed's arsenal. "There should be just enough going on in the background where you hear something," Ed says, "but you're not sure exactly what the thing is." There is a history of burying sounds in the background of Beelzebubs recordings. On *Shedding*'s "You Can't Always Get What You Want" one can almost make out the name Guang Ming—a notorious Beelzebubs fan and a reviewer for RARB. It's comical maybe, but is this any different different from Brian Wilson adding dog whistles over the intricate harmonies on the landmark 1966 Beach Boys album *Pet Sounds*? Brian Wilson used the studio as an instrument. Weren't the Bubs doing the same thing? (This is not a rhetorical question.) Still, it can get disturbingly out of hand.

Ed hits PLAY on "Mystery Tour." "We should add a bong noise here," Ed says, mimicking the sound of bubbling water. Lucas Walker auditions his bong noise for the Bubs, and they unanimously approve, sending him into the booth. He gives it a good shot, but Ed interrupts. It turns out that—like the sound of tapping individual teeth—the sound of water bubbling actually has a pitch. You can do a bong noise on a G or an A or an F-sharp.

"Do it again," Ed says. "But pitched higher."

Lucas suggests adding "tickles" to the track. And so in the second room the Bubs tickle Nick Lamm for thirty seconds. Ed records it, tweaks the track, adds an echo, and then plays it back in reverse.

"It sounds like seagulls," someone says.

"Try it without the echo."

Someone questions why the laughs are in reverse. "Is that weird just to be weird?"

"Isn't *just weird* the point?" Ed says, his right eye twitching—a sign that he's concentrating. This is "Magical Mystery Tour." The Beatles weren't singing about candy canes and rainbows. Ed plays the laugh back again behind the seagulls and Michelson's "Mary Had a Little Lamb." The group is unconvinced.

"We're beating a dead horse," Ed says.

"It doesn't sound *backward*," someone says.

To recap: Seven people have just spent twenty minutes debating the merits of a laugh track that is more or less inaudible to the naked ear. Ed had worried about the Bubs not being invested. Perhaps they were *too* invested.

They move on to Peter Gabriel's "Diggin' in the Dirt." Someone says the emotion is missing, that the track "needs a raw human factor." "Can we get someone to cry into the microphone?" Lucas asks.

There were moments of levity that week, including dips in the Vaill family hot tub, not to mention an elaborate parlor game involving Tim Vaill's electric dog fence. (In short: Two Bubs would each strap on a collar—you know, the one that not so gently zaps a dog when he's strayed outside the property line—while the rest of the group would place bets on who could creep farther away without getting tasered.) But mostly it was a lot of hard studio work, and on the final sunset at Squam Lake, Ed looked the worse for wear, with big, heavy bags under his eyes and a few pounds on the waist.

The Bubs settled on a title for the new album, *Pandaemonium*, inspired by Milton's epic *Paradise Lost* (from which the Beelzebubs also derive their name). Pandaemonium was the capital city of Hell and the title was meant to be ironic, a commentary on their music, which was (unlike hell) controlled chaos. Though, considering how the year began, *chaotic* sounded about right.

On the final night at Squam Lake, Ed Boyer sat down with the Bubs and played a rough mix of the album. And the group seemed pleased with what they heard, though Ed has his reservations about the album, describing it as "brighter" than the past few. "It's too choral for my taste," he says. "It sounds like a big group of guys singing, and to me, that aesthetic doesn't change enough." It was a valid point. Would this new organic sound come across as progressive, or would it sound like an a cappella album recorded twenty years ago? "We try not to think about the reviews," Alexander Koutzoukis says, though he admits the pressure is there. There was a more immediate problem in that the album was still missing a closer. The Bubs debated using "Living on the Edge" or "Ruby Falls" but neither felt quite right. When this conversation resumes two months later—during a spring-break trip to San Diego, no less—the Bubs will settle the matter by locking themselves in a room for eight hours.

Perhaps the Bubs were right to debate these questions so heavily. Lord knows there were plenty of people bowing at the altar of the Beelzebubs. Bruce Leddy was one of those people.

Herein, an a cappella true Hollywood story.

While the Bubs were recording their new album, Bruce Leddy was trying to sell his movie, *Shut Up and Sing*—a *Big Chill*–type story (costarring *Saturday Night Live*'s Molly Shannon) set against the backdrop of a collegiate a cappella group reuniting for a friend's wedding. The film opens with a flashback to the fictional a cappella group back in college, onstage at their final concert before graduation. They are singing Phil Collins's "Take Me Home." Or lip-synching really—to the Beelzebubs' recording of "Take Me Home," no less, arranged by Travis Mitchell, produced by Ed Boyer, with a solo by Mike Flynn. The recording appeared on *Code Red*, not to mention the BOCA 2004 disc, which is where Bruce Leddy found it while doing research for his film.

"There was no way I could do better than that recording," Bruce Leddy says. "The record and the arrangement were spectacular." When *Shut Up and Sing* went before the cameras, Bruce enlisted Sean Altman (late of Rockapella) to coach his actors, to give their performances some measure of authenticity. But he had his heart set on using the original Bubs recording. And so, before filming began, Bruce Leddy e-mailed Ed Boyer requesting permission. The two worked out a deal: If anything ever happened with *Shut Up and Sing*, if it ever found its way to theaters or DVD, the Bubs would get a thousand dollars—plus royalties on any album sales. Bruce didn't yet have a distribution deal for *Shut Up and Sing*, but, yes, he was already thinking about a possible soundtrack. He thought the album could mimic the success of the soundtrack to the Coen brothers film *O Brother, Where Art Thou?*—which sold more than four million copies. "People didn't know they liked bluegrass music until they saw *O Brother*," Bruce says. "It could be the same with a cappella."

Shut Up and Sing premiered at the HBO/Aspen Comedy Festival in March of 2006, where it won the audience award (despite the fact that *Variety* called the film "trite"). To promote in Aspen, Bruce flew in a pro a cappella group called Extreme Measures, which stood around in the cold wearing SHUT UP AND SING hats and trying to coax people into the theater. The film played at eight or nine film festivals that year but still hadn't sold.

Not surprisingly, Bruce Leddy was himself a singer. Years ago, as a student at Williams College, he was a member of the Williams Octet. "There were more than eight of us," Leddy says, repeating a popular a cappella joke. Leddy graduated in 1983 and moved to Manhattan, where he and some friends continued to sing together, every now and again, under the name the Lemmings. They'd sing at a wedding once a year, maybe. Or they'd put on a little show for friends and family at Michael's Pub on Fifty-fifth Street (the same watering hole where Woody Allen plays with his jazz combo). The experience inspired the screenplay for *Shut Up and Sing*.

This was not Bruce's first foray into Hollywood. He'd had some bad luck with the Hollywood studio system (he wrote a script for Paramount that's still sitting on a shelf somewhere in the bowels of the building) and so when it came time to produce his a cappella script, he decided to go the indie route. "I was worried if I took it to a studio," Bruce says, "they would have asked me to make it, like, a hip-hop group or something."

Much like the Bubs, the Williams Octet had developed their own shorthand, their own vocabulary. Their big running joke was *Shut up!*, which had become their universal greeting. They'd call each other on the phone. When the other guy picked up, the caller would shout, "Shut up!" The joke evolved from there. Soon it became "Be quiet!" (Eventually, though no one knows when or how, the greeting was reduced to *"Die!"*) Hence the title *Shut Up and Sing*. Now, this is where the story goes all wonky. Bruce Leddy's film *was* called *Shut Up and Sing*. Until, that is, Harvey Weinstein bought a little movie out of the 2006 Toronto Film Festival, a documentary about the controversial politics of the Dixie Chicks, a movie called *Dixie Chicks: Shut Up & Sing*.

Bruce Leddy was incensed. "We'd been out for six months with that title," he said. "And the title is intrinsic to the plot of my movie." He sent an e-mail to that other film's director, Barbara Kopple, a two-time Oscar-winning documentarian. She was sympathetic to a point. "We're going to have that title," she wrote. "It's worse. Harvey Weinstein wants to drop *Dixie Chicks* from the title." Now there were two films called *Shut Up and Sing*. And only one had a distribution deal.

Bruce found an intellectual property lawyer who wanted a forty-thousand-dollar retainer fee to take on Harvey. "We've got an open-and-shut case," the guy said. "We'll nail them to the wall." But an hour later the guy called back to say that, on second thought, Bruce Leddy didn't have a shot in hell. Harvey Weinstein had waited until the last minute to announce the title change for a reason, the lawyer explained. "They've already spent millions on advertising buys and prints so they can win this argument," the lawyer said. "It'll cost you a hundred thousand dollars by the end of the week." The whole film didn't cost much more than that.

Bruce Leddy sent an e-mail to some friends asking them to suggest a new title for his movie. "What about *The Wedding Weekend?*" someone replied. Bruce eventually settled on *Sing Now or Forever Hold Your Peace*. Why? "Someone I know in marketing told me we needed a title like *My Big Fat Greek Wedding*. Something so long, so unruly, that people would remember it. The name does its own marketing."

Ed Boyer and a few of the Bubs went to check the film out when it played the Providence Film Festival in 2006. They were not impressed. "They'd taken out some of the more obvious studio elements of our recording," Ed says. "But it was supposed to be six guys singing onstage and it sounded like there were at least twenty." Ed never thought the film would see the light of day.

In the midst of all this, Vince Vaughn's movie *The Break-Up* opened to a one-weekend haul of thirty-nine million dollars. That film featured an a cappella subplot involving Jennifer Aniston's on-screen brother. Bruce wasn't worried about *The Break-Up* affecting his movie's shot at a distribution deal—if anything, the a cappella exposure might help. Though, for the record, he didn't care for that movie. "I was more annoyed that it played a cappella as the butt of a joke," he says. "They made that guy out to be a loser because his hobby was a cappella. With my movie, we're bringing audiences to the theater to see a *Big Chill*–type relationship movie. *Then* they'll hear the a cappella and go, I had no idea a cappella was so cool."

Bruce continued to shop his film, *Sing Now or Forever Hold*

Your Peace. Finally, nearly a year after its premiere on the festival circuit, Bruce Leddy struck a deal with a small distributor, Strand Releasing. They would open the film that spring, on April 27, 2007, in New York, Los Angeles and, fittingly, Boston, home of the Bubs. They chose late April because that was when *My Big Fat Greek Wedding* opened.

CHAPTER TEN

THE HULLABAHOOS

Wherein the Hullabahoos travel to Los Angeles for winter break 2007 and attempt to (among other things) gain admission to the Playboy Mansion

On a Friday night in January, the Hullabahoos find themselves stuck in traffic. The boys are split between two sets of rent-a-wheels—a twelve-passenger van and a Dodge Caravan a few minutes apart. Not that it matters. The freeway, the fabled 101, may as well be a used-car lot.

Tonight, at the Staples Center in downtown Los Angeles, the Lakers are scheduled to face off against the Orlando Magic in front of twelve thousand fans, including regulars like Jack Nicholson and Tobey Maguire, not to mention the Los Angeles Laker Girls. Our beloved Hullabahoos booked this gig months ago—in fact, this whole trip to Los Angeles was built around their slot singing the national anthem at the Lakers game. (The five-day itinerary includes, among other stops, a gig for UVA alums, a tour of the Disney Concert Hall, and a couple of nights with the all-female a cappella group the USC Sirens.) The gig was Morgan Sword's baby—and he spent nearly six months trying to wear down the booker for the Lakers, Lisa Estrada. He sent a press kit. He followed up with phone calls. And now, well, here they were, staring down miles of traffic.

It is six-thirty P.M. The Hullabahoos are due to sound-check at seven. Joe Cassara calls the booker. According to Google Maps, he says, the trip is just 9.9 miles. They should still make it, right?

"We can hold the game until seven thirty-two," she says—a grace period of just two minutes. The Hullabahoos won't get to sound-check, she says, but that shouldn't be a problem. It's happened before. She repeats the time. "Seven thirty-two. That's the latest you can literally *run on*."

The Hullabahoos could see the Staples Center in the distance. After months of anticipation for tonight's gig, the stadium sits there taunting them. Patrick Lundquist suggested they run there. He was only half kidding.

The Hullabahoos had flown out to Los Angeles three days earlier. And the trip began with some emotional reverence. The founder of the Hullabahoos, Halsted Sullivan—now a television scribe in Los Angeles, last seen writing for ABC's *Carpoolers*—agreed to host the group for a couple of nights at his duplex in West Hollywood. He'd even stocked the fridge. Over the years, Halsted has kept up with the Hullabahoos canon, though he hasn't listened to much a cappella otherwise. "It's sort of like cleaning up your own baby's vomit," he says. "You'd do that, but you wouldn't clean up someone else's." He still has his Hullabahoos robe, by the way. It's hanging in his bedroom closet. "Just in case," he says, smiling. On the group's second night in L.A., Halsted took the Hullabahoos to a karaoke bar in Koreatown. At one point, Joe Whitney, a freshman, turned to Halsted. "Hey," he said, "I just realized something—*you founded the group the year I was born!*"

That was not the only time the Hullabahoos would embarrass Halsted that week. The guy wasn't just hosting the B'hoos, he'd set them up with a gig for the UVA alumni association in

L.A. too. When it came time to close that show, the B'hoos invited their alumni—founding members Halsted and Mark Lyons—up onstage to sing a song with them. Halsted's bowels sank. He'd told the Hullabahoos, specifically, that he didn't want to sing tonight. But standing there now, Halsted was pretty sure the group was about to launch into "Run Around Sue"—which had been Halsted's big undergraduate solo all those years before. Fearing the worst, Halsted made a little speech to the audience about being out of practice, about how long it had been since he'd sung with the group. He needn't have worried.

"They called Mark and me up to sing some song with them we'd never heard," Halsted says, confused. The founding members of the Hullabahoos just stood there, mouthing syllables and trying not to look stupid.

While the Hullabahoos had a number of gigs lined up, they couldn't come to the West Coast and not hit Vegas. So, bright and early on Thursday the eleventh of January, the day before the Lakers game, the Hullabahoos set out for twenty-four hours in Sin City. Morgan had bought a guidebook, the *Las Vegas Little Black Book*, which described the Rio Hotel and Casino as "down-to-earth" and "not for high rollers," which sounded about right. Hoping to save money, the seventeen Hullabahoos would cram into two standard rooms, which they'd booked on Orbitz. When it came time to check in, Morgan and Joe approached the front desk—while the Hullabahoos milled about behind them. It was fairly obvious what was going on here.

"How many keys do you need?" the receptionist asked. Morgan looked at Joe. Joe looked back at Morgan. Both turned to the receptionist. "Uh, four?" Joe said.

"Actually, make that *eight*," Morgan said. "We'll probably lose a couple." Joe nodded. "Yeah, we'll probably lose a couple."

The Hullabahoos were conspicuous everywhere they went. They managed to get into one casino undetected (it's twenty-one and over to gamble in Vegas), but when Morgan sat down to play blackjack, there were ten Hullabahoos standing right behind him watching. To make matters worse, they all wore matching coats and ties. The dealer looked at the B'hoos and said—brutal, concise—*"You boys should leave."*

It turned out to be a good night for Morgan and the elder Hullabahoos, anyway, to visit Vegas. Their trip happened to coincide with the annual AVN Expo—the weeklong trade show and convention for the porn industry. Chad Moses (the group treasurer) and Morgan sat down to play a few hands of blackjack at the Luxor.

"Where you boys from?" a man in a cowboy hat asked.

"Oh," Chad said, "we don't know each other. We just met."

"Oh," the man said. "OK. What line a work you in?"

"I'm in the adult industry," Chad said, smiling confidently, all dimples and teeth.

"Oh," the man said, tipping his hat. "I thought you looked familiar."

"No," Chad said. "I'm not in front of the camera. I'm a casting director."

"You here for the convention?" the man asked.

"Yup," Chad said, taking a sip from his free drink. (Free drinks!)

The man in the cowboy hat turned to Morgan. "You in the adult biz too?" he said.

"Nah," Morgan replied. "I'm in the Internet business. I founded Facebook."

"What's that?"

"Forget it."

Though no one got much sleep that night, the Hullabahoos were up bright and early, heading back to Los Angeles.

The Lakers game was that night. But first, they had a reservation for lunch—at Spago, Wolfgang Puck's fabled eatery in Beverly Hills.

Still dressed in their blazers and khakis from the night before, the B'hoos descended on the restaurant, sipping wine in their own private dining room. It was a lazy lunch, far from the UVA cafeteria. Here they ordered off a personalized menu that read WELCOME HULLABAHOOS. "I don't even know what this bread is," Matt Mooney, a freshman, says, reaching for the plate beside him, "but it's *awesome*."

How the Hullabahoos ended up at a tony spot like Spago is simple enough: Julie Neupert Stott, their benefactor, the woman who'd flown the boys out to Portland a few months earlier, had arranged the lunch—and generously paid for it. Sitting in Spago, Morgan proposed a toast. "To Patrick's arranged marriage!"

Mrs. Stott was nothing if not detail oriented. She even called the maître d' in advance, asking him to point out any celebrities who might be dining in the restaurant that day. "I thought it would be fun for the Hullabahoos," she says. There was, in fact, at least one celebrity there that day—Paul Allen, the cofounder of Microsoft and one of the world's richest men.

As the meal was wrapping up, Myles "Harry Potter" Glancy went to the bathroom. He was standing at the urinal when he heard a voice over his shoulder, a voice that belonged to none other than Paul Allen.

"Where are you boys from?" Paul Allen said, standing at the sink.

"The University of Virginia," Myles said.

"What brings you out here?"

"Oh, we're an a cappella group. We're singing the national anthem at the Lakers game tonight." Myles zipped up.

"Good luck with that," Paul Allen said, making his way

toward the door. He paused to look back at Myles. "Be careful," he says. "You don't want to wind up like that group from Yale."

It was a flip comment from the billionaire, all things considered. *That group from Yale* would be the Baker's Dozen. And much like the Hullabahoos, the Yale boys were also out in California for winter break that week. The Baker's Dozen, founded in 1947, had been coming to Los Angeles every Christmas for nearly twenty years. It was one of their favorite traditions not least of all because of Bruce Cohen's annual Yuletide party—which was sometimes held in January but always featured a celebrity guest. Bruce Cohen graduated from Yale in 1983 and had himself been a member of the Baker's Dozen. "Yale divided pretty quickly into those people who love and obsess about a cappella singing," he says, "and those who want to take a gun and shoot everyone involved." Bruce fell into the former group. After graduation, he went on to have a hugely successful Hollywood career, producing *American Beauty* (for which he won an Oscar). He never thought he'd see the BDs again. "In my day," he says, "you kept in touch with your friends, but there were no reunions. You wouldn't be caught dead going back to the BD Jam. You went on with your life." But in January 1992, Bruce got a call from a friend: The BDs were singing at a school in Pasadena.

"This was shocking to us," Bruce says. "That the BDs could afford a plane trip in our day was unimaginable. We went to Florida—and we drove! From Connecticut! In vans!" It turned out that, in the years since Bruce Cohen had left New Haven, the West Coast tour had become an annual BDs tradition. Bruce was overcome with nostalgia and in 1993 he invited the BDs to perform at his annual Christmas party. The location would change over the years—from a Los Angeles nightclub to Bruce's house in West Hollywood, the one above the Chateau Marmont with

Keeley McCowan (front) and the ladies of Divisi perform on campus at the University of Oregon on one of the first Friday afternoons of the 2006–2007 school year.

Michaela Cordova and the women of Divisi power through "You Had Me" onstage at the 2007 ICCA quarterfinals.

Marissa Neitling, CharliRae McConnell, Megan Schimmer,
Andrea Lucia, and Meghan Bell (from left to right) sing "Hide & Seek"
onstage at the Hult Center in Eugene, Oregon, for the
regional quarterfinals of the 2007 ICCAs.

Rachelle Wofford applies her war paint.

The original lineup of Jumbo's Disciples: The Beelzebubs in 1964.
The mustaches were part of a barbershop routine.

Matt McCormick (as Super Mario)
sings "City of Blinding Lights" at
Bubs in the Pub in April 2007.

The Beelzebubs old and new sing
"Brothers in Song" at Tim Vaill's
home in November 2006.

Ed Boyer '04 (seated foreground) and the Beelzebubs record
Pandaemonium in founder Tim Vaill's cabin on Squam Lake,
New Hampshire, in January 2007.

Chris Van Lenten reaches out for some support as
the Bubs rehearse at Squam Lake.

Lucas Walker blows the pitch pipe as the Bubs perform the national anthem at Fenway Park in May 2007.

Ben Appel performs with the Bubs at the Fall 2006 Homecoming Show at Goddard Chapel, days before he'll take a leave of absence from school.

Patrick Lundquist (front) and the University of Virginia
Hullabahoos perform at Rotunda Sing.

In October 2006, the Hullabahoos were treated to an
all-expenses-paid trip to Portland, Oregon. A chauffeur-driven stretch
Hummer escorted them around town.

The Hullabahoos pose in front of the Santa Monica pier
after a lucrative afternoon of busking in January 2007.

In a stirring moment, seniors Morgan Sword, Joe Cassara, and
Alan Webb sing Ben Folds's "Still Fighting It" at Big Spring
Sing Thing XIX in April 2007.

Kyle Mihalcoe, Pete Seibert, Chad Moses, and Morgan Sword of the Hullabahoos pose with President Bush at a fund-raiser in June 2007.

views all the way to Catalina—but the BDs have become a constant presence, singing two sets at every party. "They do a coherent set at nine-thirty," Bruce says. "Then they take an hour break. And when they come back they do a trashed, sloppy set." Still, even if the kids are enjoying a little eggnog, Bruce maintains order among the guests. The BDs are not a novelty act. "I have a strict complete-silence policy during the performance," Bruce says. "You can clap and enjoy the show. But you can't be *talking*—even in another room." He's not kidding.

Jim Carrey was at Bruce's Christmas party in 1993, the first to feature the BDs. Carrey was on *In Living Color* at the time and was prepping *Ace Ventura: Pet Detective* with Bruce's buddy, director Tom Shadyac. In 2005, Hilary Swank was there. Marisa Tomei is a veritable Christmas party regular. "I fell into the trap of presenting celebrities to the BDs," Bruce says. "It's a *thing* now. I feel like I have to deliver a big name." But, he acknowledges, it's easier than one would think to wrangle stars. "It's a two-way street," he says. "They come as a favor to me, but when they get here and they go into the bedroom and get a private concert from the BDs, they're loving it. Hilary Swank fell in love with them!"

In January of 2007, Bruce snagged a last-minute "set piece" for the BDs, a young actress named Amanda Bynes. "I didn't know her personally," Bruce admits. He didn't even know who she was. But the BDs, who'd grown up with Nickelodeon's *Amanda Show* and a bunch of the actress's teen movies, certainly did. "You can pull movie stars for days," Bruce says. "But I've never seen the BDs so excited. Amanda Bynes. I was a big hero."

But if Bruce Cohen was nervous about the party this year, it had nothing to do with Amanda Bynes. A few days before the Baker's Dozen had made international news. "People were e-mailing me from all over the world," Bruce Cohen says, his voice suddenly grave. The *San Francisco Chronicle* reported extensively on the incident. This is what happened:

The BDs had been invited to a New Year's Eve party at Rose Dawydiak-Rapagnani's house. The girl was a sophomore at Willamette University and she'd planned the party with her childhood friend Stephanie Soderborg, then a sophomore at Yale. Rose's parents were remodeling their three-story Edwardian home in San Francisco's Richmond District. The house was mostly empty, which made it a great space for a party, and the night was to be something of a reunion for the girls and their friends from St. Ignatius College Preparatory. But Stephanie was tight with the BDs and knew they'd be in town for winter break, and so she invited them to join in the revelry. (The e-vite read: A NIGHT OF MAYHEM.)

The girl's father, a retired police sergeant, and her mother (a sergeant out on disability) had vacated the house for the night, taking a room at the nearby Grand Hyatt. They'd locked the liquor cabinet and arranged for relatives next door to check in. "I had been a risk manager for the legal division of the police department," Rapagnani told the *San Francisco Chronicle*. "The last thing I wanted was kids served alcohol at my house."

The relatives did drop by, though they would later deny seeing any signs of alcohol. (Guests at the party insist it was essentially an open bar.) The Baker's Dozen, dressed in blazers and khakis, arrived at ten-thirty carrying, of all things, cheesecakes. At midnight, many of the revelers, including the BDs, locked arms and sang "The Star-Spangled Banner." An uninvited guest, dressed in a Santa Claus hat, declared this scene "the gayest shit I ever heard. What a bunch of fags."

A handful of BDs retreated to the back porch. That's when Sharyar Aziz Jr. of the Baker's Dozen was struck in the face with what he described to the *Chronicle* as "an open-handed slap." The party supposedly ended there, and Santa Claus and friends left. But twenty minutes later, as the BDs walked out the door, a blue-

and-white van pulled up outside and ten or twelve young men jumped out.

It took five minutes for a police car to arrive. Witnesses heard the gang yelling about "being in the four-one-five"—the San Francisco area code. One of the BDs was thrown to the ground where, in the fetal position, he weathered a series of blows. When the dust settled, Aziz had suffered a fractured jaw and nerve and tooth damage. He returned home and was treated at New York Presbyterian Hospital. His jaw was wired shut for eight weeks.

Rose Dawydiak-Rapagnani's parents were called shortly after midnight. They did not come home, believing everything to be under control. At ten the next morning they went down to the police station to investigate. The police told them (incorrectly) that no one had been hurt. Television crews descended. Truth be told, the case was hard to resist. A Yale singing group accosted outside a New Year's Eve party? Sean Hannity from Fox News even got in on the action, offering a ten-thousand-dollar reward for information leading to the arrest of the suspects. It's not that he was an a cappella fan, but this was an issue of national pride. These boys had been attacked for singing the "Star-Spangled Banner."

The media depicted the Yale kids as, ahem, choirboys. The truth is more complicated. Of course no one deserves to be on the end of a beating like that. But at Yale, a campus with at least fifteen a cappella groups, the Baker's Dozen are known as "the drinking group with a singing problem." They've had an on-campus house for nearly a decade and the BDs regularly throw Yale's first big party of the school year. "I think people are surprised to arrive at a party with hundreds of people and learn that it is being thrown by an a cappella group," says Brian Smith '01, a BD alum. From 1999 to 2003, the police were called to the BDs house at 235 Dwight Street twenty-eight times, according to *The Yale Daily News*.

Gavin Newsom, the San Francisco mayor, gave an interview to a KGO-TV reporter. "People are hiring attorneys everywhere and there's a lot of PR and spin that's been provided," he said. "So I'm hoping everyone tempers things, we have a professional investigation, investigations don't happen overnight and they certainly don't happen in the media. Why were these kids—they're all underage—why were they in a home with a lot of liquor, how'd they get the liquor, what the heck were they doing down there, why is everyone hiring an attorney, who's culpable, who's not?"

In March 2007, Sharyar Aziz Jr. filed suit against five men: Richard Aicardi and Brian Dwyer (both nineteen); Aicardi's twin brother, James, and twenty-year-old brother, Michael; and Marino Peradotto, twenty. He accused them of committing a "brutal ambush." Peradotto is a Marine lance corporal stationed overseas. A separate criminal suit was brought against Richard Aicardi and Dwyer. According to the suit, Aziz's doctors say that his jaw was broken by either a blunt instrument or "a blow by a professionally trained fighter." Still, it is doubtful that anyone will face jail time—a mix of alcohol, conflicting identifications, and the ages make it hard to seek incarceration. Even though Dwyer allegedly admitted in his statement to police, "[I] kicked someone on the ground. I kicked him hard and I meant to hurt him."

If there is a lesson to be learned from all this, it's not about class warfare, or even underage drinking. It's about dedication. It's also about jealousy—and the attention paid to a cappella singers. For all of the ink spilled, the media largely ignored the fact that the BDs *continued* their winter tour. Just a few days later, black eyes and all, dressed in their standard coats and ties, the BDs showed up for a previously scheduled gig at one of San Francisco's toughest public high schools. The school has seven full-time security guards and one full-time police officer (armed). One of the BD alums, Lance Alarcon '93, is a teacher at the school. Following the show that morning, Lance sent a message to the alumni listserv of the Baker's Dozen. "Our cop literally felt the need to personally escort the group—when he saw them arriving in their coats and ties—because he feared for their safety." It was a triumphant performance. "Despite what all these guys went through, with several of them sporting black eyes, that BD magic absolutely transcended socioeconomics, race, clothing style, culture, musical taste," Lance wrote. "It is not an exaggeration to say that it was more than a concert for our school. Our most badass security guard—he does 'scared straight' seminars at San Quentin with young juveniles—told me it was 'a beautiful experience.' Months later I still have students and faculty asking me about the BDs."

The BDs showed up at Bruce Cohen's annual Christmas party too. "They were in a little bit of denial and they were closed off," Bruce says. "On the one hand, they wanted to pretend it hadn't happened and go on with their tour. On the other hand, they didn't want to trivialize it and say, 'We're over it. And we're fine.' Because they weren't. I think they really didn't know what had happened, how to contextualize it. Was it a bunch of college boys in a brawl that got carried away? Or was it something much darker and more serious?" Amanda Bynes was a nice distraction.

In comparison, what happened to the Hullabahoos wasn't so newsworthy. Though it certainly felt like they'd been kicked in the face.

Our fabled Hullabahoos were on their way to the Staples Center to sing the national anthem at the Lakers game—a gig that had been on the books for months. Joe Cassara had just gotten off the phone with his contact at the Lakers. He had a pretty good poker face, and tried not to let on just how dire this traffic situation was. If they somehow missed tonight's performance, Matt Mooney, a Semitic-looking freshman with perma five o'clock shadow and frogs on his robe, would be particularly crushed. At a dorm picnic on the first night of school a few months ago, Mooney had made the mistake of admitting to Chad Moses, the Hullabahoos' treasurer who (as luck would have it) was also the kid's resident adviser, that he'd come to UVA *specifically* to join the Hullabahoos. Chad already knew this about Mooney because, earlier that afternoon, while Mooney was unpacking his things, the kid's mother had cornered Chad to grill him about the Hullabahoos. Chad's first thought? "Oh, shit." Mooney wasn't just one of Chad's advisees. The two were neighbors. "We share a wall," Chad says. "Awkward!" It would have been a long year had Mooney been tone deaf. Luckily, the kid could sing.

Sitting in the van, Joe Cassara was thinking back on the day they'd just had. The thing is, it had been a lazy afternoon. After lunch at Spago, the Hullabahoos spent hours lounging around. They took showers. They fell asleep on the couch. They watched television. They warmed up their voices. One sentence kept running through Joe's mind: *We could have left earlier.* That's when Morgan (in the minivan) called to say, "We gotta stop for gas." The gas gauge was reading close to empty.

"What?" Joe said.

"We gotta stop for gas."

"I heard you."

Pause.

"We don't have time to wait for you," Joe said. "Give me the directions to the Staples Center."

Morgan passed the phone to Pete Seibert, who'd lived out in L.A. last summer interning for Warner Music. "I think I remember how to get there," Pete told Joe. For all the time spent putting this gig together, no one had bothered to print out directions.

Joe looked around the big white van. It was six-forty. He was fairly certain the minivan, once they stopped for gas, wouldn't make the show. The twelve Hullabahoos in the white van began to rehearse the national anthem. "We have all the voice parts," Joe said. "We could do it."

They wouldn't get the chance. The Hullabahoos pulled up to the Staples Center at seven thirty-five. Joe Cassara was cursing, loudly. The Hullabahoos had officially missed the gig and Joe took his aggression out on a phone booth. Morgan, driving the Dodge Caravan, pulled up a few minutes later. No one was smiling. And for once, the Hullabahoos were dead quiet.

"It was poor planning," Joe said to no one in particular, shaking his head. He takes count of the group. "Where's Dane?"

Dane Blackburn hadn't wanted to come on this trip to begin with. "I wanted a break," he says. "It's called winter *break*." He saw enough of the Hullabahoos on campus. But the group had pressured him to come. Dane had some family in Los Angeles, and so he relented. He'd come for the Lakers game. With that obligation erased, he took off.

"His aunt just picked him up," someone said. "He said he'd meet us at the airport."

"What?" Joe said. "That's it? It's *Thursday*. We won't see him again until Sunday?" Joe dialed Dane's cell phone. It was a tense conversation. "We'll talk about this later," Joe said.

"Are we still going to the game?" Matt Mooney asked.

Brian Duhon, a baby-faced sophomore, sat fifteen rows behind the backboard. These seats had a face value of a hundred dollars. He looked like he might cry. "Seeing how big this place is makes it worse," he said. He did not crack a smile for over an hour—even as the Laker girls danced to "Fergalicious."

This was not the only disappointment for the B'hoos that week. They'd come to Los Angeles with dreams of hanging out at the Playboy Mansion—swimming in the Grotto, flirting with Hef's girlfriends. And darn they were going to try. So one afternoon, they pulled up to the front gate of the Mansion and innocently rang the bell. Brian Duhon talked into the video intercom.

He told the voice on the other end that they were an a cappella group from UVA. He wasn't getting anywhere. In a hail mary bid to prove their worth, Pete Seibert blew the pitch pipe and the Hullabahoos sang "One" into the intercom. When it was over, some say they heard clapping on the other end. Others insist it was merely the crackle of the intercom. Regardless, the gates did not open.

Postscript: Despite what Lisa Estrada—the first director of the Los Angeles Laker Girls and the game entertainment coordinator—told the B'hoos, in the six years she's been with the Lakers, no one has ever missed a performance of the national anthem. "Never," she said. On the night the Hullabahoos were scheduled to perform, the organist subbed in. "At least *he* was happy," she says.

CHAPTER ELEVEN

DIVISI

Wherein Divisi comes face-to-face with some Note-worthy ladies in the semifinals of the ICCAs

In January, Divisi took first place at the ICCA regional quarter-finals in Eugene, Oregon. They'd also earned fourteen thousand dollars from hosting that show. They wouldn't have to hold a single bake sale, let alone one demeaning car wash, to get to the regional semifinals in San Francisco. Still, if they stood any chance of winning once they got there, they would need to tweak their set. The girls pored over the judges' scoring sheets from that first round. There were some positive comments. "Nice intonation," one judge wrote. "Good 'tude," wrote another. But when it came to "Don't You Worry 'Bout a Thing," the troubled Stevie Wonder song, one judge was refreshingly critical. "Don't bury the soloist in the lower register," he wrote. Translation: You just couldn't hear Betsy Yates. It wasn't the girl's fault. And it certainly wasn't the fact that she'd had her tonsils taken out a month before the ICCAs. One of the highlights of Divisi's repertoire has always been the theme song to television's *Full House*. And Betsy kills it every time, because she's talented, and because the song falls comfortably in the sweet spot of her voice. But with "Don't You Worry 'Bout a Thing," the solo lived in that awkward space between her head voice (what guys call falsetto) and her chest voice. In short: great soloist, wrong song.

The scores only confirmed what Sarah Klein and Peter Hollens (the group's godfather, who was now engaged to Evynne Smith, one of the original Divisi Divas) already knew. If Divisi stood a chance of defeating the one-two Mormon punch of BYU's Vocal Point (the reigning ICCA champions) and Noteworthy ("We're wearing *green* ties and black shirts," their director said) come March, they'd need to cut "Don't You Worry 'Bout a Thing" from their set.

Sarah didn't waste much time, broaching this sensitive subject at one of the group's first rehearsals in February. "I spoke to Peter," she began gingerly. "He thinks—and we should *discuss* this—that it would be best to drop Stevie." Betsy Yates had known this was coming. She'd heard the chatter. She tried to stay out of it. "I want you to do what you think is best for the group," she allowed, and that's pretty much all she said. It would be a tense two hours. There was very little eye contact; some girls never looked up from the floor. Andrea Welsh—the den mother—was adamant that Divisi keep the song. "We've worked so hard on the choreography," she said. She blamed the tepid performance at the quarterfinals on nerves. It was like arguing in a vacuum. The girls hadn't yet seen the video of the quarterfinals. And when they did, a week later, Andrea was relieved she'd lost that round. "It's interesting to think you look and sound one way onstage," she says. "Then you see the video and it's like an entirely different group. We weren't crisp. We weren't sassy. I was totally off-base."

The problem then became: What would replace the Stevie Wonder song? And this question blew open the tragic flaw in a cappella competitions, and Adam Farb's biggest fear: Divisi had spent so much time perfecting those three songs that they hadn't learned much else. They had, of course, a repertoire of ten or so songs, but those were standard fallback tunes and certainly not competition-worthy. "Every week we were singing the same songs at the EMU," Emmalee Almroth said. There were just two songs on the table: "Sunday Morning" by Maroon 5 and a Guster tune, "Two Points for Honesty," which this incarnation of Divisi sort of learned but never bothered perfecting, because the soloist, Marissa Neitling, had spent last semester in the school play.

"Sunday Morning" was a slow burn, and it would be a risk to open their set with something so quiet. Plus, Maroon 5 was fast becoming the new Coldplay of collegiate a cappella—everyone was covering their music. But at least Divisi had performed that song. They didn't have time to start from scratch and so it was settled. There was something sweet about the decision. Keeley McCowan was the soloist on "Sunday Morning," and she was one of just two girls who'd performed at Lincoln Center almost two years ago when Divisi was robbed of the ICCA title. It was fitting she'd get a chance to make things right.

Still, there was a matter of choreography. Erica Barkett, the Divisi alum who'd drilled the girls a few weeks ago, somehow agreed to choreograph "Sunday Morning." She couldn't fly out to Eugene, though. Instead, she called Megan Schimmer and taught her the steps—over the phone. At rehearsal, when the girls wanted to know how a certain difficult dance move went, Megan threw up her hands and just said, "This is what it sounded like on the phone."

The girls had four weeks to prepare for the next round of the competition. If they won the regional semifinals in California, they'd return to Lincoln Center. That Divisi could start from scratch, essentially, with a new squad and *still* be the best—that was the goal. That would confirm that the Divisi name meant something. And these were tense rehearsals. Jenna Tooley had recovered from mono (and had her braces taken off) but was still missing rehearsals, still mysteriously absent. Rachelle Wofford was one of the first to speak that night when Divisi—as a whole—

confronted the girl. "If you don't want to be here," Rachelle said to Jenna, "I know a thousand girls who would take your spot." There was a lot of back-and-forth. Some of the girls just felt like they needed to speak—it wasn't that they had anything new to add to the conversation, they just wanted to air their resentment. Jenna pledged her allegiance to Divisi, and the matter was settled. Sort of. Jenna would remain in the group, provided she could handle the constant rolling of the eyes from the other girls every time she opened her mouth to speak.

Musically, Divisi was making progress. "Hide and Seek" had matured, as every swell, every note, every bit of the understated choreography was ironed out. On some deeper level, they'd connected with the music. "The group realized that every part of a song needs to go somewhere," Keeley says. "Even if it's a two-beat rest it's important. Even if there's no sound coming out, you need to keep that intensity." It had finally sunk in. "There's nothing in a piece of music that wasn't deliberately put there. And that includes a rest."

The week before leaving for San Rafael, California, Betsy Yates invited her new boyfriend to watch Divisi's regular Friday-afternoon performance at the EMU. The girls call him "Underwear Guy," and he showed up with Emmalee's boyfriend, better known as "Short Hot Guy." Divisi was happy for the support—even though the two men showed up drunk. When Betsy asked her boyfriend why he'd show up drunk to an *a cappella* show, Underwear Guy shrugged his shoulders. "Sometimes we like to preparty before a concert," he said.

Noteworthy—the Mormons who'd e-mailed Divisi about the dress code, throwing down the a cappella gauntlet—was heading into the West Coast semifinals with the highest point totals in the nation (an arbitrary number, which Divisi still obsessed over).

But they were not resting on their laurels. In fact, as Divisi was working on "Sunday Morning," Noteworthy was upgrading their own set.

They are a curious group, this Noteworthy. The girls from Brigham Young a cappella have a Web site—noteworthyladies .com. It's a risqué domain name for an all-female Mormon a cappella group, sounding a bit like a porn site. "That actually never occurred to us," says the group's music director, Catherine Papworth. "The only reason it's noteworthyladies.com is because noteworthy.com was taken."

Noteworthy was started in 2004 by Esther Yoder with Dave Brown and Dan Dunn, members of the all-male BYU Vocal Point. Groups at Brigham Young have a history of membership retention struggles. "That's what happens when people get married," Catherine says. Noteworthy first competed in the 2004–2005 ICCAs. They sang "Survivor" by Destiny's Child and a Bulgarian standard designed to demonstrate their range, and while they made it to the semifinals, they were ultimately crushed by Divisi's all-star team. The memory of that night is burned into Noteworthy's collective identity.

"We weren't as creative with our choreography as we should have been," their music director says. "We hadn't learned how to play it up, so that it went well with the mics. Some groups just bounce around. But Divisi"—she pauses—"they work together in this uniform effect with the music." She remembers seeing Divisi a second time at a Stanford event, singing "Fever." "Their hand movements," she says. "They were simple, but..." She's speechless.

When Divisi and Noteworthy first met in competition back in 2005, Catherine admits her girls had been intimidated. "I didn't feel like we owned the stage," she says. Part of it was their clothing. Shortly after that show, Noteworthy dropped the green teal striped shirts, black skirts, and dowdy vests that had made up their uniform. When they returned to competition next Note-worthy was sleek, in black shirts and green ties. "Divisi owns red-hot," Catherine says. "But green is our color."

Noteworthyladies.com proclaims the group's mission: to up-lift people and spread joy through the power of music. After the quarterfinals in 2007, Noteworthy's Kaitlyn Maguire gave an in-terview to the BYU NewsNet. "I felt like a tool in God's hands," she said of the show. "I could see the faces of some of the people in the crowd, smiling and nodding."

Though Divisi chose their competition set in early Septem-ber, Noteworthy didn't finalize their own song choices until Jan-uary, just before the quarterfinals. They hadn't even prepared very hard for that first round—despite their big showing. It was a weaker region, and they felt confident they'd be in the top two groups, which was all they'd need to advance to the semifinals. Their tight, four-song set consisted of "Don't You Worry 'Bout a Thing," the spiritual "How Great Thou Art," a Bulgarian song, "Ergen Deda," and Stevie Wonder's "Signed, Sealed, Delivered." But since that first round of the ICCAs, Noteworthy had added a costume change to their set—plus a full-on hip-hop dance routine.

Divisi had seen Noteworthy's quarterfinals set on YouTube. Though it was a solid showing, certainly, they felt the girls had gotten lucky. Going into the semifinals Divisi suspected Brigham Young's all-male Vocal Point would be their main competition, and with good reason. Vocal Point were the reigning ICCA cham-pions. And people were still talking about their performance at the 2006 finals, which went a little something like this:

The nine men of BYU's Vocal Point stood onstage at Lincoln Center, huddled close in their signature blue shirts, khakis, and yellow ties. Few had ever performed for a crowd this size, and certainly not in a venue with such a rich history. But if they were intimidated, they hid it well. As the lights came down, Jimmy Dunn stepped up to the microphone, which he put, more or less, in his mouth. What happened next was like a small earthquake, this rumble that came up from the bottom of the floor through your seat. There were no fancy digital effects at work there. It was all Jimmy, or rather what he was doing with his mouth and the microphone. (It's called a lip buzz.) The khaki-clad boys behind him joined in with a *whooo* building to an angelic *aaaah*. This *whoooooaaahhh* lasted all of seven seconds, but the audience was applauding wildly. Then it dawned on you. You had heard this thing before. They were imitating the THX sound effect, that instantly recognizable roar that plays in front of movies to let you know THIS THEATER IS EQUIPPED WITH THX SPEAKERS. *Whoooooooaaaaaaahhhhhhh.* Then something even more magical happened. That *aaaah* chord rang out two octaves above, an echo seemingly floating above Avery Fisher Hall. Musical scholars call this an *overtone*, and while surely there was a scientific explanation for its sudden appearance—something about a sinusoidal wave, acoustics, and angles—maybe it was divine intervention. What's more impressive is that they were just nine guys—yet their arrangements were complex, meaning each guy might have been singing his own part. (The bigger a group, the more distinct parts one can throw into an arrangement.)

Vocal Point had earned a berth in the finals twice before, but on both occasions the competition fell on a Sunday. And the BYU boys wouldn't compete on their Sabbath. They'd long felt they were the best group in the nation, and in 2006—their fifteenth anniversary year—they finally had a chance to prove it. When second place was awarded to the group from Oxford, Out of the Blue, the boys from BYU started to sweat. Had the Rutgers University ShockWave, an all-female group, won? Having formed just eight months earlier, Rutgers was the underdog. A win for them would have been the equivalent of Tatum O'Neal snagging an Oscar at age ten. And who could resist an underdog story? In the end, they needn't have worried—Vocal Point was awarded the 2006 ICCA title. And the crowd was stomping their feet in approval.

While it's customary to take the year off after winning the ICCA title, there's nothing customary about Vocal Point. They're the rare collegiate a cappella group whose music director is an alum. (James Stevens, who oversaw the 2006 win, is again in charge.) All of their members are over the age of twenty-one and have completed year-long missions for the Church of Jesus Christ of Latter-day Saints. But there was reason to believe they were still hungry for the trophy in 2007. Much like Divisi, they'd weathered extensive turnover. And while they wouldn't admit it, all the attention being paid to their sister group, Noteworthy, was likely starting to grate on them.

In March of 2007, Vocal Point, Noteworthy, and Divisi—each with something to prove—headed to the West Coast semifinals of the ICCAs. Only one group would leave with an invitation to Lincoln Center.

Marin County is just north of San Francisco, across the Golden Gate Bridge. Most nights it's a sleepy nook. But as Divisi takes over the Days Inn, it's anything but. The boys from Oregon State (who placed second in Divisi's quarterfinal round) are staying here too. The words BEAT THAT BOX K-LOWE are written across the window of OSU's big white van, which is parked in the motel lot. It is the night before these ICCA regional semifinals and Divisi—most wearing Divisi T-shirts, black with a pair of red lips on the shoulder—gather in Sarah Klein's room, overtaking the two double beds and any available floor space. Jenna Tooley sits down next to what may be the world's largest wicker basket—an endless cornucopia of grapes, beef jerky, apples, and more. The basket was a gift to Divisi from Jenna's parents. (They also do- nated five hundred dollars.) It's unclear whether the girl's parents know how tenuous Jenna's position in the group has been. And if the couple wasn't so genuinely sweet, so obviously proud of Divisi's accomplishments, the fresh produce might have read as a calculated peace offering on their daughter's behalf.

"Here's some tea for you!" Jenna says, handing a box of Throat Coat brand tea to Andrea Welsh.

"Thanks," Andrea said. "How did your parents know this was my favorite?"

Andrea and Rachelle Wofford sit on one of the double beds listening to "Hide and Seek" on an iPod. "We've been having a problem singing the word *here*," Andrea says. The girls correct each other. It should be he-*ere*. Not he-*are*.

The girls run through parts of their set. Megan Schimmer stands on the bed, supervising the choreography. She says something about the importance of forty-five-degree angles. Marissa Neitling goes over the hand movements for "Hide and Seek." The lyric is, "You don't care a *bit*, you don't care a *bit*." The move calls for small figure-eights over their mouths.

They run the beginning of "Sunday Morning." It's the set opener, which may be a problem. The song begins with the altos, alone, singing *doom doom doom*—before the sopranos come in on *bop*. If the sopranos *bop* on the wrong note, the rest of the group will sing in the wrong key. "I'm hella nervous," Meghan Bell says.

But at ten-thirty the rehearsal ends. "The things we've been picking apart," Emmalee Almroth says, "it's like, *one word* of *one song*. Where our head hits in the choreography on *one word*. Think about how far we've come."

Sarah Klein steps in. "People have been asking me," she says, "can we win this? There's some stiff competition. We need to work hard tomorrow. But we've done the work. We're prepared. We're focused. We didn't spend an hour the other night talking about what the songs meant so that we could get up there and forget the dynamics. We need to bring the audience to tears. We need to make them joyful and scared." The girls are nodding their heads. It's getting late. "Just remember to *bring it*," she says.

The following afternoon, at the Marin Center, the groups gather in the hulking auditorium to draw straws to determine the show order. Well, everyone except Noteworthy. While one wants to give the Noteworthy ladies the benefit of the doubt, they pull a second stunt—showing up thirty minutes late. The seven other groups sit waiting. There is minimal interaction. For these students from different schools, it's not about getting to know each other. It's not uncommon for two students, mindlessly beatboxing to themselves, to pass each other in the hallway and barely acknowledge each other. And Jen Levitz, the ICCA West Coast producer, inadvertently makes an already tense situation worse. When the women from BYU finally do arrive, filing into the auditorium Jen announces, "There they are! With the *highest point totals in the country*, Noteworthy!"

Divisi draws—they'll perform fourth. Noteworthy, meanwhile, will close the show. This is not a good sign. When it seems like it can't get any worse, on the way out, Marissa Neitling finally comes face-to-face with her ex-boyfriend's sisters, Catherine Papworth and her sister, Kristin, both of Noteworthy. Marissa has been dreading this confrontation, and she hopes her face doesn't betray her. It's awkward at first. Marissa smiles at them. She asks about their family. And then, without warning, the girls hug Marissa. "They told me they loved me," Marissa later tells Andrea Welsh. Still, Marissa would be lying if she said she didn't want to bury Noteworthy.

The boys from Vocal Point likely feel the same way. Outside the building they stand under a tree, several of them holding long ropes. Vocal Point had been assured the auditorium would be equipped with wireless microphones. (It isn't.) And so they work their set, tweaking the choreography, the ropes standing in for microphone wires.

Backstage, in the too-hot, too-small dressing room they've been assigned, Divisi once again comes back to the circle. There will be no revelations of drug abuse today. They are all business. They touch up their makeup. They refine their choreography. They sing the *Full House* theme song to calm their nerves. Six months of preperation come down to this moment.

The Marin County Veterans' Memorial Auditorium is a massive space, and the back rows feel miles from the stage. Attendance is spotty—there were likely more fans at the quarterfinal round in Eugene, Oregon. But there are clumps of fans scattered throughout and the OSU contingency is easy to spot, what with their faces painted orange. Then there are the women in DIVISI MOM T-shirts.

The competition opens with Raagapella, a South Asian–focus a cappella group from Stanford. (Yes, Raagapella is a pun—a takeoff on the famed a cappella group from the Folgers commercial, Rockapella.) The group's debut album was called, fittingly, *Raags to Riches*. Though they're proud of their South Asian heritage, they have a sense of humor about the culture. Their spring show featured the skit "Pimp My Bride" (a takeoff on MTV's *Pimp My Ride*). How exactly the judges will compare Raagapella's set—which includes "O Humdum Suniyo Re"—to the other groups' isn't clear. Not that it matters. The competition is very clearly a Brigham Young versus Oregon showdown.

For all the talk of Vocal Point's polish, the Brigham Young set feels sloppy. The men step out in their French-blue dress shirts, khakis, and yellow ties. They sing Michael Jackson's "Thriller," which has been in their repertoire for years—though it's easy to understand why they've gone back to that well. They stole the gloved one's choreography, and it's tough to argue with nine men pretending to be werewolves. The hour spent working with the ropes has paid off. Unfortunately, the music just isn't there. The song sounds hollow in parts and the soloist's voice cracks, Peter Brady–style. "I think they sacrificed the music for the choreography," says Julia Hoffman, one of the night's judges and the administrator of the Contemporary A Cappella Recording Awards. "More than anything, this is a *music* competition." However, they recover nicely with the spiritual "Nearer My God to Thee."

Vocal Point's biggest asset is their feel-great attitude: They are undeniably entertaining and loose. They're clearly having fun up there. And they score the night's only genuine laughs with "No, Not Much," a barbershop tune from the fifties originally recorded by the Four Lads. Tonight, four lads from Vocal Point step out, put their hands in their pockets, and sway back and forth innocently as they sing, *"I don't want my arms around you"*—then, wagging their fingers at the crowd and mugging wildly—*"no, not much."* They are crowd favorites, clearly, but they've made the mistake of performing as if this were just another gig. They may win. But they've left the door open for a spoiler.

Divisi steps out onstage next, walking briskly to their spots for the opening of "Sunday Morning." *Doom doom doom—bop!* Crisis averted. The group is in tune, sturdy. Keeley McCowan is not a born performer. Her movements are wooden, and the white lights make her already pale skin seem translucent. But she uses her body language to her advantage, and the song suits her. "Sunday Morning" is a jazz tune at its heart. And so she keeps her arms by her sides like an old-time supper club singer. "Got the flower in your hair," she sings, tapping at her hair as if she had a bouffant. She sings: *"Sunday morning rain is falling and I'm calling out for you,"* putting her hand out as if to catch the drops. It helps to have Betsy Yates on the beatbox. It's sort of perverse, really. If the audience is going to be distracted by someone *pfing* and *spitting*, that person may as well be one of the more attractive girls.

"Hide and Seek" is crisp, the dynamics strong, the choreogra-

phy on point. The song is already something of a collegiate a cappella cliché. But after the show, one judge will say it's easily the
best she's seen. And Divisi's Robert Palmer look only completes
the feeling of unity. By the time Andrea Welsh makes her way
around the group, singing, *"Hi-ide a-and seek,"* more than one
member of the audience is in tears. "There was something about
the emotion up there," Marissa Neitling says later. "I've never
felt such a connection to the song."

The set closes with "You Had Me." The song begins with Divisi in the power stance—legs shoulder-width apart, arms at their
sides. They look angry, determined. But it's not all sheer force.
Michaela Cordova, the soloist, has learned to inject some subtlety
into the verses, and the contrast makes the choruses all the more
striking. There's a soft vibrato on the early verses: *"I don't want
no part in your next fix // Someone needs to tell you this is it."*

But it builds to a strong defiance. Michaela pulls at her
tie, banging on her chest, singing: *"Vodka and a packet of cigarettes // that's all it used to be // but now you're sniffin' on snow
when you're feeling low // suffocating dreams that could have //
Maybe for a minute I'll be down with that // but it didn't take
long for me to see the light."*

The crowd is roaring. That Michaela's father is in the audience tonight makes the comeback that much sweeter.

After intermission, Divisi sits in the back of the auditorium,
watching the second half of the competition, waiting for Noteworthy. Finally, the ladies from BYU step out in their gray slacks
and black tops. Their green ties are tucked into their shirts (like
restaurant waiters sometimes do). The women of Divisi shifted
uncomfortably in their seats. "You could see it in their eyes,"
Rachelle says. "They wanted it."

Noteworthy opens with the Bulgarian tune "Ergen Deda."
And it is a feat of complex musicianship—perfect intonation,
flawless phrasing. But it is also stunningly out of place, a move

designed, it seems, to demonstrate the breadth of their talent as opposed to entertaining the crowd. To some, it just sounds like a lot of shrieking—as if they're beating the judges into submission. (For the record, here's what the shrieking was about. The lyrics of "Ergen Deda" translate to: *The old man decides he wants to go to the dance, so he dresses up as a young man. But when he arrives, all the young girls run away, except for the littlest one, Angelina. Poor Angelina.*)

Any lingering doubt Divisi may have had about dropping "Don't You Worry 'Bout a Thing" evaporates the minute Noteworthy begins their version. The choreography may feel tired (think Spider-Man on a surfboard) but it doesn't matter. Courtney Jensen, the soloist, picks the mic up out of the stand and wails—full voice. Where Divisi was stiff, these girls have found the salsa beat in the original. Sarah Klein turns to Keeley: "So, we've got some competition." A spiritual, "How Great Thou Art," is equally stirring.

It's not just the music—the whole package is polished. There are even quick costume changes. Noteworthy pulls the neckties out of their shirts for "Don't You Worry 'Bout a Thing." By the time they get to "Signed, Sealed, Delivered," Noteworthy have untucked their black dress shirts, pulling down on the T-shirts underneath to reveal the hint of a fuchsia accent.

Courtney Jensen isn't Noteworthy's only standout soloist. Kaitlyn McGuire—compact, with her hair pulled back—is a pint-size Kelly Clarkson. Noteworthy follows through on the promise to add in a hip-hop dance routine to "Signed, Sealed, Delivered," which closes their set. One minute and thirty-five seconds into the song the girls remove their shoes, shouting *"Remix!"* The song ends with them hoisting a girl in the air like some high school cheerleading squad. *Here I am, baby—huh!—signed, sealed, delivered, I'm yours.*

Divisi bristles in the stands. "They were trying to pull off something like 'Yeah,'" Rachelle Wofford says. "But it just *wasn't.*"

Sitting together way up in the back row, nervously pulling at their red ties, Divisi felt the heat. They'd performed their best tonight. "But we weren't sure it was enough," Betsy Yates said.

It was nearly an hour before the judges returned to the stage. A pro a cappella group, Hookslide, entertained in between. The wait was interminable. When, after thirty minutes, the judges still hadn't returned, someone from the audience actually shouted, "Free Bird!" Finally, the groups were called back to the stage. And Divisi returned to their familiar onstage huddle, clawing one another. Divisi took home the award for best choreography. And they were feeling pretty good, until Noteworthy scored the best arrangement prize for "How Great Thou Art."

Jen Levitz, the West Coast producer, spoke. "It was very, very, very tight," she said. "Any of these groups could be going to New York. But only one will get to go."

It happened quickly, a merciful end to Divisi's storied comeback. "The second runner up," Jen said, "with three hundred eighty-one points—Divisi!" Sarah Klein walked out to receive the award, and the girls clapped. But they were crushed. Vocal Point was named the first runner-up, with 394 points. Onstage, Haley Steinberger of Divisi turned to Rachelle. "Noteworthy just won," she said under her breath. Rachelle whispered back, *"You need to put your hands together and clap right now."* They were not the only ones disappointed. One of the Vocal Point members actually walked offstage, pulled out his cell phone, and made a call: "Noteworthy just beat us!" he could be heard barking offstage. So much for the Latter-day Saints.

Noteworthy, with 426 points, was headed to the ICCA finals at Lincoln Center. While they performed their encore, Natasha Bedingfield's "Unwritten," Divisi returned to the too-small dressing room to collect their Aqua Net. Sarah Klein looked over the score sheets. One judge placed Divisi first, two placed them second, two slated them third. It could have gone either way. "Find more variety in your performance," one wrote. Some loved "Hide and Seek." One called it "pitchy." The score sheets, however, should have been a comfort to Divisi. Choreography, style of dress—that's subjective. But intonation isn't: You're either on pitch or you're not. (Music is, more than anything, mathematics.) But the judges couldn't even agree on that. Not to mention that the judging panel was rife with conflict of interest. Bill Hare, the well-known a cappella producer, was brought in as a last-minute judge—and he had mixed Divisi's last album, *Undivided*. Deke Sharon was also judging (he ranked Divisi first)—and Divisi had bought professional a cappella arrangements from Deke's side business, Total Vocal. Not to mention the fact that Sarah Klein had more than once e-mailed Deke for advice on her own arrangements. It was a bit incestuous.

Divisi could not see this—they were so blinded by their desire to win this competition. And their singular focus was disturbing.

The thing is, Divisi had come a long way—not just musically but as women. Surely this was more important. Plus, wasn't a cappella supposed to be fun? Had they really gotten into this to learn three songs, perform them well, and then be sent home from San Francisco—without even seeing the Golden Gate Bridge, let alone much beside the courtyard at the Days Inn?

At the first rehearsal back on campus following their defeat at the semifinals, the girls are already discussing whether or not to compete the following year. There were mixed reactions. Andrea Welsh was thinking about going abroad. Others suggested touring instead. But they watched the clips on YouTube and the matter was decided. It wasn't about the alumni this time. "We weren't satisfied with our performance," says Rachelle Wofford. The women of Divisi were looking forward to a new regime, and a new music director. "I love Sarah [Klein]," Rachelle says, which is what women always say before insulting a friend. "But she wasn't a leader." Sarah's biggest weakness was opening the floor to discussion where she should have been decisive. "We're fourteen girls," Rachelle says. "Everyone has their own opinion." Michaela Cordova didn't say much that night. When she looks back on the competition at the Marin Center, singing "You Had Me," she says, "That's the last time I really felt like myself." A few weeks later she will withdraw from school.

CHAPTER TWELVE

Wherein we peek inside the nefarious world of the Contemporary A Cappella Society, a feud is born between two companies—Primarily A Cappella and Mainely A Cappella—and the NCCAs go international

At various points in its history, the Contemporary A Cappella Society would be run out of Deke Sharon's dorm room, an apartment in the Bay Area, and finally a condo Deke and his wife bought on Polk Street in San Francisco. At its highest point, CASA had close to ten thousand paying members.

CASA was, and continues to be, a nonprofit entity whose mission is clear, and true: to promote harmony through harmony, and to support and disseminate a cappella music. When the music changed, and collegiate a cappella exploded, with new groups popping up at universities in the South and Midwest (schools that had never had a cappella before) CASA was there to help. "The biggest problem with starting a group," Deke says, "is that they have nothing to sing. It was really a matter of these kids thinking they had to reinvent the wheel." Deke and Anne Raugh took steps to change all that, compiling twelve songs—including standards like "In the Still of the Night"—into a book, *Contemporary A Cappella Songbook*. A second volume followed, as did a Christmas edition. Hal Leonard Publishing later offered to distribute the series. And Deke says they've sold over a hundred thousand copies, to high schools and collegiate a cappella groups.

(Hal Leonard wouldn't confirm the figure, saying: "They're above average for choral music.")

With the advent of the Internet, CASA was able to do even more, launching the arrangement library, an online, easy-to-use archive of SATB (soprano-alto-tenor-bass) arrangements that a cappella groups could download for free. It was extensive—anything from "Blue Moon" to Maroon 5's "She Will Be Loved." While many undergraduates arranged music themselves, some groups just didn't have that talent. After all, a cappella was becoming a bit like Major League Baseball. The increased number of franchises was diluting the talent. And for them, thankfully, there was CASA. For a while, anyway.

The problems, it seems, started in 2003 when Jonathan Minkoff, a lawyer and the recently installed president of Contemporary A Cappella Society of America, moved to shut down the arrangement library, an on-line archive of a cappella sheet music. He argued that the library was likely illegal. Deke Sharon (who had been the CASA president on and off for years) was livid. He felt the library was vital for new groups just getting off the ground. And so Deke consulted several copyright lawyers, who, he says, "made it clear that the library wasn't clearly illegal." "Limited numbers, educational organization, fair use," he says. "They also made it clear that no one in the industry would come after us even if they had a legal case." There just wasn't enough money in a cappella. But Minkoff forced the issue, using what Deke calls *scare tactics* to pressure a majority of the CASA board into shutting the thing down. Minkoff implied that individual members of the board could be sued by music conglomerates.

Unfortunately, just as the library was coming down, the CASA Web site was undergoing a much-needed overhaul. A few readers e-mailed, wondering if CASA had been permanently shut down. "These were tough years," Deke admits. "The stripping away of programs and stripping down to the foundations hap-

pened before the rebuilding." Paid membership, once in the thousands, dropped to the low hundreds. Some say it actually dropped
to almost zero.

Without the arrangement library, it became unclear what
CASA was for—except to stroke the egos of its board members,
all collegiate a capella alums. "We have this conversation all the
time," says Mike Mendyke, CASA's treasurer. While CASA is a
nonprofit organization, everyone on the board has his or her own
for-profit a cappella side ventures. And everyone is pushing his or
her own agenda. In early 2006, Don Gooding—the proprietor of
a-cappella.com, an alum of the Yale Whiffenpoofs, and the owner
of the ICCAs—made a decision: "I was going to resign from the
CASA board. I was tired of people *talking* and not *doing*."

The CASA board had become a parody of itself, a soap opera
of onetime collegiate a cappella singers. It was like some *Best in
Show* spoof—but hyperreal. Jonathan Minkoff, the president,
was in no way above the fray. He runs the annual East Coast A
Cappella Summit—a three-day weekend of performances and
master classes. "It used to be an *event*," Mike Mendyke says. He
talks about the landmark 1997 summit, where the Blenders, the
Persuasions, the House Jacks, and Acoustix all performed at the
New England Conservatory. "It was a watershed moment," Mendyke says. In recent years attendance has risen modestly while
interest in a cappella has skyrocketed. Some say, because Minkoff
continues to hire his own group, Blue Jupiter, to headline.

"A cappella isn't so much about money," says Julia Hoffman,
who runs the Contemporary A Cappella Recording Awards. "It's
about bragging rights." The East Coast Summit, some say, had
become Minkoff's masturbatory, narcissistic parade writ largeish.

As collegiate a cappella exploded, and its alumni spread forth
like spores, a number of businesses popped up targeting the burgeoning market. In some ways, it was like Motown all over again.
And somehow all roads led back to the indomitable Don Gooding.

Herein, the infighting, presented as a (dark) comedy in three acts.

I. Don Gooding versus John Neal

Don Gooding, an alum of the Whiffenpoofs, graduated from Yale in 1981 and went on to have a successful career as a venture capitalist, working for Accel Partners in Princeton, New Jersey. However, he felt unfulfilled. In 1991, he and his first wife were visiting her folks in Maine. They drove by the L. L. Bean headquarters (birthplace of the popular catalog), which gave Don an idea for his own business. In January of 1992, Don incorporated the Primarily A Cappella catalog. The first edition offered some one hundred and fifty CDs plus sheet music, and Don hired a friend to run the operation out of a spare bedroom in his Princeton home. It's worth noting that Don's tax returns for the side project actually read UNITED SINGERS INTERNATIONAL. "I had grandiose plans," Don says. "But I was losing money hand over fist." He needed a business partner. This is where things get interesting.

John Neal was a tough-talking British expat living out in the Bay Area. He'd started out as a theater producer and a talent manager. He was also the owner and operator of the Harmony Sweepstakes—like the ICCAs for professional a cappella groups. There were negotiations. John Neal agreed to run the Primarily A Cappella catalog in exchange for a whopping sixty percent ownership of the company. Begrudgingly, Don Gooding agreed, retaining forty percent for himself. "John Neal was the only game in town," Don says. In October of 1993, Don got on a plane and hand-delivered his entire inventory of CDs—of the Blenders, the Bobs, the Real Group—to John Neal out West.

Don had, in time, become a partner at Accel. But he was burning out on the venture capital game. "Venture capital is about manipulating people," Don says (and, in light of his a cappella dealings, what comes next will strike some as ironic). "It took many years and a bruised ego to realize I wasn't good at this. I'm really an entrepreneur at heart." In 1997 he quit the firm entirely and turned his attentions to Primarily A Cappella, which Neal had taken good care of in his stead. In fact, Primarily A Cappella was just starting to make money. You can see where this is going.

"Now that I was focusing on the a cappella business full-time," Don says, "I could no longer ignore the human being that is John Neal." Some say Neal regularly skimmed a little off the top from his collegiate a cappella groups—claims that he denies. (Adam Farb describes John Neal alternately as a "scumbag" and "hilarious." "John is like every record producer in Hollywood," Adam says. "Just a little less tactful. That's why he's in this small subculture and not in Hollywood. But he's no more of a freak than I was or Deke is.")

Regardless, Don Gooding tried to take back ownership of Primarily A Cappella. John Neal still remembers their last conversation. "Our last conversation that didn't involve lawyers, anyway!" he says. It was a disagreement over collegiate a cappella groups. John Neal was tired of the turnover in college groups. "I'd spend a year training a business manager to do his job," Neal says, "and then they'd graduate." The new business manager would want to know why the group hadn't been paid. "I don't care that you're so-and-so from whatever Yale group," Neal says, "you didn't send an invoice!"

When those talks dissolved, Don Gooding's wife suggested he start a new company. And so he did. He called it Mainely A Cappella. It's not a typo. "We live in Maine," he says. Both companies sell sheet music and a cappella paraphernalia, plus CDs and MP3 downloads of collegiate recordings. Two firms, Primarily A Cappella and Mainely A Cappella, doing the exact same thing. Was there room for two companies? "No," Don Gooding says flatly. In 2006, Don Gooding's company did $1 million in business—from a-cappella.com and from an a cappella storefront run out of a strip mall in Maine.

John Neal declines to comment on the earnings at his own Primarily A Cappella. "Don Gooding is a businessman," he says. "Me, as long as the lights are still on and I can pay my employees and I've got my house, I'm not concerned with what the bottom line is."

II. Don Gooding versus Mike Mendyke

Mike Mendyke and Don Gooding, both CASA board members, had issues dating back nearly a decade. To make a long story short, in the late nineties, Don Gooding started an a cappella record label, Hot Lips Records. He'd briefly signed the Boston-based pro group Five O'Clock Shadow. Mendyke, a longtime member of Five O'Clock Shadow, was soon forced out. Blame that old rub—creative differences. Mendyke sued FOCS. (Don Gooding funded the FOCS defense.) The group had been paid just north of ten thousand dollars to record 1998's *So There*. It was a standard record deal. The money wasn't really theirs—it was an upfront payment against future royalties. Mike had written an original song for the album and was never paid. It was just one symptom of the mismanagement, Mendyke claims. "He didn't know how to run a record label."

Don Gooding isn't amused. "Mike Mendyke has been a thorn in my side for ten years," he says. "And he was fired because he couldn't sing on pitch. He cost me ten thousand dollars in legal fees." In Mendyke's defense, if he couldn't sing, he hid it well. Mendyke would go on to sing in a part-time a cappella group with Dick Van Dyke called (yes) the Vantastix. (He later buried the hatchet with Five O'Clock Shadow, and even joined the group on stage at a reunion show to serenade his five-year-old daughter with "Baby of Mine.") Still, Don Gooding shuttered Hot Lips Records after releasing just a handful of titles.

The two would clash a second time in the fall of 2006 when Mike Mendyke launched acaTunes—The Digital A Cappella Music Store. The site is exactly what it sounds like: iTunes for a cappella with individual tracks selling for one dollar. Mendyke's business partner was Freddie Feldman, a computer science guy and an alum of the Northwestern Purple Haze—also a CASA board member. Feldman owns an a cappella recording studio in Evanston and once helped a friend record an a cappella version of the entire Pink Floyd *Dark Side of the Moon* album. (At the launch party for the album, they played the a cappella disc alongside *The Wizard of Oz*. It synced up perfectly.)

Don Gooding saw acaTunes as a direct attack on his own business, Mainely A Cappella. "Mike Mendyke," Don says, "he's sort of got a Don Quixote thing—going after me in six different ways over ten years." (A charge Mendyke laughs at. "I define my own successes," he says. "A cappella is about music and friendships, not lawsuits.") But Don quickly started selling MP3s in response. "Competition keeps you on your toes," he says.

Though acaTunes worked brilliantly, business was slower than Mike and Freddie had projected. Still, they soldiered on (acquiring distribution rights to a popular a cappella podcast, A Cappella U, hosted by the infectious superfan, Joey C, aka Joseph Campagna). In December of 2006, the proprietors of acaTunes sent a mass e-mail out to users: *We've sold 1,000 tracks!*

"So what!" Don says. "So in six months they made a thousand dollars. That's not a business, that's a *hobby*."

The final straw was Mendyke's investment in an a cappella competition with designs on challenging Don Gooding's own ICCAs. "With thousands of a cappella groups, there's room for a Burger King-McDonald's situation," the good-natured Mendyke says. The competition was conceived by Mark Surprenant, a former member of the University of Michigan Compulsive Lyres.

"The Compulsive Lyres," Don Gooding says. "That's fitting!" At CASA board meetings (which took place monthly over the Internet), Mike Mendyke pushed his agenda hard, desperate for the organization's imprimatur on this just-launched competition, feeling it would help them attract participants. In the end, it wouldn't matter. After one successful year as a competition, receiving praise from high school teachers across the country, the first collegiate outing of Surprenant's experiment would fold abruptly—one month before a planned May 2006 finals at Epcot Center.

III. Don Gooding versus Adam Farb

In 1998, after three years at the helm of the National Championship of Collegiate A Cappella—the competition he'd willed into being—Adam Farb wanted out. It wasn't just the traveling. Though it was that too. (He was producing twenty-five a cappella shows in two and a half months, and the miles quickly wore him down.) He was running BOCA on the side, having started a small a cappella record label, Smokin' Fish Records (named for an inside joke with the Brown Derbies), to distribute the disc. Farb hired Liana Tang, an alum of NYU's APC Rhythm, to assist him with the NCCAs. "I couldn't run the show out of Kinkos anymore," he says. In the fall of 1998, he called Carnegie Hall and Lincoln Center—both were booked for April. Farb was lost. "If I did the show that year," Farb says, "I was either going to kill myself or someone else." And so he cancelled the finals. In a cappella circles, 1999 would become known as the Lost Year. "A lot of people were pissed at me," he says.

Both Farb and the NCCAs were at a crossroads. The show had momentum, but like any burgeoning business, it needed capital: a hundred thousand dollars by Farb's own estimation. The NCCAs needed their own equipment, plus a big marketing push. Farb wanted to staff up. And to make matters worse, the constant turnover (read: graduation) among the competitors wreaked havoc on the system. "What's unique about a cappella is that there's no institutional memory," Farb says. "Every year kids graduated and you had to start over." Farb didn't have the money or, frankly, the drive to continue. "I was fried," he says. When Don Gooding offered to buy him out, Farb was thrilled. Don had been a venture capitalist and a member of the Yale Whiffenpoofs. "He could bring the infrastructure the organization needed," Farb says. In 1999, Farb agreed to sell his stake in the NCCAs and the BOCA compilation to Don Gooding. It would not be a smooth transaction.

Don Gooding says he bought the rights to both for a flat fee of twenty-five thousand dollars.

Farb says Don promised him close to seventy thousand (which included a "declining stake in future profits" from the competition). The deal was contentious—and very nearly litigious. The frustration ate away at Farb. To make matters worse, he watched as Don did little to improve the NCCAs. "I thought he had plans," Farb says. "But I just think he didn't know what to do with the thing." Eventually Farb stopped caring, and he gave up all attempts to rectify the financial disparity. "At some point, I just said, Fuck it. I've got better things to worry about. You have to move on." By 2001, Farb had dropped out of the a cappella scene entirely. He even tried to give his collection of a cappella recordings away to his alma mater, the Brown Derbies. They declined the gift. "Even Deke didn't want them," Farb says.

If the a cappella crowd had its own version of *Us Weekly*—and clearly it warranted one—it would be the forums at rarb.org, the Recorded A Cappella Review Board. "It's the gossip column of a cappella," says Dave Sperandio. He would know. He's banned from posting to the RARB message boards. (More on that soon.)

It started innocently enough. Like most Web sites worth their column inches, RARB was launched from a dorm room back in

1993, the brainchild of Washington University students Seth Golub and Chris Tess, both onetime members of the all-male a cappella group the Pikers. Seth, now a Google employee working on artificial intelligence, built the site. And the concept was simple—almost altruistic. It was a place where collegiate a cappella groups could have their albums reviewed by professionals (mostly collegiate a cappella alums and members of CASA) on a scale of one to five (five being the best). In the first year, nearly thirty albums were reviewed. These days it's closer to a hundred annually. And it's deadly serious business. Groups know the veteran RARB reviewers by name and even request specific reviewers. Elie Landau and Rebecca Christie have been reviewing since the late nineties. "They tend to prefer a more natural sound," says Ben Stevens, the RARB coordinator. "The newer reviewers— Robert Dietz, Ryan Joyce—they're from the Bill Hare school."

For all the talk about RARB, the nonprofit has an operating cost of twelve dollars a year—for Web hosting; reviewers are paid in albums. But the real genius—or the real curse—of RARB isn't the reviews, but rather the forums, where some thousand registered members discuss the reviews (among other things) ad nauseam. Upward of twenty thousand messages have been posted since 1998, on close to two thousand topics. It's Ben's job to (among other things) police the forums, which tend to spike around the ICCAs and the BOCA announcements. For example, when Divisi lost in the finals of the ICCAs in 2005, it inspired pages of back-and-forth talk on the judging.

In 2003, producer Dave Sperandio really did lose his posting privileges, after referring to RARB founder Seth Golub as a "slack ass" in an online argument about why RARB didn't yet offer emoticons and avatars in the forums. In late 2007, someone posted a note saying they missed Dio on the forums, and could a resolution be reached. Which is sort of funny because Dio cops to posting under an assumed name since the smackdown.

If there was any doubt, collegiate a cappella had become a serious business. Perhaps nothing underscored the incestuous, self-destructive nature of this subculture more than the Wikipedia pogrom of February 2007. The bloodletting was initiated by a Dartmouth University student named Shane Avidan, who was working as a part-time administrator for Wikipedia. He began deletion proceedings against a smattering of a cappella stubs, including entries for Andrew Chaikin (a beatboxer who goes by the name Kid Beyond), the House Jacks, BOCA, CASA, the ICCAs and, yes, even Deke Sharon himself. The administrator argued that the a cappella community was bordering on a pyramid scheme. Julia Hoffman from the CARAs was one of the few people to see the humor. "It's rare you encounter a cappella terrorists!" she said.

The crisis was ultimately averted. But for a second there, it appeared that Rockapella would be the lone survivor. Because even a Dartmouth student on an a cappella jihad was prepared to acknowledge the relevance of Rockapella's legacy as the house band for *Where in the World Is Carmen Sandiego?*

CHAPTER THIRTEEN

THE BEELZEBUBS

*Wherein the Beelzebubs travel
west for spring break*

Unlike most a cappella groups, the Beelzebubs begin each rehearsal with the historian (an elected position) telling an
old Bubs story—some dating back to the group's founding. These
legends cover the derivation of words in the Beelze-lexicon, a
continuously updated dictionary of terms the Bubs have invented
(and use frequently). Other stories recount road trips of yore.
There's a by-product to all of this self-study—and it's expectations. When the Bubs traveled to Los Angeles on spring break
in March 2007, Doug Terry (who'd organized the trip) had a
plan: the Bubs would talk their way onstage during a live taping
of CBS's *Late Late Show with Craig Ferguson*. "We thought it
might happen," Doug says.

Why was he so sure? Because it had happened before.

On May 20, 1999, a Beelzebub named Jeremy Cramer came face-
to-face with David Letterman—yes, that David Letterman. The
confrontation aired on national television, and though it didn't
last very long, Letterman did manage to get in a few zingers.
"Letterman called me a *squirrelly little kid*," Cramer says.

For all the talk of a late-night war, Jay Leno regularly trounces Letterman in the ratings. In 1999, in an effort to boost market share across the country, Letterman's people implemented a plan. It was fairly simple: They'd fly hundreds of Bostonians in for the night, give them tickets to the show, and promote it back in Bean Town as Boston Night. (Some eight thousand Bostonians sent postcards to Letterman, hoping to win tickets.) Rob Burnett, an executive producer of *Late Night with David Letterman*, is a Tufts alum. He wanted to do his part for his alma mater, and so he called the Tufts PR office and sent over twenty-five tickets. The university, quite smartly, gave fifteen of those tickets to its best ambassadors—Jeremy Cramer and the Tufts Beelzebubs.

A Bubs performance at Logan Airport—as the New York–bound Letterman flights boarded—was caught by a CBS affiliate. And lo and behold, the Bubs—dressed in Tufts gear, no less—found themselves seated in the front rows of the Ed Sullivan Theater for the taping. That night's guests: Natalie Portman and the newly reunited J. Geils Band.

Before the show begins, as is customary, Letterman comes out in his gray double-breasted suit. He fiddles with a button. He says hello to the audience, makes a Boston joke, and asks if anyone in the crowd has any questions. A few hands go up. Letterman calls on Jeremy Cramer. "I'm here with the Tufts University Beelzebubs, the university's oldest all-male a cappella group," Jeremy says. "Natalie Portman goes to Harvard and we'd really like to serenade her with—"

Letterman abruptly cuts him off. "Shut up, kid," he says. "I run the show here. I don't have time for your *a cappella* music." Letterman wasn't kidding, Jeremy says. "He was *nasty*." Jeremy Cramer sits back down with the rest of the Bubs. He's pretty embarrassed about the whole thing. Oh, had it ended there.

Letterman retreats backstage and the taping is about to begin.

Paul Shaffer strikes up the CBS Orchestra. "Live from New York—where everyone in the audience is from Boston!" the announcer says. "It's the *Late Show with David Letterman*."

Letterman comes out for the opening monologue and immediately deviates from the script. "Good evening, ladies and gentlemen," he says. "Welcome to the show. Had a *fascinating* conversation with a kid from the audience before the show began." Here Letterman affects a high-pitched nerd voice. "Ah, yes, Dave, we're part of an a cappella singing group. *What we'd really like to do is come up onstage and sing for the audience.*" The camera flashes to Jeremy Cramer. Letterman says, "Here's what you do…you get Regis to invite you to his show—you can sing all you want."

The show comes back from commercial break and Letterman is seated at his desk. He wipes his lip with an exaggerated gesture, and starts in again. "Thank you very much," he says. "Good evening, ladies and gentlemen. Welcome to our big Boston show. We've been thinking this over—before the program a kid, a frankly, a *squirrelly little kid* stands up, and he says, Well, we'd really rather just sing. And I tried to explain to him, well, we have a show lined up for you already. And I don't know that there is a position in the show for"—Dave uses air quotes for emphasis—"*a cappella* music."

Cue audience applause. The camera cuts to Jeremy Cramer, who blows Letterman a kiss. "Not very *Ivy League*, is it," Letterman says, mimicking the air kiss. "Hi, how you doin? Kind of hip, Beverly Hills a little. So, we're trying to work these kids into the show, because what television show would be complete without a little"—he pauses again—"a cappella music. Paul, you have any suggestions?"

PAUL SHAFFER: "For an a cappella piece?"
LETTERMAN: "Yeah."

PAUL: "I think whatever he wants. You know. Don't you think?"

LETTERMAN: "Wait a minute. I assume you have something prepared? OK, all right, well, you sit there, let me think it over."

Letterman is relentless. Between bits about Michael Dukakis, and the Top Ten List—Boston Mayor Thomas Menino read "Things you don't want to hear from a hot dog vendor outside Fenway Park"—he continues to berate Jeremy Cramer. Letterman jokes with the crowd: "Are the kids ready? Are the kids ready?" The audience is eating it up. All Letterman has to do is say *a cappella* and they lose their lunch. Jeremy cannot believe this is happening. During the commercial break, one of the producers comes over to Jeremy Cramer and the Bubs. He's asking them whether they can really sing. And the negotiations begin. "The producer would say, Well, maybe we can do something with a crowd shot," Jeremy says. "But, because we're the Bubs, we keep pushing. *What if we run out onstage*, that sort of thing."

Meanwhile, Natalie Portman comes out and does her thing, promoting *Star Wars*. And when the show comes back from commercial, Letterman says to Paul: "We have the brotherhood of music. I'm putting you in charge of the fourteen a cappella singers, all right? You figure something out."

PAUL: "Should I confer with them?"

LETTERMAN: "Yeah, whatever you can do for them."

The show goes to commercial again. Now, the Beelzebubs are looking at one another. Is this going to happen?

Minutes later, Dave says to the audience: "When you have a television show like this, often the best part is when members of the audience beg to be on the show. And that's the situation we find ourselves in here tonight. And, Paul, you're taking charge of this. What do you know about the group you are about to present?"

> PAUL: "I know that they are called the *Beezl*, the Beelzebubs. And I know their names. And that's all I know. And I know what they're going to sing. They're going to sing their own arrangement of a Stevie Wonder composition, 'Signed, Sealed, Delivered.' May I introduce them?"
>
> LETTERMAN: "Yes, please do."
>
> PAUL: (*looking down at a note card in his hand*) "Ladies and gentlemen, from Tufts, Jeremy, Adam, Alexander ..."

The camera pans to the audience, in time to catch the Bubs jumping up from their seats and running onto the stage. Paul Shaffer's band plays an E. Jeremy does a quick count-off, two-three-four, and the Bubs launch into the song. The intro sounds a little like this: *Nunga nung a nung a nung nung nunga nung a nung.* It is both amazing—the Bubs are on *Letterman!*—and impossibly embarrassing. They're dressed, almost uniformly, in ill-fitting Tufts sweatshirts tucked into khakis. The camera zooms in and pans across the group. Paul hasn't told them how long they should sing, so they just keep going. Eventually, after a minute, the camera cuts to Letterman, who looks confused. "OK there," he says. "How about that?" The Bubs sing for another few seconds. The camera returns to Letterman. "Ladies and gentlemen. Still going....We'll be right back with the J. Geils Band." As the show fades to commercial you can hear Paul Shaffer and the CBS Orchestra pick up "Signed, Sealed, Delivered."

In 2007, Doug Terry wonders: Could lightning strike twice?

When Matt Michelson pictured spring break with the Beelze-bubs—an eleven-day trip to Los Angeles and Mexico—he couldn't have imagined the scene that awaited him at the Backpackers Paradise Hostel in Inglewood, California. Perhaps the seventeen-dollar-a-night fee should have tipped him off. Though the Web site did describe the place as "centrally located." (Inglewood is, of course, many things—homicide up thirty-eight percent from 2005 to 2006!—but centrally located? Nope.) Matt had no one to blame for the accommodations but himself. "I booked it," he says. "My bad."

The hostel was, judging by the clientele, a stopping-off point for some bizarre mix of Euro tourists and runaway teens. The pool was kept at a warmish temperature (perhaps better hospitable to bacteria and STDs?). An elaborate system of electronic gates had been installed to keep the guests and their automobiles safely inside. No one dared sit in the pleather mechanical massage chair, the one located perilously close to the pool. The hostel's saving grace was supposed to be the room itself. The receptionist at the Backpackers Paradise had promised the Bubs their own private oversize dorm. But when the Bubs unlocked the door—revealing a long, dank barracks with twelve identical bunk beds—there were two guests already inside. The first was a female Japanese tourist who told the Bubs she'd been living in that room for a month; the second was a hotel maid who'd taken up residence.

"Do we have to stay at this shitty hotel?" Lucas Walker said. The Japanese tourist giggled. Unfortunately the Bubs had pre-paid for the hostel—five nights.

A few of the Bubs, making the best of a not-great situation, sidled up to the hostel bar. "Can we have a drinks menu?" Andrew Savini asked the surly Eastern European barmaid. She didn't move, just stared back at him blankly. Finally, slowly, she spoke.

"We have red wine," she said. "One dollar. White wine—one dollar. Frozen margarita—one dollar. Beer—one dollar." Pause. "Oh, and da hot dogs."

"Let me guess," Andrew said. "One dollar?"

A Rastafarian seated a few stools over suggested the frozen margaritas.

Andrew looked back at the bartender, who suddenly remembered one last item: "Oh, and we have lick-*war*."

"What?"

"Lick-*war*." She pointed to a few bottles of bottom-shelf liquor on the mirrored bar behind her.

The next morning the Bubs abruptly checked out of the Backpackers Paradise Hostel and into a nearby econo-chain, negotiating a severance package with the hostel.

When it came time to visit the *Late Late Show with Craig Ferguson*, the Bubs—as planned—made their move. Matt Michelson attempted to negotiate with the producers, much as Jeremy Cramer had done with Letterman's people back in 1999. But Ferguson's team was less receptive. And the Bubs were shut down fairly quickly. The Bubs would have to settle for smaller, local numbers—agreeing to sing "Cecelia" for the studio audience before the taping began. If it was any consolation, Craig Ferguson must have heard them from back in his dressing room, because when he came out to deliver his monologue, on air you could hear him whistling "Cecelia."

The Bubs' eleven-night tour of the West Coast would include (among other stops) a gig at Disneyland and a detour to Mexico, where they sampled Cuban cigars. Maybe Craig Ferguson hadn't worked out, but there was another high-profile gig on the Bubs' docket, this one at a rock club, of all places.

But first there was business to attend to. This may have been spring break, but it was far from a vacation for the Bubs.

———

It was ten o'clock at night when, just a few days after checking out of the Backpackers, the Bubs locked themselves inside a Super 8 in San Diego for a meeting on *Pandaemonium*, which was scheduled for release five weeks later at Bubs in the Pub, the group's final show of the year. Ed Boyer had e-mailed a rough mix of the album to Matt Michelson. Tonight, the Bubs would listen together and air any concerns. In a few weeks, Matt and Alexander Koutzoukis would fly to San Francisco to mix the album alongside Bill Hare and Ed Boyer, where they could advocate for the group's interests.

Which is how the Bubs ended up taking this room hostage, comandeering two double beds, a rollaway cot, a handful of standard-issue chairs, and whatever floor space wasn't taken up with luggage. For a while there, anyway, it was smooth sailing. Though the Bubs played the tracks on Michelson's laptop, it didn't sound half bad. Minor elements were missing, like the percussion on "Ruby Falls." But the Bubs were happy with what they heard. Until, that is, they came to "Come Sail Away."

It would be seven hours before the Bubs would leave this room.

Before hitting PLAY, Michelson prepared the group. Ed hadn't had a chance to work on the song yet, which meant parts were still out of tune. Also: The solo hadn't been recorded yet. Still, the Bubs couldn't get past the imperfections. It wasn't just that it was out of tune. The Bubs weren't sure it had earned its place on the album. Two hours into the argument, Michelson (who was leading the discussion) tabled the talk. The fight over "Mama, I'm Coming Home," meanwhile, would quickly turn into nothing short of a debate over the soul of *Pandaemonium*. Michelson played two mixes of the song—one with a vocal percussion track and one without. This argument had been raging since Squam Lake in January. Lucas Walker was against using percussion. He felt that dropping the drums here was somehow *progressive*.

"The drums don't sound organic," Lucas said. "We have a chance to do something no one has ever done before." Which wasn't remotely true but certainly sounded good.

Alexander Koutzoukis argued for the opposing side. "Without percussion," he says, "it sounds like a wall of Auto-Tune. It's like we were slapping people in the face with the arrangement; you could pick out every separate line, every bit of movement." In short, every *dim dim*. He felt there was no energy without the percussion. Unfortunately, where Lucas would argue lucidly and with specificity, Alexander would begin every statement by insisting, *"There's no way you're going to make me vote for not having percussion."* The kid's closed-minded tactics were infuriating. Alexander wanted to be cutting edge, to respect the Bubs tradition. But this wasn't about making a statement. "The song sounds better with percussion," he said. "And the point is to put out the best album we can."

At five in the morning the Bubs adjourned.

Ed Boyer doesn't find this conversation surprising in the least. He isn't concerned with the amount of time the Bubs spent discussing the album in a small Super 8 motel room on spring break; he's concerned with the decisions born from these marathon arguments. "When the Bubs get together they make terrible decisions," he says. "When they came out of that meeting, the consensus was that they'd use percussion on 'Mama'—but it would be *mixed quietly* into the background. That's like wearing half of a winter coat in the snow." Still, he understood the impetus. "A couple of the guys had an idealistic, nonpractical view of what they wanted the song to sound like," he says. "They wanted this captivating choral thing that didn't need percussion and was going to be pure and fine on its own. If they were the King's Singers or Take 6 and their voices were amazing you could get by with having nothing but the tenor-one part."

The kicker was, none of this really mattered. Ed Boyer—and

Bill Hare—had already decided to use percussion. "The reason we pay Bill Hare is because he's mixed hundreds of a cappella albums," Ed Boyer says. "He's not taking notes from fifteen kids who've never mixed an album before."

Ask a member of the Beelzebubs why they do this—why they have these marathon arguments—and they'll tell you it's because it's always been done that way. The Bubs breed a culture of self-obsession. When Adam Gardner from the rock band Guster was a freshman singing with the Beelzebubs, he was subjected to a long car ride with Danny Lichtenfeld '93. Danny felt Adam didn't know nearly enough of the old Bubs music and so, for hours, they listened to the limited-edition twenty-fifth anniversary Bubs tape, the one featuring Gerald James's rendition of "Take You Back." Adam Gardner, meanwhile, felt that the Bub lore was being forced down his throat. The indoctrination would come to a head later that year on a trip to San Francisco. The Bubs have a hand signal they use—discreetly—onstage, to remind a Bub to smile. It's easy: Give the thumbs-up, extend your index finger and cock your eyebrows. Onstage in San Francisco, Danny looked over at an exhausted Adam Gardner and gave him the thumbs-up. Just as discreetly, Adam mouthed back "Fuck off."

All of this indoctrination, all of this history that each kid has at his fingertips—the gig at Letterman, past soloists, Bub words—drilled into him on countless car rides, comes with a price. The group is guided by a set of expectations (real or heavily imagined) that dictates every one of their actions. It tells them where to travel and when. It tells them it's OK to drive through the night to sing a five-song set at Duke—on consecutive weekends. One worries they're not making their own jokes and experiences but rather are destined to relive those that came before them. Surely, this is not what Tim Vaill would want for his Beelzebubs.

It had been a busy spring even by Beelzebubs standards. In February, the Bubs performed at the grand opening of the Granoff Music Building at Tufts. They went to Georgetown for the annual Cherry Tree Massacre, an a cappella festival put on by the all-male Georgetown Chimes. In Michigan, they were the guest group at the Midwest ICCA quarterfinals where, postshow, the Bubs invented a new drinking game, the Tour de Franzia, which involved pouring boxed wine down one's throat. Later, in Ohio, the Bubs performed with Ed Boyer's dad and his barbershop group. Somewhere amid all of this was StAAg Night, the annual Bub alumni dinner that ends late in the evening with hours of drunken singing they call *woodshedding*. (In barbershop terms, *woodshed* means to sing without arrangements, inventing harmonies on the spot.) StAAg Night is an incredible feat of continuity, both physical and historical, when an alum from the sixties can reasonably expect to sing his old solo backed by fifty voices spanning generations of Beelzebubs.

The Bubs were occupied seven of eight weekends leading up to the trip to Los Angeles. On their lone free Saturday they drove ninety minutes to a state park, traipsing around in the snow for two hours—a photoshoot for their forthcoming album *Pandaemonium*. The Bubs also managed to learn a handful of new songs for their spring show, including "Come Sail Away." When you are a Bub, your time is not your own. Which begs the question: When is it all too much?

Perhaps because of this traveling, Chris Van Lenten '08 nearly failed out of school. Or maybe it's because of his prodigious Nintendo Wii habit. Regardless, at the last minute he decided to skip spring break in Los Angeles entirely. Which pissed the group off. "We're not the Bubs when we're missing even one person," Matt Michelson likes to say.

However, a few weeks later—when the Bubs returned to campus—it would be Matt Michelson who needed to miss a show.

The backstory: Way back in October, the Bubs hosted a visit from the Silhooettes, a rowdy all-female group from the University of Virginia, who nearly drank the Bubs under the table that night. The two groups had an honest-to-God *sing-off* at Doug Terry's house and the stomping that accompanied the Sils' version of K. T. Tunstall's "Black Horse and a Cherry Tree" literally shook the foundations. There was drinking. There was beer pong. Later that night, everyone hit a frat-house toga party. When the sun came up, Matt Kraft was still cuddling with Olivia Bloom— the Sil with a passing resemblance to a young Meg Ryan. The Bubs were supposed to return the favor, traveling to UVA in April for the final Sils show of the year. The gig was on the Bubs' calendar for months. The two groups were even supposed to do a duet together, an arrangement of "Wait a Minute," by the Pussycat Dolls. The Bubs never learned the song. And four days before the trip, they canceled. It was the first gig the Bubs would miss in at least four years. But Matt Michelson and Matt Kraft had been training for the Boston Marathon—also scheduled for that weekend. And then there was the matter of Adrian Dahlin, a freshman, nearly seven feet tall, with a mop of big red hair. His e-mail is JollyRedGiant, and he was generally visible in the back row— except when he missed a show for the track team, of which he was a proud member. He'd missed more track meets than he would have liked that semester. Worse: Even when he did skip a track meet for the Bubs, the group *still* needled him about it. Well, Adrien had a track meet that weekend, and when a couple of Bubs got sick, the group pulled the trigger and canceled the trip to UVA.

The Bubs did not take the decision to cancel lightly; rather, it was fraught with e-mail exchanges and investigations into last-minute airline flights (so Matt Kraft and Matt Michelson could fly back to Boston in time for the marathon). "We never cancel shows," Doug Terry says. "It's unprofessional." Which is sort of the point and maybe even their tragic flaw: The Bubs *aren't* professional musicians. They're students. They've been using the word *professional* as a noun, when they should have been thinking of it as an adjective. And for the first time all year the Bubs were forced to contend with the fact that they were students—mortals, even—just a group of guys with disparate interests and priorities.

But the weight of their phenomenal success has made them, at times, shockingly myopic. They don't need music from their alumni—what they need is *perspective*. After Los Angeles, the Bubs were asked to perform at a rally for Senator Barack Obama, held at the five-thousand-person arena on the Boston University campus. The Bubs sang "America the Beautiful." But they didn't actually get to meet Obama.

"We *would* have," Matt Michelson says, "but we had to leave for a gig at a private school. It was really far away."

The Bubs had double-booked themselves, and the only person to raise a serious objection was Andrew Savini. It wasn't just that Obama had gone to Savini's high school. "Obama is the man," he says. Surely the private school would have understood? Perhaps it could have even been rescheduled.

Did any of the Bubs suggest canceling the private school gig? "I said that thirty times," Andrew Savini says. "Obama might be the next president!" And then, just when a Bub seems curious about the world outside of the Bub room, Savini concedes the true reason for his disappointment: "The Bubs would have had another PR picture with a president!"

The Bubs lacked self-awareness. Perhaps no story demonstrates this more than spring break 2007, the night the Bubs performed at a rock club in Venice Beach.

On a chilly March night, a stone's throw from Venice Beach, the Beelzebubs park their big white van outside a Los Angeles dive bar called Good Hurt. Andrew Savini goes in to do a preliminary sweep of the place. He reports back with some unfortunate news: "I didn't see any waitresses dressed as nurses."

"We were told there'd be *nurses*," Lucas Walker says, indignant. "I thought that was the *theme*." Not that it matters. It's uncertain the Bubs will even get inside. Out in the crisp air, the very big, very broad bouncer looks the Bubs up and down. He is staring at fourteen guys all dressed in some iteration of baggy jeans and wrinkled shirts. "How many of you are under twenty-one?" the bouncer asks. The majority of hands go up. "No, I can't have that," he says, shaking his head.

Lucas tries to reason with the man. "We're performing tonight," he says. "What if the under-twenty-one guys wear *X*'s— on their *foreheads*?"

"What band are you with?" the bouncer asks.

Just then, Dave Iscove, a Bub circa '94, comes out of the bar, accompanied by his brother. "These are the Bubs!" Dave Iscove shouts, pointing.

"I know," his brother says. "You can spot them from a fuckin' mile away."

Iscove sees the Bubs are shivering. He apologizes for the situation with the doorman, says he called the bar, says he spoke to someone.

"Let's go warm up," Alexander Koutzoukis says. And with that, the Bubs walk toward a vacant parking lot across the street, passing their van along the way. Matt Michelson stops dead in his tracks. He looks at the van. He looks back at the Bubs. "I thought you meant *warm up*, like, get in the van and warm up," he says. "I'm fucking cold."

The Bubs circle up next to a Dumpster. "Listen," Alexander says. "We have to take this gig seriously. It's one thing to be an a cappella group singing at a bar. It's another to be a *shitty* a cappella group singing at a bar." He hits a note on the electronic pitch pipe, and the Bubs warm up, harmonizing on the syllables *benny benny benny benny benny benny benny benny blaaaaack.*

It's true, the Bubs are on the bill at Good Hurt tonight. They're scheduled to open for Iscove's band, an alt-rock outfit called All Rise, at twelve-thirty in the morning. It is an odd scene—an a cappella group performing at a club— and the irony is not lost on the Bubs. "This is how that Yale thing happened," Alexander says to the group.

Lucas implores the Bubs to lose the Pips-like choreography on "Smiley Faces." "It doesn't make sense at this venue," he says. "Don't do it." He stresses the importance of looking cool. "The bouncer asked me what *band* we were with," he says. "We have to act like a *band.*"

Suddenly, amid the scales and vocal warm-ups, a strange (possibly disturbed) man makes a beeline for the Bubs, pushing his way into the circle. Tim Conrad looks like he might soil himself. The confusion quickly dissipates, however, when this man joins the Bubs in singing a vocal warm-up, which goes something like this (in harmony): *"You can suck my balls."* This strange man is Jeff Murphy, Bubs class of '94. Most of the Bubs have never met Murph before (he lives out west). He plays bass in Iscove's band, All Rise. He tells the Bubs how excited he is to see them perform tonight, and just as suddenly he disappears.

Alexander runs through that night's set list. They'll open with "Inaction," he says. "It's the loudest rock song we have." While that may be, it's also sung by the wispy Doug Terry, who tonight wears a peach-colored button-down, open wide to reveal a Crest-white undershirt.

This will be the Bubs' second gig today, by the way. They are, perhaps, the only band to have played the Plaza Gardens Pavilion at Disneyland and Good Hurt in the same day.

The Bubs—most with *X*'s on their hands—finally gain admittance to the club. It is after midnight. The place is dark, which is a relief, judging by the stank. It's a thirtysomething crowd, a mixed bag of pool players and women begging to be hit on. The Bubs survey the space. Their faces betray their deepest fears: Singing at a rock club may just be a terrible, terrible idea for an a cappella group. But it is too late. The ska band onstage finishes up their set and Iscove jumps up onstage. "We have something super-different for you tonight," he says. "Remember in college how a cappella was the biggest thing. These guys here"—Iscove points at the Bubs, now lining up in front of the stage—"they are the *fucking shit*. The national champions. You guys are in for a treat. Straight from Boston, the fucking Tufts Beelzebubs!"

The Bubs jump up onstage, clumsily arranging themselves into a tight space. If nothing else, they've gotten the room's attention. The bartenders are looking over. The pool table has gone quiet. The basses begin: *Dinna-inna-inna-inna Dinna-inna-inna-inna*. The tenors come in: *Get it! Get it! Get it! Get it!*

It is clear, from the first notes, that "Inaction" was a bad call to open the show. Doug solos on this one, and he doesn't sing so much as spit with intention: *Call on the fates // this'll take a second // While I fall on my face // like everyone else*. It may be a rock song, but it's an obscure rock song—worse, an obscure rock song sung by an obscure (for these parts) chorus of a cappella kids.

"Get off the stage!" someone shouts from the back.

Chris Kidd, a Bub alum along for the ride, tries to be supportive, though he looks mortified. He would have opened with "Magical Mystery Tour," he says. "At least people know that song." A guy at the pool table takes the pool cue and plays his best air guitar.

While Doug sings the bridge, in the background the Bubs repeat *No! No! No! No!*—shaking their heads in time. The microphones are not helping. The Bubs need dull area mics, not hot solo mics. Iscove, oblivious (or just that damn fired up), is front and center, giving the devil's horns.

"They're like the Polyphonic Spree," someone says.

"You suck!" someone shouts. The set is mercifully short—four songs total. Savini steps up to the mic. "We've got one more song for you," he says. "You've been a lovely audience this evening."

CHAPTER FOURTEEN

THE HULLABAHOOS

Wherein the Hullabahoos' relaxed attitude finally catches up with them while Brendon Mason reports back from a Lexington, Virginia, jail cell

When the Hullabahoos returned to campus in late January, following the embarrassment of missing the Lakers game, they considered keeping that little story to themselves. The national anthem wasn't televised and, well, who would know if they told one little white lie? The Hullabahoos are the group, after all, whose Web site boasts of performance requests from the White House, the Kennedy Center, and NBC's *Today Show*. What it doesn't say is that the B'hoos were *invited* to the White House and to *The Today Show*, but didn't actually perform in either place—scheduling conflicts both times. "We were *invited*," Morgan Sword says.

A lull had set in. The Hullabahoos would elect new officers that Sunday night—generally a brutal exercise. It was still March, though. Why elect new officers so soon? "The group has a tendency to lose momentum in the spring and we need time for the officer transition," Joe Cassara, the outgoing president, says. The Hullabahoos were learning new music, but all was quiet on the West Lawn front. Well, for everyone but Brendon Mason, maybe. It started with the Justin Timberlake concert. Six months before, Brendon had bought a handful of tickets for the Charlottes-ville stop of Timberlake's *FutureSex/LoveShow*. Brendon wasn't planning on treating his friends to the concert. Rather, he just wanted to control his environment. So he bought up the seats around him and sold the tickets off to a well-curated group of coeds. And for six months he counted down the days until the concert. And then the night before, Brendon took part in some-thing called the Case Race—a drinking game in which indivi-duals attempt to finish an entire case of beer (twenty-four cans). No one ever finishes, though as with most drinking games, Bren-don will tell you, everyone's a winner. Unfortunately, Brendon was so hungover the next day he couldn't lift his head off the pil-low, let alone attend an eardrum-killing Justin Timberlake con-cert. Brendon is not shy. He loves to share stories of his drunken exploits; the ones that end with him blacking out are some of his favorites. The Justin Timberlake story, however, was somehow more embarrassing. Perhaps because it had consequences.

Consequences. It's a good word and one the Hullabahoos—and Brendon—are about to learn the meaning of. The B'hoos had spent much of the year trying to up their game, enjoying a free trip to Portland, putting on a sold-out Christmas show. Yes, they'd missed the Lakers game—which should have been a career highlight. But they'd felt on top of their game musically, at least. Until now. It had been a quiet couple of months on campus and the Hullabahoos were getting lazy, not to mention cocky—a terrible combination.

Our story begins upstairs in the Hullaba-house on Wertland Street.

"Is this everyone?" Pete Seibert says. It is four o'clock on Friday afternoon when the Hullabahoos convene at the house before a gig. Pete surveys the room. It does not look good. The Hullaba-hoos have been invited to perform at Washington and Lee for the second annual (and creatively titled) A Cappella Festival, put on by that school's coed a cappella group, General Admission. Normally, this is the kind of gig the Hullabahoos would have turned down flat. It wasn't a particularly big show (the crowd wouldn't top three hundred), nor did it pay anything. The B'hoos didn't have any friends in the host group. And Lexington, Virginia, wasn't far enough away to justify staying the night, but at two hours was just enough of a drive to be an inconvenience.

Joe Cassara booked this gig despite resistance from the Hullabahoos—or rather *because* of it. When the girl from Washington and Lee called to invite the B'hoos, Joe asked who else would be singing. When she told him that Exit 245, the all-male group at James Madison University, would be there, that was all Joe needed to hear. He jumped at the chance.

The Hullabahoos had never thought much of Exit 245. But last semester the boys from JMU had been the guest group at a Silhooettes show on campus at UVA. Many of the Hullabahoos had been in the audience that night (some of their best friends are Sils) and Joe Cassaro for his part was caught off-guard. Exit 245 wasn't just technically solid, they were entertaining. And unlike most visiting all-male a cappella groups, these boys actually appeared to be cool. (Brendon Mason's best friend from home, Dave Kidd, is in Exit 245.) "The Hullabahoos weren't as bothered as I was about the competition," Joe says. And he wanted to strike fear in the hearts of the Hullabahoos before he graduated in May. "Besides," he says, "Exit's been talking some a cappella shit."

But standing there in the Hullaba-house that afternoon, a sense of dread was creeping in. Maybe Joe had made a mistake. The B'hoos were about to leave for the gig, and four members were missing. Morgan Sword, it turned out, was with his girlfriend. "Lindsay's formal is tonight," someone said. Brian Duhon, likewise, was absent. He'd totaled his electric-blue Ford Mustang in a car crash in Canada on the tail end of winter break. Though he managed to walk away unscathed (despite all logic of physics) he had to leave what was left of the car upstate. He'd returned to Buffalo this weekend to pick up the rehabbed Mustang. Blake Segal, meanwhile, an aspiring actor, was performing in a theater piece on campus that weekend. And Alan Webb, well, he was preparing to leave for a Future Business Leaders of America conference on the West Coast. What's he doing there? someone asked. "Meeting other future business leaders," Pete Seibert said, laughing.

Joe expressed some concern about the attendance. Pete laughed him off. There was precedent. A few weeks ago they'd done a solid sorority gig under the rotunda with just nine members. "We only need five songs," Pete said, looking around the room. He announced the set list—basically, the same five songs the Hullabahoos had been performing all year: "One," "How to Save a Life," "My Love," "Lips of an Angel," and "Home."

Dane Blackburn bristled at the set list. His attitude (and patience) had grown increasingly poor since he'd abandoned the group outside the Staples Center in Los Angeles. He'd stopped suggesting songs, tired of the group rejecting R & B (his taste) for the kind of *Grey's Anatomy*–type soft rock their female fans wanted to hear. He took the driving directions Joe printed up and climbed into his car, slamming the door.

The Hullabahoos, by the way, would be closing the show at Washington and Lee. Joe asked the girl from General Admission why her own group wasn't closing the concert. "Because everyone here loves the Hullabahoos!" she says. The B'hoos were actually a bigger draw at Washington and Lee than that school's own a cappella singers. The president looked at his Hullabahoos. It appeared that not a single one of them had showered that day. It would be a strictly robes-over-cargo-shorts night.

Perhaps Joe was right to be worried.

The Hullabahoos are a lot like five-year-old boys. When they pull into the parking lot at Washington and Lee's Lenfest Performing Arts Center, they meet the pretty girl who invited them—and ignore her entirely. She escorts them to the classroom where they'll warm up, and they immediately start touching things. Two Hullabahoos are writing on the chalkboard. Another is playing the piano. Another is pulling at the string attached to a pull-down screen. Desks are knocked about as the Hullabahoos walk by; it's as if they don't even see the furniture. The only one not smiling is Patrick Lundquist, who is off in the corner, head down on a desk, dramatically rubbing at his temples.

The Hullabahoos gather around the piano to warm up. They start with "One." It sounds empty. Midsong, Brendon Mason points to the ceiling, a shorthand gesture that says, *Tune up, we're going flat.* "If there are people missing on your part," Joe says, "you need to compensate." Myles Glancy comments on the group's breathing, which is entirely too visible. If the mess of them all breathe at the same time, between measures, there will be a lot of dead air—which kills the illusion that there are instruments on-stage. Because Morgan Sword is missing, Chris Brown is forced to do percussion on nearly every song, and he's winded, quickly.

Still, the Hullabahoos seem content. Sufficiently warmed up, they return their attention to drawing obscene things on the chalkboard.

The show opens, like most a cappella concerts, with an eighties tune. General Admission makes a grand entrance, walking down the aisle, singing the first chords of "Total Eclipse of the Heart." "What the fuck is this?" one of the Hullabahoos says. Sitting with the B'hoos during a show—it's sort of like listening to DVD commentary on a movie. Some of the B'hoos try to stifle their laughs. Brendon isn't so courteous. The performance is serviceable. But it's unclear why a group with two black girls would have the small Jewish girl sing lead on Roberta Flack's "Killing Me Softly."

The Hullabahoos are having a good time entertaining themselves. Until Exit 245 takes to the stage, wearing jeans, white Oxford shirts, and ties. Most of the kids carry Poland Spring bottles or plastic Nalgene bottles, but one, Chris Talley, steps forward and places a gallon jug of water at his feet. Somehow this reads as awesome. He even has the shaggy hair of an indie *rawker*, not to mention the impossibly skinny jeans to match.

"Look, it's Myles!" Brendon says. Myles leans over. "You can't make fun of me about the skinny jeans anymore," he says. "Those are *way* skinnier."

Exit 245 opens with another eighties tune, Foreigner's "Cold as Ice." Talley solos, brushing the hair out of his eyes and singing out, *"You're as cold as iiiiice // willing to sacrifice our love."* The arrangement is unspectacular—a lot of *"ba da // da da // ba da // da da // pay the price // ba da."* But it has a certain swing to it.

The Hullabahoos suddenly clam up. It wasn't just the music. The guys from Exit 245 were clearly having more fun than anyone else in the room. They sang Lionel Ritchie's "All Night Long." They sang a Disney medley, of all things. Yet it worked.

Amid the applause, the Hullabahoos file out of the auditorium, walking quickly back to the classroom to prepare for their own appearance. In the hallway, they catch the sweaty members of Exit 245 just as they're exiting the stage. "Good job, guys," the B'hoos mutter in near unison.

"Close the door," Pete Seibert says. "We'll do the pep talk later." When Chris Brown makes a joke, Pete is quick to react. "Brown, elections are tomorrow night," he says. "You can run for this job and then you can talk all you want." Chris Brown looks stunned.

"Circle up," Pete says. "Let's try Faith Hill." He blows the pitch pipe and the Hullabahoos run thirty seconds of "Cry," which they'd recently learned. (Coincidentally, the Beelzebubs had also just learned "Cry," but had a difficult time finding a soloist. That's the challenge of alumni arranging—the old guys don't always know if there's someone in the group who can handle the solo.) Patrick took this one, and would have shamed Faith Hill herself, such were his over-the-top, self-important vocal acrobatics. "The background needs to be stronger," Pete says. "We were nine under the rotunda the other night and we sounded great. What's the problem?"

Pete announces the new set list. They had planned on opening with The Fray's "How to Save a Life." Instead they begin with U2's "One." "Cry" would come later in the set. And they'd close with Marc Broussard's "Home." It is a stronger set list, if suddenly Patrick-heavy. It was not ideal, but so be it.

The Exit 245 performance laid bare all of the Hullabahoos' insecurities—and perhaps their biggest flaw. "It's just a cappella!" Pete likes to say, though he doesn't really believe that. How else to explain his last-minute tweaking of the set. "We don't mind what anyone thinks," Joe says, "as long as everyone thinks we're the best." Pete tries to pump the Hullabahoos back up. But Brendon compounds the problem by sharing a story his buddy in Exit 245 told him: "That skinny kid has a record deal and was down in Miami over spring break laying down tracks with his band."

Joe interrupts "There's no point in coming here if we aren't going to be the best," he says.

The Hullabahoos are due onstage in a few minutes. "All aboard," Pete says, readying the group for their pre-show ritual. He blows a pitch and Patrick, stretching on the floor, starts in. *"People get ready // There's a train a comin' // Pickin' up passengers from coast to coast."* Just as they finish, Dane Blackburn walks in, having missed the entirety of the warm-up. "Just in time," Joe says, shaking his head. Dane doesn't seem to notice.

"Hands in," Joe says. "We came here to be the best. Let's kick some ass. I love you guys." The last bit was designed to make them laugh. No one did. *Unit. God. Corps. Country. Hullaba-hoos.*

Out in the auditorium, the emcee introduces the Hullaba-hoos. "They've been invited to the White House and to *The To-day Show*," she says and a hush goes over the crowd. One can actually hear people whispering, *"The Today Show!"*

The Hullabahoos walk onstage but they aren't themselves. No one is smiling. They're all business. Even Bobby Grasberger's hat seems cocked just a drop farther to the right. The Hullaba-hoos had been psyched out, Joe will later say. He wanted to push the Hullabahoos—that's why he booked this gig. He hadn't ex-pected them to cower. "I hated that," he says. "Some people pan-icked instead of rising to the challenge."

The B'hoos open with "One." It still sounds empty, but more than that, it lacks feeling. In the past, just the strains of the opening chord would be enough to get the Hullabahoos smiling (even the morning after the Lakers game, at the Disney Concert hall, performing "One" for the tour guide hours after that embarrassment). But tonight it feels forced. When they arrive at *"Have you come here to play Jesus?"*—this is where the group drops out, and Brendon and Patrick harmonize on the word *Jesus*—something goes wrong. The entire stage is quiet, which is what makes the harmony stand out generally. But to-night the harmony is spectacularly off. And when it misses, there's nowhere to hide that note. Patrick and Brendon look at each other, and the look exchanged is one of utter confusion, a look that says, first, What was that?, and then quickly turns to blame, as in: *That unspeakable offense to mankind must have been your fault.*

The set drags—it feels like an eternity. There's minimal in-teraction with the crowd, and worse, no discernible energy. Joe does a long (not funny) intro about the origins of the robes. The problem (one, anyway) is that the Hullabahoos are performing as if there's no audience. Patrick destroys the Faith Hill song. It works despite (or rather because of) the arrangement, which is entirely egregious—and nearly identical in structure to Pete's "I Can't Make You Love Me" arrangement (or "One" for that matter). Which is to say the song builds to a climax, the group gets suddenly quiet, and Patrick comes back in (generally a half-step up), belting out a note that hits you in the gut.

Joe Cassara was right about a lot of things. The main one: The Hullabahoos don't know how lucky they are to have soloists like Patrick and Brendon, not to mention Chad Moses, Myles Glancy, and Dane Blackburn. But even with a great soloist, if the group isn't emotionally invested, you're dead.

Dane closes the show with "Home," leaving his sunglasses on for some unknown reason. "I got confidence issues," he says to the crowd, pointing to the shades. What the audience doesn't know is that halfway through the song the sunglasses fog up and Dane can't see a thing. The show's saving grace: Myles will be happy to know that when he steps out to sing "How to Save a Life," the entirety of Exit 245 will turn toward their own singer in skinny jeans, Chris Talley, patting him on the back and pointing. "It's you! It's you!"

There isn't much time to worry about what's just happened onstage. Because the girl from General Admission has just wandered over to invite the Hullabahoos to the after-party. Or, rather, after-*parties*. "There are two parties," she says. "One house has beer. The other one has liquor. It's going to be pretty crazy." Outside, Joe asks one of the girls how to find the party. She points indiscriminately up the hill and says they can't miss it. Which of course they do. Suddenly the B'hoos are standing in front of a house with a red porch light. "Is that it?" Joe Cassara says. "Brown, go knock on the door."

"And say what? *Is this the a cappella party?*" Chris Brown is relieved when no one answers the door.

The Hullabahoos eventually find the party. And one girl from General Admission—who sang backup on "Killing Me Softly"—is close-talking to Pete. She is drunk, already, and she keeps referring to Pete as *Keith*.

"You're killing me softly," Pete says to her.

One of the girls gives Matt Mooney a compliment, sort of. "I was sitting next to this, like, fifty-year-old MILF," she says. "When you sang, she was like, 'Don't you think he's handsome!'"

"Moms like me," Mooney says.

The music director from Exit 245 corners Pete in the kitchen. He compliments Pete on the group's tone, then proceeds to call him out on his arranging style. "The arrangements are all pretty much the same," the kid says. It might have been awkward if they weren't distracted by Brendon Mason, who is standing in the next room, leading a housewide chant of *"Frats! Frats! Frats! Frats!"*

Brendon singles this out as the moment he should have left town, along with the other Hullabahoos who departed for Charlottesville, pulling into campus around two in the morning. But he didn't. None of the Hullabahoos would see Brendon Mason again for close to twenty-four hours. The next day at UVA there was some e-mailing among the Hullabahoos. "Did Brendon get arrested?" someone wrote.

Brendon Mason wanders into the Hullaba-house the night after the show at Washington and Lee, wearing his trademark Hanes undershirt and flip-flops. Elections will be held momentarily. The group is begging for the story—a story, Brendon says, he would like to tell just once, and so he waits for everyone to arrive. Finally, dramatically, he begins:

It had started innocently enough. Brendon and his childhood buddy, Exit 245's Dave Kidd, had been growing tired of the a cappella festivities. After the other Hullabahoos left town, one of the girls mentioned something to Brendon about an after-party at a nearby fraternity house. And so the foursome stumbled over to the festivities—a party Brendon says was unlike any he'd ever seen. "I was *grinding*," he says, smiling, as if he'd invented the term. The lights were off. He was sweating so much, he says, he "should have been having sex." He'd been to many fraternity parties in his time, but this was something else. It was like a movie, he says. The night could not end there.

Of course, it *could* have ended there. Brendon could have gone back to Charlottesville with the rest of the Hullabahoos hours ago. He could have sat with the B'hoos eating Gus burgers at the White Spot on the Corner, safely back on campus. But instead, when the frat party ended, Brendon Mason—former Disney child star, celebrated offensive lineman of the Hullabahoos B football squad—stumbled outside with his buddy Dave Kidd and eventually came upon an off-campus house party. Upstairs, the two found a handle of low-budget gin, from which they sampled liberally.

As the four o'clock hour approached, Brendon and Dave Kidd were walking in the street, still holding the handle of gin, which they were chasing with a bottle of Gatorade they'd picked up along the way. That's when someone caught sight of the LEXINGTON COUNTY SHERIFF'S OFFICE sign. At the time, it seemed like a good idea to *steal* this sign. And so Brendon put the gin and Gatorade down and he and Dave Kidd started clawing at the metal. They were able to unhook one side before Dave Kidd yelled, "Run!" Brendon's reaction time was—not surprisingly—piss poor. And a cop car appeared. The officer stepped out of his car. "What are you trying to do to my sign?" he said.

"Nothing, sir," Brendon replied.

"Do you know that person running down the street?"

"No, sir."

"Is that your alcohol?" he said, pointing to the handle of gin in the grass.

"My *what*?"

Brendon Mason was fingerprinted, handcuffed, and thrown in the drunk tank, where he fell asleep on the concrete floor of the cell. "I blew a point three," Brendon tells the Hullabahoos proudly. "It's off the BAC card." In the morning—after a breakfast of prison biscuits, which Brendon reports are quite good—Dave Kidd picked him up.

Upstairs at the Hullaba-house, one of the B'hoos asks the obvious question: "Did you get raped?"

"No. I had my own cell."

"We're all very proud," Blake Segal says, shaking his head.

It was a throwaway joke from Blake, but in some ways, it spelled out the operating principle behind the Hullabahoos. That story—the biscuits, the handle of gin—was much more important than what happened onstage with Exit 245. In fact, no one ever really mentioned that gig again. Because it happened in a vacuum, which is to say, off campus. If they were embarrassed, at least no one was there to hear it. They were still the Hullabahoos.

When it came time for the elections that night, heart won out over organizational skills. Which is entirely fitting. Missing the Los Angeles Lakers game had been an embarrassment. But it was also a great story. And that's really what the Hullabahoos were all about. The elections only affirmed what it meant to be a Hullabahoo.

Going into the night, Patrick Lundquist was the wild card; he was running for president. He talked about "the Patrick Lundquist idea box"—a collection of great ideas just sitting around waiting to be implemented. He was insufferable. And this gave the group license to air every grievance—every emotional snub—they'd felt this year. Patrick sat in front of the firing squad.

"A big check mark on the president's to-do list is managing the personalities in the group," Morgan Sword said.

"Are you asking about the diva thing?" Patrick said.

"It's kind of funny that you don't know what I'm talking about."

"That it's all about me?"

"The truth of all of this is we're seventeen people who are not of equal talent when it comes to singing," Morgan said. "And it creates this artificial hierarchy. It's silly. But people act according to it. It's always been somewhat intentional that Joe and I, who aren't the best singers, have been running things."

There is a delicate balance of power at work in these a cappella groups—a sort of self-correcting meritocracy put in place to account for the fact that the best singers inevitably get the most attention. It's the reason bands have broken up since time immemorial. When it comes to planning big-ticket gigs, Patrick would have been the best president. He is a dominating personality whose good looks alone have led to gigs like the fall 2006 trip to Portland. He is also the one who reached out to Howard Spector, the man who booked the B'hoos for the Republican National Convention three years ago, in a quest to get back in the men's talent stable. But Patrick can be humorless, sitting in the corner by himself before a show. It's no surprise that he was shot down tonight. Electing him president would have given the guy free rein on the mic. They imagined the concerts, with Patrick—as he was wont to do—mimicking that movie trailer voice (a favorite joke of his): *"In a world where the Hullabahoos come to Rotunda Sing…"* The Hullabahoos would have imploded.

It's Chad Moses—the candidate least likely, on paper anyway—who is elected president of the Hullabahoos. A story: One weekend last semester, when Joe Cassara was away at a job interview, he left Chad (then the group's business manager) in charge. And the B'hoos very nearly missed a gig that weekend. At a children's hospital! Perhaps it shouldn't have been a surprise. As business manager, Chad had earned a reputation for both forgetting to retrieve mail from the Hullabahoos' mailbox (leaving checks uncashed) and spending too much of the group's money on beer. The children's hospital incident just confirmed the group's suspicions about Chad's leadership skills. They pulled into the hospital that day with ten minutes to spare. Unfortunately, it was the *wrong hospital*. Chad turned to the group and made his now famous declaration: "Let's get the crap out of here." By the time they found the gig, they were thirty minutes late for the kids.

Musically, 2007–2008 could be their best ever. Not a single soloist was graduating, and Pete Seibert had agreed to stay on as music director for his senior year. Facing the Hullabahoos at elections, Chad had said the exact right thing: He talked about ownership. "I don't always have the best ideas," Chad said. "I am going to rely on you. This is a group. And every member of this group should feel responsibility for it." Patrick would have been a dictator. And so the Hullabahoos elected the guy who liked to get drunk and spend the group's money on beer. (They refer to those drinking nights as Hullaba-funded.) If this year had been about playing on the level of a group like the Beelzebubs, the Hullabahoos just unanimously decided that it wasn't worth it. One needs to be invested. There should always be stakes. But not to the detriment of all else.

The elections actually relieved a lot of Joe's Cassara's anxiety about how the Hullabahoos would fare without him next year. (Joe and Morgan Sword are known in the group as the Team Dads.) Graduating seniors don't vote on officer positions. So he and Morgan sat back and listened to the deliberations. "It was nice to hear them talk," Joe says. "They care!" After an hour, Joe Cassara finally called the candidates back upstairs.

"You can't wear those shorts next year," Joe said. "And you have to get rid of the chin strap. Chad, take a few victory laps and start working off that gut. Congratulations."

CHAPTER FIFTEEN

Wherein the ICCAs goes international, the man behind Mainely A Cappella quits the scene, and we meet Merv Griffin's favorite a cappella group—which not surprisingly turns out to be the a cappella equivalent of the cabana boy

As collegiate a cappella became less of a novelty act, the stakes seemed to rise exponentially. There were rivals to BOCA, the Best of Collegiate A Cappella compilation, sprouting up every year, it seemed. One, *Voices Only*, was a two-disc compilation founded in 2004 by Brock Harris and Corey Slutsky. Another compilation, called simply *sing*, catered to the burgeoning a cappella scene in the South and Midwest but also included professional a cappella groups. (*Sing* would be entirely superfluous save for the fact that its second edition was called *sing 2: eclectic boogaloo*—an excellent eighties reference.) Dave Sperandio, the man who was banned from the message boards at RARB, and his organization, the Alliance for A Cappella Initiatives (AACI), had also launched their own one-day collegiate a cappella competition held annually at an a cappella conference he'd started in the early aughts called SoJam.

The thing is, in 2007, even Don Gooding—the owner of Varsity Vocals, the proprietor of a-cappella.com—decided it was too much, that it was time to get out of the business. After buying the NCCAs from Adam Farb in 1999, Don hired Jessika Diamond, a Canuck, one of the few people in a cappella who never actually *sang* in an a cappella group, to run the competition. (She also happened to be Farb's ex-girlfriend.) It took a lot of legwork to revive the competition after the Lost Year. Jessika got in touch with the groups who had competed in recent years to find out what they liked (and what could be improved) about the NCCAs. She soon uncovered a secret: Adam Farb was not a popular guy. The Golden Overtones at UC Berkeley had hired Farb to produce a CD—which they received. Unfortunately, he handed them just one copy. They had been expecting five hundred. There was a disagreement over who was going to pay to print the discs, and when the university bursar wouldn't cut Farb a check, he disappeared. The Men's Octet at Berkeley, who'd won the NCCAs in the 1997–1998 school year, never saw the advertised prize money, Jessika says. (Farb doesn't have the records anymore, but says the organization had plenty of money and would have surely paid the winner.) Such was the resistance that Don Gooding went so far as to actually post photos of the entire NCCA staff on his Web site just so people could see that Farb was no longer on the payroll. In three years, Jessika Diamond managed to restore the competition, and in 2001 she launched the first international show at McGill University in Toronto. The next year the competition was officially reborn as the International Championship of Collegiate A Cappella, the ICCAs. "Deke used to call me the queen of a cappella," Jessika Diamond says.

Jessika ran the ICCAs for three years. And from the outside, anyway, it seemed like everything was in order. In her final season, she'd received two hundred tapes from various college a cappella groups hoping to compete. But now Don Gooding wanted out. "The ICCAs lost money every year that Jessika ran it," Don Gooding says.

Jessika sighs. "There's going to be a lot of finger pointing here," she says.

Jessika Diamond, who'd had her hand in so many a cappella projects—from CASA to the ICCAs—parted ways with Don and largely retreated from the scene. She was, however, still running the Contemporary A Cappella Recording Awards (the CARAs). She would leave that behind, as well, but not before a stint in the hospital. "I developed shingles over forty-five percent of my body," she says.

The CARAs had been haphazard at best. Here's how the nominations worked. Jessika would have listening parties at her apartment in the Bay Area. Five people would come. There would be stacks of a cappella CDs around the room. Together they'd nominate in thirty-three categories, including best female collegiate soloist, best professional a cappella group, that sort of thing. They'd listen to thirty seconds of each track. People would go to the bathroom. People were drinking. They'd skip whole categories while eating chips in the kitchen. Still, at the end of the session, they'd emerge with a final list of CARA nominations. From there, Deke Sharon (who'd started the awards in 1992) would make cassette tapes of all the nominated music, which he'd ship out to qualified voters. But as the numbers grew—some one hundred and twenty collegiate albums alone are released every year—this became cumbersome. Soon, voters were receiving three-cassette sets in the mail. Who was even listening to cassettes anymore? Besides, the nominations were something of a joke. The nominators rarely listened to an entire track; they just didn't have the time. Once the committee actually nominated a track that had a piano on it.

At what would turn out to be her final listening party, Jessika's skin started to burn. She was lying down on the floor, scratching her back. She couldn't stop. Eventually she had to kick everyone out of the house. "I literally had to take my pants off," Jessika says. "And I didn't know any of those people well enough to do that in front of them." The next day she went to the doctor. By the end of the week she was hospitalized.

Julia Hoffman, an alum of the Stanford Harmonics, stepped in to run the CARAs. Maybe "stepped in" isn't right. "We had a coup," Julia says.

Don, meanwhile, hired Amanda Grish, an alum of the University of Illinois a cappella group No Strings Attached, to run the ICCAs. In her new role she's had several surprising phone calls. "I've had parents call me to ask, Of the schools my child is applying to, what are the places with good a cappella?" she says. "The parents are desperate. They say, My kid wants to sing, and I want to know where he'll have the best chance."

In 2007 Amanda Grish bought Don out. "I'm forty-nine," Don Gooding said. "I've been at this for sixteen years." He's selling a-cappella.com as well (though he'll retain a small stake in future profits for five years). He wants to get involved with the centennial celebration of his old Yale Whiffenpoofs, set for 2009. "Besides, I have the constitution of an entrepreneur," he says. "Once businesses are up and solid I lose interest in the day-to-day operations. I like to reinvent myself." More than that, it was about the music. "I'm hoping to sing again," Don says. "It's the old saw about the cobbler's kid not having any shoes. I'm the a cappella guy who isn't singing."

The thing about collegiate a cappella is, no one wants the party to end. That's the buried—but not too deep—emotional hangover of all this CASA infighting, lawsuits, and shingles. It shouldn't be surprising. Isn't collegiate a cappella just another *Behind the Music* story? But in place of Grammys and world tours, it's CARAs and spring break trips to Mexico. The emotional scar may be proportional. Leif Garrett winds up homeless and in rehab for heroin. The a cappella idols just graduate, forced to weather sudden anonymity and BlackBerry slavery. Most adjust. For others it's like being cast out of Eden. You can't really blame these adults for mourning the loss of their campus fame— even thirty years later.

If there truly is an a cappella Garden of Eden, it might just be on Martha's Vineyard. This is the story of Vineyard Sound—a summer job that celebrates all that is holy in a cappella: sex, music, and camaraderie.

In the early nineties, Townsend Belisle was a student at Skidmore College in Saratoga Springs, New York, majoring in music and economics. In his free time he sang with the university's all-male a cappella group, the Bandersnatchers. (The name, among the best in a cappella, comes from a Lewis Carroll poem, "The Jabberwock.") In the summer of 1991, while his friends were pursuing résumé-padding internships, Townsend waited tables at the Seafood Shanty on Martha's Vineyard, the tony playground of the Kennedys, among other notable families. Townsend loved the sea air. He loved Captain Parker's chowder. Life was good. It would turn out to be a formative summer. Upstairs at the Shanty, you see, there was a makeshift cabaret where a bunch of Yale kids would perform for cash. Townsend had an idea.

Townsend called up his buddy Chris Bettencourt, a member of Connecticut College's all-male CocoBeaux. He had a proposition: I want to create a ten-member all-male a cappella supergroup made up of guys from the Wesleyan Spirits, the CocoBeaux, and the Bandersnatchers. Martha's Vineyard was surely starved for entertainment, he said. "We'll learn *Sesame Street* songs for the kids," Townsend told Chris, "and Sinatra for the older crowd. We'll call ourselves Vineyard Sound." He didn't have to work very hard. Chris was in. It would be the a cappella equivalent of being a cabana boy.

Over spring break in 1992, Townsend took the ferry to the Vineyard and, with the help of a broker, found a spectacular house for that summer—a three-bedroom on the Bay of Edgartown with hardwood floors, cedar siding, and a hot tub. The landlord was nervous about renting to a bunch of college kids. But Townsend, a self-described mama's boy, convinced him to do the deal and Townsend signed the lease that day. The rent on the house: sixteen thousand dollars for the season.

Back at school, Townsend and Chris recruited for Vineyard

Sound. And for the first two weeks of the summer, the group rehearsed eight hours a day, learning some twenty songs. To introduce themselves to the locals, the Sound set out on a listening tour. They'd walk into a restaurant, find the manager, and ask to sing a song for the patrons. That song was usually "Taking Care of Business." "It was upbeat," Townsend says. "And most people couldn't imagine it being sung that way." By *that way*, he means without instruments. On the way out, Townsend would hand a Vineyard Sound business card to the restaurant's manager.

Their big break came at the Seafood Shanty, where Townsend had seen the Yale kids perform the summer before. Townsend negotiated a regular gig at the Shanty. They'd charge a five-dollar entry fee, collecting additional tips in a bucket that read FINANCIAL AID. But for the most part the gigs were slow in coming. They would cover the cost of the house, but Townsend couldn't guarantee the guys would go home with any money. It was a disappointment—most of them had to get other jobs, some at the Yacht Club, others at the grocery store. The lucky ones were lifeguards. But there was momentum.

The members of Vineyard Sound would never need a second job again.

That second summer—all ten original members returned—the Vineyard Sound expanded their repertoire. They even booked a few regular gigs in advance. They were also back at the Seafood Shanty—with one slight change. That first year, the boys had fought with the waitresses. "They'd disrupt our set," Townsend says. It wasn't pretty. He had an idea: Why didn't the men of Vineyard Sound just serve the tables themselves? In place of one long set, the Sound would do several short sets, serving drinks in between. Tips skyrocketed. Even better, chatting up diners between sets, they got to know the locals, which led to more gigs. Eventually they were performing at the Shanty three nights a week, not to mention church gigs and community center events.

Townsend graduated in 1993 but went back for one last summer with the Vineyard Sound. That's how he met Merv Griffin.

It was the summer of '94 and Vineyard Sound was performing upstairs at the Seafood Shanty. One of Townsend's buddies from Martha's Vineyard happened to be Merv Griffin's pilot. Townsend asked for an introduction. And so, one night after dinner, the guy brought Merv Griffin and his six-member entourage down to the Shanty to watch Vineyard Sound perform. Merv was sitting at a table, chomping on a cigar. "Merv was shit-faced," Townsend says.

Billy Joel's "Lullaby" was a big part of the group's repertoire that summer. Garth Ross, a founding member of the Sound and an alum of the CocoBeaux, remembers that night Merv Griffin showed up. (In 2008, the self-same Garth Ross would organize a ten-day a cappella festival for the Kennedy Center, called Singing Solo.) When the Sound came to the end of "Lullaby," it was dead quiet. In that breath of silence before the audience begins to applaud, one husky, cigar-stained voice could be heard way in the back. "Beautiful," Merv Griffin said. *"Beautiful."*

"That sound, *Beaaauutiful,* is ingrained in all of our minds," Townsend says. In fact, they printed it on a T-shirt.

That would not be the last Vineyard Sound saw of Merv Griffin. The pilot took a Vineyard Sound business card and passed it on to someone in Merv's camp. And, lo and behold, three days later Townsend Belisle was standing in the Vineyard Sound house when the call came through. He signaled to the guys to quiet down. "It's a guy from Merv Griffin Entertainment," Townsend whispered, pointing at the phone. The Sound gathered in close.

The man wanted to hire Vineyard Sound to open for Paul Sorvino at Merv's property in Atlantic City in the fall. "He kept saying to me, 'What's your fee?' " Townsend says. Generally, if the Sound made five hundred dollars for a gig they were thrilled.

But this was Merv Griffin! Townsend was stalling. "Well," he said, "a lot of us have significant others. Can we bring our girl-friends?" Yes, the man said. He even agreed to pay for travel. Again, he said, What's your fee? Townsend blurted out five thousand dollars. "Done," the man said.

And so, in the fall of '94, Vineyard Sound reunited in Atlantic City to open for Paul Sorvino. "We sang three songs," Townsend says. There was a big discussion over what three songs to sing, though today no one actually remembers what those three songs were. What they do remember is how bad the show was. First, they were poorly mic'd. Also: It was Atlantic City. "Three-fourths of the crowd was over seventy years old," Townsend says. The show was over in less than fifteen minutes.

Merv was in the audience that night, however. And after dinner, as the Sound went to hit the tables, Townsend ran into the entertainment director for Merv Griffin Resorts International. "Let's go back into this room over here," the guy said, taking Townsend by the arm.

Suddenly, Townsend found himself in a small private room with Merv Griffin, the actor Robert Loggia, and Barbra Streisand. Merv Griffin was eating his favorite frozen yogurt—chocolate, always. And everyone was talking about the yogurt! "Barbra Streisand, Robert Loggia—they were gushing over Merv Griffin's frozen yogurt. They were kissing his ass," Townsend says.

"What do you want to do with your life?" Merv Griffin asked Townsend.

"I want to learn marketing within the entertainment industry," Townsend said, smart enough to take advantage of this very bizarre introduction.

A few months later, Merv Griffin hired Townsend to be one of his six personal assistants. "I was a scout," Townsend says. "I was always three days ahead of Merv's traveling schedule. I had to make sure his yellow pillows were warm and fluffed and that we could find the right brand of chocolate frozen yogurt."

Townsend meanwhile had bigger dreams for Vineyard Sound. He liked the formula. The guys were having fun. And by now they were making good money—more than four thousand dollars *each* for the summer (all expenses paid). Townsend felt they could re-create the magic on nearby Cape Cod. And so he found a two-family house in a shady part of town, close to a strip mall and a U-Haul rent-a-center. "If there was such a thing as a ghetto on Cape Cod," he says, "that's where it was." But the house was within walking distance of the action and it had a big backyard with a volleyball court. He christened this new group Hyannis Sound.

While the Vineyard Sound was strictly made up of members of the CocoBeaux, the Bandersnatchers, and the Wesleyan group, there would be open auditions for this new venture. In the spring of '93, Townsend went on a mini–college tour, scouting guys from the Hullabahoos, the Bubs, and elsewhere for a new group to perform that summer on the Cape. It was the same business model. Except that Hyannis Sound would have one advantage: population. Where Martha's Vineyard was made up of six towns, Cape Cod comprised some twenty-three towns.

On the first night, Townsend sat down with the boys of Hyannis Sound to lay out the group's mission statement. This was not *The Real World: A Cappella*. "This summer, you're looking to grow as much as possible in musicality and stage presence," he said. "You'll also grow personally. You'll make some money too." He appointed two music directors. He assigned house responsibilities. "The best thing you can do," he told the ten men of Hyannis Sound, "is to put yourself in front of an audience. Learn five songs and knock their socks off." Musically they were probably better than Vineyard Sound. But they weren't motivated. On the weekends, Townsend would take the ferry to Cape Cod to check in on the newbies. "They'd say, *We're not making enough money*," Townsend remembers. "Well, there are probably sixty empty cases of beer on the porch. Why don't you go return those bottles and make some money?" They were loving the volleyball court, though.

Both groups began doing community outreach work, stopping by the local schools at the start of every summer to conduct music workshops (which were really advertisements for both Sounds disguised as goodwill). Needless to say, women everywhere fell in love with them. Both Sounds were invited to family barbecues. They were doing a hundred shows in ninety days.

Fairly quickly, the groups took on their own personalities. In a reverse, Vineyard Sound embraced a laid-back spirit. Meanwhile, improbably, Hyannis Sound became something of the overachiever. They moved out of the house with the volleyball court and began recording albums—a live album every summer, and a studio album every two years. (The Vineyard would only do live albums.) But both were thriving enterprises. The Hyannis Sound albums sell close to two thousand copies each—and the money goes right back into the group. They even performed the national anthem at Fenway Park.

And then Townsend got cocky. In 1995, the year after launching Hyannis Sound, he set his sights on Newport, launching, yup, Newport Sound. It flopped. Early in the summer the group scored a one-night, eight-thousand-dollar gig on a yacht. And then they didn't work for two weeks. "The gigs were too inconsistent," Townsend says. And so Newport Sound folded.

Ed Boyer of the Bubs was a member of Hyannis Sound and recorded their 2006 album, *Route 6*. This is what he remembers of his time on the Cape: "The house was not well maintained," he says. And the house parties were frequent. "Every Friday night," Ed says. "Sometimes more. Inevitably a handful of girls would crash on the couch." This was actually a good thing, and not for the reasons you'd expect. "I'd wake up in the morning," Ed says, "and these eighteen-year-old girls would be *cleaning our house*." What? "Cape Cod is full of old people," Ed says.

"Except for us ten guys. We were the only market in town, literally."

As the empire expanded, Townsend—who by now had left Merv Griffin Enterprises and was living in New York—set about legitimizing the operation. Formal auditions for Hyannis Sound were scheduled annually in Boston. (The only restriction was age: Auditions were open to anyone from the summer they'd graduated high school until the summer after leaving college.) In 1998, a formal board of directors was put in place. In 2003, Hyannis Sound became an official 501c3 nonprofit in Massachusetts. They've got an accountant, a lawyer, and all the trappings of a nonprofit.

The corporation is there to ensure the group's continued existence, but the summer is student run—by design. Every summer Townsend sits down with the boys on both forks and gives what's come to be known as the Speech. The one that begins: "We are handing this to you on a silver platter. You're in the public eye. All we need is one person to sleep with a seventeen-year-old and this is over." Townsend trains the new business managers every year and then walks away. "I learned so much from negotiating with Merv Griffin's people," he says. "I want these kids to have that kind of experience. It's priceless." Townsend himself had learned the most important lesson of all in a cappella: when to walk away.

In the spring of 2006, Townsend Belisle got a call from one of the Hyannis Sound guys. They'd been having trouble finding a house for the summer. Finally they'd found something with promise. "It's in walking distance of everything," the kid said. "It's kind of in a sketchy part of town, right near the U-Haul. But it's perfect for us. And there's a volleyball court in the backyard!"

CHAPTER SIXTEEN

DIVISI

*Wherein personal tragedy becomes triumph
in the spring of 2007*

In a mirrored dance studio somewhere in downtown Eugene, Divisi primps for their spring concert. For the night's first set, they've forsaken their black shirts and red ties—Divisi's signature red-hot—in favor of a little individuality. The color palette remains the same, but the girls are mostly in dresses, some with halter tops, some with big red belts tied at the waist. The girls run through a bit of complex choreography, some counting the steps to themselves. Andrea Welsh applies bronzer to her legs. "Why won't my boobs stay separated?" Haley Steinberger asks, staring into the mirror.

Outside, the auditorium is filling up. Peter Hollens and Evynne Smith—the founders of On the Rocks and Divisi, respectively—mill about. They talk about their upcoming wedding—on campus, near the Student Center, fittingly, where they performed on so many Friday afternoons. If this were *Grease*, they'd be the Danny and Sandy of Oregon a cappella; he's even wearing a leather jacket.

Divisi walks out onstage in two lines and assumes an attitudinal pose, all hands on their hips, weight shifted to one side. Marissa Neitling steps up to the microphone. And she sings: *"I got the stuff that you want // I got the thing that you need // I got more than enough // To make you drop to your knees."*

Marissa sings, beautifully, clean: *" 'Cause I'm the queen of the night..."*

Those who know Marissa couldn't help but see this performance as a triumph.

Marissa Neitling had been mindful of keeping her story to herself this year. "Whatever is going on," Rachelle Wofford says, "Marissa always leaves it at the door." But the week before this final concert, Divisi showed up en masse for the performance of Marissa's thesis, the one-woman show she'd been working on all year. They were unsure of what to expect. They knew it would be personal, that it had something to do with the ex-boyfriend who was now married (with a child on the way, no less). But they were not prepared for the seething, raw anguish on display that afternoon.

Marissa stood before the audience in the seventy-two-person black box theater, so small up there. True to herself, Marissa had written a play that was both theatrical and precise. Moving about the space, she told the story of her father—of his drug abuse, of his breakdown, of the anger—in exacting, matter-of-fact detail, making eye contact with the members of the audience. She was not intimidated by her father's childhood friends who were in the audience, the ones who'd accused Marissa and her mother of being (in her mother's words) "the bad people." She talked about the night she and her mother had to leave their home in fear, because her "father was a good shot."

Marissa talked about the calm she'd found. No, *calm* wasn't the right word, because this thing would still devour her if she wasn't careful. But she was learning to let go—not because she wanted to, but because she needed to. It had been over a year since she'd spoken with her father. He wasn't the same man anymore. No, the father she had known was buried inside, in some unreachable place. She didn't say much more. What would have been the point?

What this year had been about, she said, was learning to grieve for someone who was still alive—there but not there. She had come to this quiet understanding. When Marissa was a child, her father had rarely been without a videocamera. And when he left, she found the tapes—hundreds of them. He'd always said, These tapes will be my gift to you. In the end, it was a greater gift than he could have ever imagined.

"We still have the memories," she will tell you, of the magic tricks he used to do around the house, of him dressing up in costume with his daughters. "We still have so much."

The ladies of Divisi sat together, wiping tears from their eyes. Marissa, however, remained strong, her voice unwavering. Until she told this story. The lights dimmed in the theater and a projection came on behind her. It was a video from when she was eight years old. Marissa Neitling is Greek, and growing up, her grandfather was always called Papou. It was Christmastime on-screen, and there was Papou—dressed as Santa Claus, placing gifts under the tree as he did every year. Marissa's younger sister, Mackenzie, was at the age, five, when she didn't necessarily believe in Santa anymore. But Marissa—herself still a child, really—was desperate to preserve that innocence for her sister.

"Santa looks like *Papou*!" Mackenzie says in the video. "Why does Santa look like Papou?"

Marissa grabs her sister by the ponytail and yanks hard. "Leave him alone!" she says. "It's Santa! It's Santa!"

Marissa stops the video and turns to the audience. When she looks back on that moment, she's still not sure where it came from. But Marissa turned to her little sister, pulling on her ponytail even as the little girl repeated, again, "Why does Santa look like Papou!"

"Because Santa looks like the people you love," Marissa said.

It was the one moment in her life, Marissa says, when she said exactly what she felt. When she didn't analyze, and worry, and rethink. She wanted to find that place again as she moved forward with her life. Marissa's sister was sitting a few rows back in the theater, alongside their mother. That's when Marissa's voice broke. She could no more protect her sister than she could bring their father back from the abyss.

Growing up, Marissa's mother had a saying. In tough times, she told her daughters, you had to *Put on your boots and tromp through the muck.* Marissa used the line onstage. Throughout the show, a bright pair of Wellington boots was visible off to the side. At the end of the show, Marissa sat down, looked out at the audience, and put on her boots.

In that moment, Keeley McCowan cried too. "We cry when the people we love cry," she says.

It had been an emotional spring for Divisi. But the girls who came in all those months ago, with their sloppy habits and worse intonation, had found their voice. "We weren't the old Divisi," Keeley said, "or the new Divisi. We were just Divisi." The disappointment over the ICCAs had subsided somewhat. Though there was a pang of regret when the girls from Brigham Young's Noteworthy not only went to Lincoln Center for the finals but were crowned the champions. It wasn't even close. Julia Hoffman, who'd been a judge at the West Coast semifinals and later emceed the ICCA finals, summarized it best. "Any of the top three groups from the West"—Divisi, Noteworthy, or Vocal Point—"could have won at the finals," she said. "The West Coast semifinals has become the real finals."

Divisi's singular focus on the ICCAs, meanwhile, had let Michaela Cordova hide the troubles in her own life. Always a thin girl underneath those hoodie sweatshirts, Michaela was losing more weight. She was a vegan—and the intricacies of what a vegan could and could not eat gave her license to pick at beans on a plate in broad daylight and without appearing conspicuous. But a few weeks after the semifinals, the girl who'd walked out of a hotel room in Alaska less than a year ago, rather than share some bit of herself, found the courage to let these women know her, to confront her own demons head-on.

At rehearsal one night, Emmalee Almroth sat down with Divisi, as they had done so many times during this difficult and oftentimes remarkable year, and she read a letter from Michaela. She'd been suffering from an eating disorder for seven or eight years, the note explained. And she was worried about herself in a way she'd never been before. She couldn't be at rehearsal—not tonight, not for some time. She checked herself into a residential treatment center forty minutes from Eugene.

Divisi would not see her for six weeks. It was not easy for anyone. "She's such a strong part of the group," Keeley says, "and all of a sudden she was gone." But not forgotten, certainly.

Peter Hollens put together practice tapes so Michaela could learn the new music for the spring show from her room at the treatment center. Megan Schimmer would drive forty minutes out to the center to run the choreography with her. Later, when Michaela was able to leave the center for a few hours of supervised watch, Divisi worked additional rehearsals around her schedule.

On the afternoon of Divisi's spring show, Michaela stands onstage at the sound check trying to pick up the last elements of the set. Her mother is in audience. Michaela is not allowed to be alone—that's part of the deal. Still, she is there, present in a way she's never been before. "I've never really tried to deal with my emotions and my past hurt," she says. "I know that I'm changing now. I'm becoming better. I'm becoming the kind of person who can start to experience life rather than going through the motions."

Following intermission, Divisi returned to the stage—this time dressed in their customary red ties and black shirts, paint-thick red lipstick, and pearl earrings. Michaela sailed through Michael Jackson's "I Want You Back." Next it was Jenna Tooley's turn to shine. The blond girl who'd missed the first round of the ICCAs with mono, the girl who'd nearly been kicked out of the group, had landed a solo. *"Oh what a night!"* she sang. *"Late December back in '63."*

A few weeks before, Divisi had rented a houseboat, of all things, a few hours from campus. It was something of a spring retreat, a chance to learn some new music away from the confines of campus. Jenna's best friend in the group, a fellow alto named Meghan Bell, missed the trip. For the first time, Jenna was on her own musically and socially. "She really earned our respect that week," Rachelle Wofford says. Jenna knew all of her music, and she sang confidently.

At that final show, Divisi reveled in the new material, including songs like "Truth No. 2" by the Dixie Chicks (which Haley Steinberger sang with sass appeal). It was Keeley's idea to bring back the Divisi medley—once the group's signature performance piece. Lisa Forkish had arranged the medley, which opened with the familiar choral strains of Madonna's "Like a Prayer," the girls holding their hands together in devotion, staring up at the sky. There was intricate choreography and key changes but tonight, the song progressed, effortlessly, through Donna Summer's "Hot Stuff," Marvin Gaye's "Let's Get It On," and even the Spice Girls' "Wannabe."

Evynne Smith was sitting down front with most of the original Divisi members—save for Lisa Forkish, who was in Norway with her boyfriend. (Her thoughts, however, were with Divisi. On the morning of the show, Lisa Forkish turned to this man and said, "This is going to be a tough day for me. Please take care of me.") Keeley hadn't told the alums that they'd be bringing back the medley. Sarah Klein and Keeley quietly taught the girls the music. Megan Schimmer watched an old video of Divisi to familiarize herself with the choreography. When Divisi put their palms together and began to sing, they could hear the alumni whispering to one another in the front row. By the time the song ended, as Rachelle did the rap on "Wannabe," Evynne Smith and the Divisi alums were on their feet.

CHAPTER SEVENTEEN

THE BEELZEBUBS

Wherein the Beelzebubs unleash
Pandaemonium *on the world*

In 1973, a handful of alumni from the Tufts Beelzebubs got to talking. One thing became clear: Everyone missed performing. The matter was broached with the Beelzebub Alumni Association (The BAA), whose members in turn proposed an annual on-campus talent show where Bub alums could perform. Gene Blake in '73 was heavily involved. They called it the Beelzebub & Friends Coffeehouse—and the first show included guitar playing and women performing but not a lick of a cappella music. Peter Gallagher, later of *American Beauty*, sang to piano accompaniment. "The show was developed to highlight that there is musical life after Tufts," Blake says. And it became an annual tradition held every spring in the Dewick-MacPhie Dining Hall, which (in less litigious days, and before the drinking age went twenty-one) the university regularly converted into a pub on weekends. In time this show would become known as Bubs in the Pub.

From time to time, Tim Vaill '64, the founder of the Bubs, would perform at Bubs in the Pub alongside his side project, Peking and the Mystics. "The current students loved to see these gray-haired Bubs up there singing," Vaill says. But The BAA would give up ownership of the show in the eighties when university rules about who could—and could not—rent campus venues changed. With the undergraduate Beelzebubs now planning the show, selling tickets, securing the venue, it seemed only fair to invite them to perform. It was a decisive moment. Over time the show became less and less about the alumni and more about the current group. "Peking would say they'd do twenty minutes," Deke Sharon says, "and they'd do forty-five." In 1991, Deke Sharon (the only one willing to take the fall) officially told the alums the party was over, wresting Bubs in the Pub from those liver-spotted hands.

Long after the actual pub closed, the show would continue to be their final concert of the year and a send-off to the graduating seniors. The Dead Guys—that's how the Bubs refer to the alumni—were no longer invited to perform. And while some of them have never gotten over this affront, in late April 2007 some twenty-five Dead Guys—ranging in age from twenty-two to sixty-two—turn out for Bubs in the Pub, to bid farewell to Andrew Savini, Matt Michelson, Arkady Ho, and Matt Kraft. And the crowd is full of familiar faces from the group's travels.

While Tufts closed the pub when the drinking age went twenty-one, the concert is still held in Dewick-MacPhie Hall. There is no hint that it was *ever* a pub—no sepia-toned pictures of long-haired Tufts students from the seventies hammered, no neon Budweiser sign. Actually, the place looks like Folsom Prison. Ed Boyer takes his seat in the audience, just behind Chris Kidd, who'd spent a day at Disney with the Bubs over spring break a few months earlier. Danny Lichtenfeld '93 is in attendance as well. Though he's been largely absent since having kids a few years ago, he has a wedding nearby the next day and is happy to make the show. He hugs Jeremy Cramer '00, who, as far as David Letterman is concerned, is still a squirrelly little kid.

Sometime in the eighties, the Bubs started dressing up for

Bubs in the Pub. Dressing up—as in Halloween, not black tie. Tonight the Beelzebubs are backstage warming up and behind them one can't help but notice garbage bags full of disparate—and elaborate—clothing. When Deke Sharon was a senior, the year he put the kibosh on the alumni talent portion of Bubs in the Pub, he came out dressed as a Pez dispenser. As with everything the Bubs do, there is an elaborate set of rules to the costumes. To wit: If any one of the Bubs—living or dead—should discover another's costume prior to the performance, said costume must be scrapped entirely. Arkady Ho, one of the seniors, was a Vietnamese prostitute his freshman year (his words), then a hula girl (with grass skirt and coconut bra), and, finally, Cupid. There is good money going that he will again be showing skin.

Andrew Savini's parents are seated in the pub, a few rows back from the small stage. Minutes before the show they are chatting with Doug Terry's mom. "DID DOUG STAY AT MY HOUSE?" Mrs. Savini asks. (She is a lovely woman, but she speaks in all caps.) One year the Bubs traveled to Hawaii for spring break and bunked up with the Savinis. "I NEVER SAW SO MANY BOXER SHORTS IN MY LIFE!" Before Doug's mom has a chance to respond, Mrs. Savini pulls out the concert program. "LET ME LOOK AT HIS PICTURE AND THEN I'LL KNOW." She looks. "OH, I *LOVE* DOUG!"

Eric Valliere, Bubs Class of '91, materializes onstage to introduce the Bubs. "I'm just glad the fire marshal isn't here," he says, looking out into the capacity crowd. He pauses awkwardly before blurting out: "The Bubs told me to whip you into a *frenzy*. So, welcome the Tufts Beelzebubs!"

"This is really weird," Chris Kidd says to his girlfriend. That's common the first year out—that first time you're in the audience instead of dressed as Pez.

This should have been Ben Appel's biggest night as music director—Bubs in the Pub, the release of *Pandaemonium*. But he was not on stage; rather he was seated in the audience. In fact, he wouldn't return to campus full-time until January of 2008—eighteen months after taking medical leave. In that time, he attended classes part time at Temple University near home, did landscaping to make some cash, and focused on his treatment. He'd kept up with the Bubs, even recorded a solo for *Pandaemonium*. When he showed up at Ed Boyer's place in the Bronx to record, he was fifteen pounds heavier, buried beneath a big army coat with a hulking pair of headphones around his neck. When Ben Appel looks back at what's happened to him, he would never blame the Bubs. But the culture didn't help. He tells a story:

There comes a point in every Bubs audition where the group opens the floor to questions. Inevitably one freshman will ask about the time commitment. *Can we still go abroad, can we play a sport,* that sort of thing. "The Bubs always say, you can definitely do those things," Ben says. They'll point out how so-and-so played football, and so-and-so was on the basketball team. But that last time Ben was in the room, just before he left for school, he felt like a liar. "I wanted to pull each kid aside and tell them the truth," Ben says. "When you join the group, there is this amazing sense of having joined something incredible and prestigious—and it is. But it sucks you in through total commitment and complete dedication. And it sets up this mentality, this insider mentality, and you begin to view the rest of college as a choice between Bubs and non-Bubs." It's not a surprise that the Bubs get you as a freshman, he says. The Bub speak, that lexicon of words they've invented—words like siv, hook, roll—it all serves to separate you from everyone else on campus, Ben Appel says. "If your friends ask why you're always away on weekends, the Bubs say, 'They just don't understand.' The Bubs never want to hear that it doesn't have to be done this way." He's talking about the all-night drives. He's talking about the commitment. "As a freshman," he says, "you don't know any better. They're wrapped up in the allure of it. But the responsibility falls on the alumni to tell the group that they don't have to be so strict with traditions. That it doesn't have to be this way."

Even Matt Michelson, when pressed, will agree. "I wouldn't trade being in the Bubs for anything," he says. "But did I miss Tufts? Did I miss college? Yeah."

When it came time for auditions in the spring of 2007, in the days before Bubs in the Pub, one couldn't help but wonder: Was becoming a Beelzebub the best thing that could happen to a kid or something more complicated?

Jon Miller was a soft-spoken, good-looking kid whose family moved to Newton, Massachusetts, when he was in the first grade. Growing up, his dad often took him to Beelzebubs concerts as a kid. "We had *The Blue Album* and *The White Album*, *The House of Blue Lights*"—Bubs albums from the seventies, he says. When it came time to apply to college, Jon Miller considered the West Coast. "But Tufts just looks like college to me," he told his dad.

In high school, Jon Miller had played the guitar. But he was looking forward to singing in college—specifically with the Bubs. He'd auditioned in the fall, a week after he arrived on campus, and it hadn't gone well. He didn't even get a callback. He hadn't realized how much he wanted it until then. That night, Jon Miller called home to relay the disappointing news. His father, Dr. Michael Miller, was uniquely qualified to field this call. Dr. Miller wasn't just a concerned parent. He was, himself, a Beelzebub alum, from the proud class of 1974.

Dr. Miller came to campus the following morning to check in on his son. The two went for a walk, passing Dewick-MacPhie, unfortunately, where they ran into Matt Kraft from the Bubs at the ATM. "It was awkward," Dr. Miller says. It got worse when Taylor Horst, a Bub alum who was now in medical school at Tufts, happened to wander by at the same moment. "There we were," Dr. Miller says, "the four of us standing by the ATM." Matt Kraft eased the tension. He told Jon that he shouldn't be discouraged, that he should audition again in the spring. "Sometimes I wish I'd had my freshman year outside the group," Matt said. "My whole time at Tufts has been defined by the Bubs."

When father and son walked away, Dr. Miller turned to his boy. "You don't have to want to be like me," he said. "You can have your own experiences." His son looked back at him. "Dad, I don't want to be like you," he said. "I already *am* like you."

Not long after his failed audition, Jon Miller called Matt Michelson and asked for a sit-down, asked how he could do better next time, asked for any scrap of advice that might help him find his way into the Bubs. Michelson suggested voice lessons. Ouch.

It was a hard semester for Jon Miller. Most of his friends from the dorm were involved in athletics and weren't really around all that much. The one person Jon Miller did see—often—was Tiny Tim Conrad from the Bubs. "He lives in my dorm," Jon says. Things were not working out as the kid had hoped. "I was worried I wasn't going to find my niche," he says.

The thing is, his father, Dr. Miller, had gone through much of the same angst thirty-five years before. Though he is now a noted psychiatrist (and a featured guest on NBC's *The Today Show*), he'd majored in English. And he nearly flunked out of physics that first year at Tufts. He started working for the Tufts Radio station, where he had his own rock 'n' roll show. "I had a good voice for radio," Dr. Miller says. He thought about pursuing a career in music. "But my parents grew up in the Depression and the idea of a musical career…" he says, his voice trailing off. And so the English major reluctantly switched gears. Freshman year was a particularly tough time for him. "I'm a psychiatrist," Dr. Miller says. "Without going into too much detail, I was depressed. I planned to go to medical school, but I was ambivalent about it."

At the end of his freshman year, Dr. Miller auditioned for the Bubs. He brought his guitar with him to the audition and played something from Carole King's *Tapestry*. "You couldn't walk by any dorm on campus that year without hearing Carole King," he says. He was accepted into the group, which took some of the weight off. "The Bubs created a focus for my time in college," he says. "It was a very engaging creative outlet."

Dr. Miller remembers getting that call from his son back in September of 2007. "He was so hurt," he says. "It was a character-building moment for both of us."

Meanwhile, Jon Miller took Michelson's advice. He invested in voice lessons. He recorded himself again and again, working to iron out the kinks in his voice. He also started going to the gym. It was nothing short of a regimented extreme makeover.

In the spring, Jon returned to the Bub room for auditions. He sang an Incubus song, "Here in My Room," which he'd gone over with his voice teacher. He'd called his father on the way to the audition that night, and again after for a debriefing. Jon Miller got a phone call that night. He was at a party, it was loud, and he couldn't make out exactly what Arkady said. But he picked up enough to know he'd gotten a call back. He was due at the Bub Room for a second audition at 10:40 P.M. "I'll never figure out why the Bubs do auditions so late at night," Dr. Miller said. But he was relieved for his son.

The Bubs taught Jon Miller the bass part to "Ruby Falls." The whole thing was surreal. "I was singing with the Bubs," he says. Finally it came time to sing in a quartet. It's an exercise to see if your voice will blend with the group. However, the Bubs don't make it easy. Rather, they actively try to throw the kids off. "The Bubs like to mimic a crowd," Jon says. "During my audition they were making crying-baby noises. And Michelson kept calling my cell phone."

At home, meanwhile, Dr. and Mrs. Miller watched the clock. His son called again at one in the morning. It would be a long night.

Dr. Miller was anxious, and he felt like he'd let his son down. "I felt some responsibility for creating the idea of this iconic experience—that if he didn't have this opportunity it would somehow leave him missing out on some crucial experience in life. I said to Jonathan, This is just a bunch of college kids singing. It's a wonderful thing. But it's not like playing the cello all your life and not making it into the New York Philharmonic. There are a lot of great experiences in life."

At three A.M., the younger Miller received a phone call from the Bubs. They wanted to see him—one last time—for what they promised would be the final round of auditions. What happened next is only for the Beelzebubs to know, but at some point in the next few hours Jon Miller fulfilled a long-standing Bubs tradition, and in the depths of Ballou Hall, he became a Beelzebub.

At six-thirty in the morning, the Bubs pulled into Bickford's—a diner—for breakfast. Jon Miller called his dad with the good news. Dr. Miller actually already knew—Michelson had called to invite him to Bickford's, in case he wanted to surprise his son; Dr. Miller declined the invite, wanting to let his son enjoy the moment. But that night, the good doctor came to campus to celebrate with his son. "I bought him a burrito," Dr. Miller says. What else could he do?

A few days later Dr. Miller came back to campus for Bubs in the Pub. Sometime in the eighties the Bubs decided that for this final show the group should sing every song they learned that school year. Tonight they perform twenty-one songs. The arrangements were uniformly solid—and varied, because they'd been done by at least ten different people (many of them alums). Unfortunately, the acoustics in Dewick-MacPhie were shameful. Worse: The Bubs, slaves to tradition, were still hiring the same guy to do the sound. The Bubs spent unheard of hours perfecting their blend. But past the tenth row, their intricate arrangements just sounded muddled.

Danny Lichtenfeld '93 sat in the audience. In regard to the venue he said: "I'd hate them to be following tradition for tradition's sake." The same could be said of elections. A few weeks prior to the show Danny received phone calls—like clockwork—from the Bubs running for president. Lichtenfeld is happy to talk to these kids and admits he'd be miffed if they didn't ring him up. But he'd be just as happy if someone called and said, "With all due respect, I'm in the Bubs now and I have my own ideas about how to run it."

Bubs in the Pub was a brutal three-plus hours. Lucas was dressed as Che Guevara. "I'm the hero of privileged suburban kids everywhere," he says. Michelson was, of all things, a flamingo, in black leggings and a pink bodice. Arkady was (true to form) dressed as a baby, in little more than a diaper. There were senior speeches—private jokes about things the audience didn't understand that went on and on. There were standing ovations from the Bub alums. During the speeches, a policewoman approached the stage. Michelson—the flamingo—bent down to find out what could possibly be so pressing. Following the speech, he took the mic: "Uh, whoever has the red Kia needs to move it."

As the concert came to a close, the Beelzebubs invited all of the gathered alumni up onstage to sing "Brothers in Song." Jon Miller, naturally, stood next to his father. And later that night, at the postshow party, father and son drank a beer together out of a funnel.

In the week after the audition, Jon Miller's in-box was flooded with e-mails from past Beelzebubs, welcoming him to the fold. He'd already picked up on some of the Bubs' language. Ask him how he feels about the whole experience, he responds as only a Bub could: "It hooks you."

Bubs in the Pub doubled as the release party for *Pandaemonium*. Though the Bubs had heard rough mixes of the new album a few months ago, they hadn't heard the final product. They hadn't even *seen* the final product. With the exception of the music director and the president, none of the Bubs is allowed to see the artwork until the group cracks open the boxes the week of Pub. (For the record, the cover art looked like the white-on-white Travis album *The Man Who*.) The only question left was: where to listen to the thing. Which is how the Bubs ended up at the Best Buy in Waltham, Massachusetts, taking over the high-end speaker room, the one with the big circular couch in the center and woofers lining the wall. The Bubs said they were shopping for a speaker for their rehearsal room. (Not true.) The salesman would stop the CD to change speakers. "Uh, can we hear the album continuously?" Matt Michelson said, interrupting the man. "I think at that point he caught on," Michelson says. Because after that he walked away.

Though the official reviews for *Pandaemonium* would not be posted for five months, it didn't take long for the message boards at RARB to light up with chatter once the album was out. Matt Emery, the music director of the Duke a cappella group, Rhythm & Blue, started the thread with a one-word entry: "Wow." Matthew Bolling, an alum of Virginia Tech's Juxtaposition, pointed out the change in the Bubs' sound. "The CD is solid," he wrote. "It has a surprisingly small amount of production and really sounds like it thrives from the raw voice. This is something that a lot of male groups could just not achieve." The conversation went on for weeks.

Almost no one mentioned "Come Sail Away" or "Mama, I'm Coming Home." Or, for that matter, much of anything the Bubs had debated internally.

Matt Michelson and Alexander Koutzoukis did fly out to Bill Hare's studio in northern California to watch the legendary a cappella producer mix the album. They brought their notes with them—this solo should be louder, this bass section is too quiet—but for all the man-hours spent arguing in the Super 8 over spring break, the two still managed to sleep through some of the mixing sessions, betraying their compatriots back home. The truth is, there wasn't much they could have done out there anyway. Ed was right. They'd hired Bill Hare for a reason. Collegiate a cappella recording had, in many ways, gotten out of hand. Still, working within that framework, the Bubs managed to record an accomplished album that was inarguably, at its deepest level, the product of the human voice. And it had nothing to do with Pro Tools, and everything to do with the music itself. Though one gets the sense that it might have been a better learning experience if they'd really produced it on their own—instead of paid for it on their own. That might be their next evolution.

At its heart *Pandaemonium*—could they have picked a better title for this year?—was something of a middle finger to the a cappella establishment and RARB itself, even. The twelve tracks on *Pandaemonium* were masterfully done—with top-tier production values and the bells and whistles you'd expect from the Bubs, but for all the polish you'd never mistake them for the original recordings (as you could easily do when listening to much of *Code Red*). "Come Sail Away" would be the album's real triumph. It begins with a little trio singing, *"Ding ding DING ding ding // Ding ding DING ding ding // dee deedl-lee-dee."* Matt Michelson's solo is clean and clear, seemingly untouched. (Ed Boyer would say the technology is *transparent*—Michelson's voice is just as computer tweaked as the rest of the album, it's just not noticeable.) Matt sings: *"I'm sailing away // set an open course for the virgin sea."* He's even got a sweet vibrato.

But then, four minutes and five seconds in, the song takes a left turn. The Bubs build to an eight-second wall of sound, a loud *aaaaaaaaahhhhhhh*, mechanical, distorted. Listen to the original song. It's there—that cluster-chord banged out on the synthesizer, modulating down. It sounds like you took both hands and slammed them down on the keyboard. To get that effect a cappella, Ed had the Bubs each sing a different note—hold it out, and then slide down. *Aaaaaahhhhhhhh*. Like the sound of a guy falling down a well. The Bubs were triple-tracked and delayed. What you hear on the album is forty-five Bubs, really, at different speeds, on different notes. With the reverb, it feels like even more.

The listener doesn't know exactly what's happened, but the chord leads into a big guitar solo. To get that Eddie Van Halen sound—that pecking out of notes—Matt Michelson sang each note of the guitar solo individually. Bill Hare then chopped the notes into pieces and each became a tap on the fret. He lined the notes up in Pro Tools, ran it through a guitar amp simulator, and, well, there you have it. Bill Hare summarizes: "The end to 'Come Sail Away' is this reminder of what the Bubs can do. That after all this great, raw singing on the album, we close with this little snippet of ear candy. It's this little spot to show that the Bubs could still do it"—could still do the *Code Red* aesthetic they'd standardized—"but they chose to do something else."

Pandaemonium had responded to the call of *Code Red*. It received straight fives—the top rating—from the reviewers at RARB. And the Bubs had predicted a changing tide in a cappella recording. When the Hullabahoos released their own new album in December of 2007, *Varsity Sing Team*, the liner notes came with a note: "On this album, we tried to stay away from what has become the a cappella standard: pushing computer production to its limits. Instead, we aimed for a more classic, natural sound that we hope will stand the test of time."

CHAPTER EIGHTEEN

THE HULLABAHOOS

Wherein the Hullabahoos reconnect with an old friend in the spring of 2007—and come face-to-face with a new one

It was months before the Hullabahoos received a reply from Howard Spector. But one day, there it was. The man who had booked the group for some of its most lucrative gigs—Burger King, the Republican National Convention—was curious to hear how the Hullabahoos sounded these days. And so it was set: Howard would drive down to Charlottesville for the Hullabahoos' Big Spring Sing Thing XIX, their final show of the 2006–2007 school year. Perhaps the time was right for a reunion. Howard's event-planning firm, Ashley Entertainment, had a gig coming up—an annual GOP fund-raiser called the President's Dinner, which, in 2006, raised twenty-seven million dollars for Republican congressional candidates. The dinner was scheduled for June. If the Hullabahoos could impress Howard enough to land the President's Dinner gig, they might have a shot at booking the lucrative 2008 Republican National Convention.

Just days before Big Spring Sing Thing, the Hullabahoos were still learning new music for the show. And they were still dealing, really, with the fallout from the gig at Washington and Lee—where Exit 245 had proved a formidable competitor to the cocky Hullabahoos. While the gig didn't do much to dent their sense of self (impossible, really), they couldn't ignore what had happened with U2's "One." A few days after returning to campus, the Hullabahoos got their hands on a recording of that show. Patrick Lundquist and Brendon Mason were eager to find out just who'd messed up the harmony on *"Jesus"*—so loudly and embarrassingly, at that. Judging from the audio, it was obvious that Brendon was to blame. He didn't take it well. In fact, he soon developed a mental block—like a major league baseball pitcher who suddenly couldn't throw to home plate. The Hullabahoos had sung "One" a few times since then, but Brendon missed the harmony every time. At one recent show he had skipped the phrase entirely, letting Patrick belt the line alone. It didn't pack nearly the same punch, and one of the Silhooettes caught the mistake, shouting, "You suck!" At a sorority gig one night a couple of the Hullabahoos asked Pete Seibert (the music director) to drop the song from the Big Spring Sing Thing set list entirely. "It was that bad," Pete says.

This is the first time the Hullabahoos have seen Brendon rattled. And frankly it's uncomfortable. "I've been walking around campus with my headphones on, listening to 'Jesus' again and again," Brendon says. Minutes before Big Spring Sing Thing XIX, he is still listening to the song, singing the note quietly to himself.

The show at Washington and Lee didn't tell Pete anything he hadn't already known about the Hullabahoos and their music. His arrangements were too similar. Even he was tired of them. "I was sick of the *shedula-shets*," he says, mocking the syllables he so frequently employs. Pete enlisted the help of his fellow B'hoos. Matt Mooney (a freshman) did two arrangements for the show: Michael Jackson's "The Way You Make Me Feel" and "Sleeping to Dream," by Jason Mraz. Myles Glancy arranged Chris Daughtry's "Home." It's not that it took so much of the pressure off

(Pete still tweaked all three arrangements) but it did introduce some variety into their repertoire. Pete even mixed up his own style, bringing in new syllables, opening Rob Thomas's "Street-corner Symphony" with *bwey-do bwaay-do*.

The group had other concerns. There were final exams to prepare for. Blake Segal, never without a book, appeared to have been entombed. Pete Seibert pulled a few all-nighters in the days leading up to the show, writing some music of his own. The conductor of the UVA orchestra had sent out a blanket call for entries to the music school. If a student submitted an original score, she said, the orchestra would play it. "I didn't have an orchestral score that I was really proud of," Pete says, "so I thought I'd better write one." He called the piece "Daybreak," because he finished it at seven-thirty in the morning. The Hullabahoos would turn out in force to hear the seventy-piece orchestra play Pete's five-minute composition. The Hullabahoos didn't know much about classical music, but Morgan Sword offered this review: "I feel like success has a lot to do with how many times you use the chimes." For the record, Hullabahoos B, the group's intramural football team, wrapped up their season then, too, finishing third in the Independent circuit. Morgan sustained a crippling finger injury in the final game, which sidelined him from two drives. But he rallied. "This was the highest known ranking for any a cappella group ever," Joe Cassara says.

If the Hullabahoos were stressed out about final exams, or impressing Howard Spector, something would happen five days before Big Spring Sing Thing to put it all in perspective. It was April 16, 2007, when Seung-Hui Cho opened fire on Virginia Tech's campus, killing thirty-two people and wounding another twenty-five before committing suicide in the deadliest school rampage in U.S. history. Joe Cassara, the president of the Hullabahoos, had gone to elementary school with Seung-Hui Cho. More distressing: Joe's younger brother was a junior at Tech. His kid brother was safe in his dorm, but too many of their peers were affected, too many felt bruised themselves. The a cappella community at large quickly responded with a two-disc compilation of local Virginia a cappella groups organized by Matthew Bolling, a Tech alum who sang with the VT Juxtaposition. The disc, *For Today, We Are All Hokies*, would go on to sell one thousand copies, making close to twenty thousand dollars for the families affected by the shooting. But the B'hoos wanted to address the tragedy at their own concert. And so, visible beneath their robes at Big Spring Sing Thing, one would see a mix of red and orange neckties—a subtle, gentle reminder that their thoughts were with the families.

In a way, the tragedy cut through all of the bullshit. In a few weeks Dane Blackburn would quit the Hullabahoos. No one was surprised. For one thing, he wanted to make his own music. And that was fine. But more than that, he didn't seem to be having fun anymore. And for all of the rehearsing, and the recording, the Hullabahoos were more of a fraternity than anything else. Morgan Sword would graduate in a few weeks and he'd miss the singing. But really he'd mourn for something else—the feeling of sitting in that room on the west side of the Lawn, never knowing which of the Hullabahoos was going to come through the door next.

Backstage, the night of Big Spring Sing Thing XIX, the Hullabahoos stand in a circle, with their arms around one another—and it brings them full circle, back to the memory of the morning each was accepted into the Hullabahoos, that morning, as tradition dictates, they were awakened in their dorm late at night and driven up to the hill at the apple orchard, where they stood just like this as one of the seniors in the Hullabahoos told them their life was about to change. And it had. Tonight, Pete blows the note and they sing, *"All aboard // get on board."*

John Stanzione and a handful of alums like Keith Bachmann, Nic Von Bank, and Russell Bloodworth sit upstairs in the balcony. Later that night, Bachmann, a med student and newly engaged, will admire the so-called Hullaba-hos, and midconversation will be momentarily distracted by the shortness of one girl's skirt. "I took anatomy," he'll say. "And we're very close to seeing her vagina." Yes, the after-party would always be a big draw for the alums, but the B'hoos were surprised to see so many alums in attendance that night. Earlier in the year, Morgan Sword had sent a letter to the old guys asking for money. "The money wasn't for anything in particular," he says. It was more of a test-run than anything else. Which was good, because the Hullabahoos received exactly one check. The alums may have spurned the group's request for funds, but they turned out en masse for the show, flying in from all over the country. It wasn't a big discussion. A few e-mails had gone across the Hullabahoos' alumni listserv. The alums just realized they hadn't been back to campus in a while and so they mobilized.

While Morgan Sword, Joe Cassara, and the Hullabahoos stand backstage warming up with "People Get Ready," a video they recorded (and edited) earlier unspools in the four-hundred-seat auditorium at McLeod Hall. The video was modeled on MTV's *Jackass*, and the familiar black screen comes up, with simple white lettering that reads: BODY WAXING. The following scene plays out:

"We're about to go to CVS and see if we can get some stuff to wax our chests," Joe Cassara says to the camera. Once inside, he find a CVS employee—a woman with a southern accent thick as molasses—stocking the shelves. He interrupts. "My friend and I want to wax an *H* into our chest hair," he says, lifting up his shirt. At first she ignores him, trying to contain a smile, but when he doesn't walk away, she relents.

"Probably the easiest thing for you to do would be to use wax strips," she says. The camera follows her to the appropriate aisle. "*Ah* you *shaw* you *wahnt* to do it?" she asks, sounding like some trailer park Blanche DuBois. He does. And so she removes the strips from the box and walks Joe through the process. "You warm them up between your hands like this," she says, "and then you peel them apart. Apply 'em and then hold this kind of tight and pull it against the hair." It's gonna hurt, she warns.

"Will there be any bleeding?" Joe says.

"No," she says, slowly, contemplatively, "but I would recommend that you only do it once. Don't do it over and over and over again."

The screen goes black. In white lettering, across the screen, it reads: "REMEMBER THAT: Only do it once. Don't do it over and over and over again."

The video flashes back to Joe, now standing on campus, a sunny day, with lots of people around him. "I love the Hullabahoos," he says to the camera. "That's why I'm getting an *H* waxed into my chest hair." With that, he lies down on the grass. An unseen body applies the wax to his chest, presses down on the strips, and yanks. Joe screams. The wax strip has pulled some hair—and skin—off, but there is no discernible *H*.

Off-screen someone shouts, "Do it again! More wax!"

The screen flashes back to the woman at CVS. "Don't do it over and over and over again," she says. Each time another attempt is made, and Joe screams, the screen flashes back to CVS, and the crowd applauds even louder. Finally, the screen goes black save for two words: HEY HULLABAHOOS! Upstairs in the balcony John Stanzione laughs.

Humor (in theory, anyway) has always been part of the Hullabahoos' DNA: "In 1994," John Stanzione says, "humor is what we were about. Music came second. We'd do a skit every three or four songs." With so much output, invariably a few skits tanked. It was awkward. The Hullabahoos would stand onstage waiting for applause—applause that wasn't coming. And so they came up with a solution. At the end of every skit (good or bad) the group would shout, *Hey, Hullabahoos!* "The *Hey* thing was a way to indicate to the audience that the skit was over," Stanzione says, "and to overcome the deafening silence of tumbleweeds when things went badly."

Tonight, the video screen disappears and the stage goes dark, with the exception of a single red light overhead. The Hullaba-hoos appear and Pete blows the pitch. Kyle Mihalcoe comes in first, singing, *"Nomina nomina nomina nomina."* It builds from there, slowly, with more Hullabahoos coming in on their own parts as *"nomina nomina"* segues into the familiar strains of "One." Pete wrote a new intro to the song, a gospel-tinged exer-cise to surprise the crowd and juice the Hullabahoos themselves. And it feels like the Hullabahoos are singing "One" for the first time. But would Brendon hit the harmony?

Patrick Lundquist and Brendon Mason (visibly stiff) stand on opposite sides of the stage as the group moves into the second verse. Brendon holds the mic tight. He isn't making eye contact with the audience. They walk toward each other.

Patrick: *"Have you come here for forgiveness?"*

Brendon echoes on: *"Have you come to raise the dead?"*

Together: *"Have you come here to play—Jesus!"*

The harmony is pitch-perfect. Brendon's shoulders relax. He and Patrick keep singing, pausing almost imperceptibly to give each other a knowing smile. And the alumni—not aware of the backstory, most never having heard the Hullabahoos sing the song before—are on their feet. When the applause finally dies down, one of the alums shouts, *"Sing it again!"*

It's Joe Whitney's turn at the mic. The microwave kid smiles that gawky smile of his and the Hullabahoos sing: *"Bwey-do bwaay-do // bwey-do bwaay do // aaaaaaaaaaahhhh."* The vocal percussion begins like a rocket taking flight, *"sssssssshhhhhhhHH-HHHHHHHHH."*

Joe sings: *"It's morning // And I wake up // The taste of*

summer's sweetness on my mind." Alex Chertok, one of the alums up in the balcony, says to no one in particular, "Who is *this* guy?" And just like that, a soloist is born.

The Hullabahoos experiment with something completely different in the second set, pulling three wooden stools from the side of the stage. Brian Duhon sits down and produces a guitar. "What's that?" someone yells from the balcony. The alumni actually start booing. "Can't you do that with your voice?" someone shouts.

The song is Jason Mraz's "Sleeping to Dream." And the worst part is that it's fantastic. It's not just that Chris Brown sings the solo with a lush sweetness, or that Pete's harmony is pretty, or that the group backs them both with the angelic *oooohs* and *aaahs* of a night around the campfire. Later James Gammon, who is producing their new album, sums it up: "The song inadvertently reminded people how silly a cappella can be. You start to miss the instruments when you hear the guitar." But only an a cappella purist would care. There's a rich history of collegiate a cappella groups from the sixties using guitar on folk tunes. Even the Beelzebubs, back in the seventies, used to have a singer-songwriter on guitar in place of a guest group.

The night's highlight, it turns out, isn't about pitch or vocal histrionics, but rather a tradition: the senior solo. It's not that Morgan Sword, Joe Cassara, or Alan Webb—the graduating seniors—sing all that well (they don't). It's the emotional reverence. Watching from the balcony, the alumni are pitched forward in their seats, as if they are holding their breath to see how it will end.

When Morgan—six foot two, quarterback for Hullabahoos B—steps up to the microphone to sing, his voice breaks. Perhaps it's the alumni presence in the audience. Or the fact that Morgan's girlfriend will be moving to Ohio in a few weeks to start a career while he goes off to Boston for a consulting gig. Maybe it's the slowly sinking revelation that this is his final time on this stage.

Earlier that day, the Hullabahoos organized a picnic for the visiting alumni—which they held in a tulip-lined garden behind the Colonnade Club grounds. One of the B'hoos alums came into the garden with his wife and a stroller. "Hey, *fat old guys!*" he yelled out. Another alum, the owner of a Gold's Gym franchise, showed up with his girlfriend, an equally jacked woman named Diesel. The barbecue had been slow in starting, cute almost. "This is like an eighth-grade dance," Pete Seibert had said, what with the alums on one side and the undergraduates on the other. Finally, the ice thawed. The undergraduates had realized the essential truth about reunions like this. What these fat old guys wanted more than anything was to meet the young Hullabahoos—to hear their stories, to share their own, to establish the kind of connection that keeps one coming back. And onstage at his own final concert, the revelation hit Morgan like a ton of bricks.

The senior solo was Ben Folds's "Still Fighting It"—a song about a father and his son, about birth (and death) really. Morgan sings the chorus, his voice cracking, the emotion finally taking hold: "*Everybody knows // It hurts to grow up // And everybody does // So weird to be back here // Let me tell you what // The years go on and we're still fighting it // We're still fighting it.*"

Upstairs the alumni are quiet. The song could have been written about them, about how it feels to sit in the balcony and not be standing onstage, and how that's both a relief and curse. It grows deadly quiet. Morgan sings, himself, in a sensitive falsetto: "*You try // and try // And one day // You'll fly // Away from me. Good morning, son.*"

For all the talk of Howard Spector, an hour after Big Spring Sing Thing XIX, there he was standing on the porch of the

Hullaba-house sipping a beer. He was joined by his business part-ner (an Anjelica Huston type) and a handsome young man he referred to as his "assistant." Howard wasn't hard to miss. In a sea of khaki shorts and flip-flops, he was a guy in his forties wear-ing a destroyed cotton blazer with embroidery and contrast stitching. "The Hullabahoos still have it," he says, smiling.

A few weeks after the show Howard Spector followed through on his promise, inviting the Hullabahoos to perform at the Pres-ident's Dinner—a mammoth fund-raiser set for June 13 at the Washington Convention Center. The gig would pay a few thou-sand dollars, but it wasn't about the money. This was a warm-up for the Republican National Convention in 2008, Howard said.

The gig was simple enough. The Hullabahoos would sing an eleven-song set after dinner. Howard didn't ask to see a set list. Just be smart, he said. "I don't want to hear anyone say 'The president sucks.' Or anything about abortion." He did have one request: He wanted Pete to arrange an invocation. "Something inspirational," he said. And so Pete arranged a pop version of "Amazing Grace," weaving in elements of "America the Beauti-ful." The B'hoos had already gone home for the summer, so they'd need to learn the music on their own. Pete recorded "Amaz-ing Grace" on his computer—part by part—and e-mailed the tracks out to the group. And then, just before showtime, Howard had one more request. He asked them to sing the national anthem—alongside country star Jo Dee Messina. "It was probably the most stressful day of my life," Pete says. There he was, working out the chords with Jo Dee's keyboard player, teaching the B'hoos on the spot. Pete was starstruck. "Jo Dee Messina was talking to me about what I thought we should do musically," he says. "Then I tripped over a speaker and she gave me a hug." Pete needn't have worried. The national anthem went off without a hitch (Jo Dee Messina blogged about it on her Web site), as did the group's stand-alone set. Later that night, Matt Mooney made off with a full set of drinking glasses with Bush's presidential seal—party favors left behind by some of the night's guests. Pete, meanwhile, reports on the night saying, cryptically, "I made some bad decisions as the group was swarmed by many hot Republican intern girls."

One story remains to be told. Did the Hullabahoos meet the president?

Before the show, Howard Spector escorted five of the B'hoos to the front of the receiving line, where President Bush was shaking hands. "We were expedited with the members of Congress and bigwigs who'd paid a hundred thousand dollars to sit on the main stage," Patrick Lundquist says. Howard tried to manage expectations. It would be a two-second deal, he'd said. Pause. Smile. Keeping walking. Well, it didn't work out exactly that way.

"We rounded the corner," Patrick Lundquist says, "and there he was, just chillin', GDUB." He's talking about the president.

"Now, who are you guys?" President George W. Bush said.

"We're the group that's singing tonight," Morgan said. "From UVA."

"University of Virginia, huh?" Bush said. "My little brother, Marvin Bush, went to the University of Virginia."

Morgan didn't exactly know what to do next. And so he just kept walking.

Patrick got in a few more words. "I hope you enjoy our singing tonight," he said to the president of the United States.

"Well," George W. said, "I'm sure I will—if I can ever get out of this line."

And then Patrick made his move.

"With the president's hand in mine," Patrick says, "I leaned in, hand on his left shoulder, and whispered into his jolly elf ear, 'Dude, seriously, I feel really bad for you right now.'"

Patrick immediately realized he'd committed an obscene (and potentially dangerous) faux pas. Worse: Of all the things he could have said to the president, he sympathized with the man about having to shake hands with donors?

And then President Bush made *his* move.

"I backed away," Patrick says, "and as I let go of his hand, he grabs mine, and my upper forearm, pulls me back in closer, looks me in the eye, and goes, 'Don't feel sorry for me. I knew exactly what I was getting into.'" The Republican National Committee took in more than fifteen million dollars in donations that night for the 2008 campaign.

In the summer of 2007, not long after Morgan Sword and the Hullabahoos met President Bush, public perception of a cappella seemed to be turning—from pop culture curiosity to mainstream pursuit. Almost.

It started with a professional a cappella group from Ithaca, New York, called the Fault Line. The five men made their national television debut on NBC's summer reality series, *America's Got Talent*. They were alums of Ithaca College, where they'd sung in an a cappella group, Sons of Pitches. Their style had matured since then—both musically and sartorially. And for their big semifinal appearance on *America's Got Talent*, they wanted to look like a band, so they dressed in tight T-shirts, tighter jeans, and studded belts. One couldn't help but notice something else one of the members was wearing.

Sitting at home in Evanston, Illinois, Freddie Feldman—a partner in acaTunes and CASA board member—was watching *America's Got Talent* when he nearly fell out of his chair. Years ago, Freddie had developed a special microphone for vocal percussionists that he called the Thumper. "It's like a dog collar with a microphone attached," Freddie says. It was designed to pick up the low tones the same way an AKG D12 mic sits in a kick drum. Freddie jerry-rigged the prototype with a tiny Shure mic, a Jansport backpack strap, and some Velcro. The thing worked like a dream. The mic has since undergone seven or eight incarnations, dropping in price from seven hundred dollars to two hundred and fifty thanks to advancements in technology, and Freddie (who never kept great records) thinks he's sold fifty or so. Apparently, one of those sales was to the vocal percussionist for the Fault Line, who was, to Freddie's shock and awe, wearing the Thumper on *America's Got Talent*.

The Thumper looked like the kind of choker a teenage girl might wear. Still, for a moment, it seemed like contemporary a cappella would finally have its day in the sun.

"Well, hello, gentlemen," Sharon Osbourne—one of the judges—said. "And what's the name of your group?"

"We are the Fault Line," the vocal percussionist said.

"What kind of group are you?"

"We're a vocal rock band," he said. "We're bringing a cappella to an edgier level."

"Do you think you're worth a million dollars?" she asked, invoking the show's big prize.

"Absolutely."

With that, the Fault Line sang thirty seconds of "Some Kind of Wonderful." The Hoff—David Hasselhoff—was one of the judges too. And when they finished, he was beside himself. He couldn't believe that what he'd just heard was a cappella. "It sounds like a track is playing," the Hoff said. "It blows my mind."

Sharon Osbourne weighed in. "Yeah," she said, "I think that you're really, really unique guys in what you do. I've never seen anybody do this before—and you do it well. I am in love with you."

Days later the Fault Line was eliminated.

One can't help but wonder: What happens to all of these collegiate a cappella singers once they graduate? Well, there is always
the world of professional a cappella groups. Blake Lewis had been
the 2007 *American Idol* runner-up, a fan favorite for incorporating his beatboxing skills into his performances. Blake previously
sang with a pro a cappella group, Kickshaw. Likewise, *Idol* finalist
Rudy Cardenas sang with a group called *m-pact*. (The two had
been at a mutual a cappella friend's wedding a few months before
the *Idol* auditions in '06, where they'd both sheepishly admitted
they were going to try out.)

But the professional a cappella circuit, it turns out, is just as
dirty and competitive as the undergraduate world. Of all the
touring contemporary a cappella groups—including Deke Sharon's the House Jacks—very few members actually make their
full-time living as musicians. In the United States, you could
count them on one hand. One of those groups is Ball in the
House—largely considered the bad boys of pro a cappella. They've
co-written and produced twenty-three lucrative Cool Whip com-
mercials. "We're on the road two hundred days a year," says
group member Aaron Loveland. At one point they were signed to
Warner Bros. Records, and hit the Billboard chart with "Something I Don't Know," an original tune. The label hoped they'd be
the next Backstreet Boys. It wasn't to be. A major marketing push
was set for, yes, September 11, 2001. "I still have the press release," Loveland says. They got some good press. A *Boston Globe*
review: "Ball in the House has everything you would expect to
find in a successful pop/rock band—the one thing it doesn't have
is instruments." But the music industry shifted.

"There's a stigma from the a cappella community," Loveland
says. He's given up on dreams of major label stardom and seems
content to be a working musician. Perhaps contemporary a cappella just isn't meant to cross over. Bruce Leddy's movie, *Sing*

Now or Forever Hold Your Peace—a cappella's answer to *The Big Chill*, featuring the Bubs' version of "Take Me Home"—finally opened in theaters on April 29, 2007. It grossed a total of $20,903.

The latest professional a cappella group to make a push at crossing over is called Mosaic. At one point, Scott Porter, the quarterback on NBC's *Friday Night Lights*, was a member of Mosaic. When he left the group for Hollywood, Mosaic took up residence in Las Vegas, where they landed a one-year deal opening up for veteran comedian George Wallace in his six-hundred-seat theater at the Flamingo. There Mosaic would thrive. At the time, Prince—yes, *that* Prince—had his own standing gig in Vegas, at the Rio. One night, Prince caught the George Wallace show, fell in love with Mosaic, and invited the boys to perform at his 2007 New Year's Eve gig.

And so, on New Year's Eve, Mosaic opened for Prince. They sang a short set, went to dinner, and never expected to hear from Prince again. "We thought, That was cool," says Mosaic's Josh Huslig. But later that night a message arrived from Prince: He wanted Mosaic to meet him at his signature nightclub, 3121, where he regularly played an intimate, late-night set. Mosaic was thrilled. Even more so when, sometime around four in the morning, Prince invited Mosaic back up onstage with him to close down the club. "Do you know any Sly and the Family Stone?" Prince whispered. Actually, they did. "How about 'Thank You'?"

Josh Huslig tells the story. "So Prince gets the guitar out and doesn't say another word," he says, reenacting what may be his career highlight. "And Prince just starts *jamming*." Six handheld microphones appear. Luckily, the band played "Thank You" in E—the same key Mosaic sings it in. There isn't much more Huslig can say. He still can't really believe it himself.

The image of that night—Mosaic and Prince—eats away at Scott Porter from *Friday Night Lights*. "That's a rock star moment," Porter says, taking a breath. "I am on this massive, amazing TV show that everyone loves, but I devoted eight years of my life to taking the next step with a cappella music, and turning something I was passionate about into a way of life. And there is a huge part of me that regrets leaving Mosaic." Uh, what? You're on *Friday Night Lights*, a show some consider to be the second coming. "I would regret it more if I was on the WB and wasn't doing groundbreaking television," Porter says. "There's no rehearsal on our set, no marks to hit. It's gorilla-style for prime-time network television. It's incredible. I'm happy where I am. At the same time, I wanted to make people go, Holy crap—a cappella. That's something *new*. I want to imitate that."

Scott Porter is right. There is some undeniable pleasure in a cappella music—something so simple about the human voice, about harmonizing with your best friends. But for every John Legend, who leaves the UPenn Counterparts and goes on to win Grammy awards, there are thousands of a cappella alums who will never sing again.

Andrew Renshaw was there at Big Spring Sing Thing XIX in April of 2007. Renshaw, a legendary member of the Hullabahoos, may just be the best soloist in the group's near twenty-year history. He went to the Philippines with Ron Puno and the Hullabahoos a few years back, when they sold out the Hard Rock and became minor celebrities. After school, Renshaw tried to make it as a musician, touring the country with his guitar, playing to small crowds in smaller bars. At one point he even considered going back to the Far East to capitalize on the Hullabahoos' name. In collegiate a cappella, Andrew Renshaw is the kind of guy one worries about.

He was hard to miss at Big Spring Sing Thing XIX—what with the crutches and all. Earlier that day, hours before the concert, he and some of the alums played a game of pickup basketball.

Renshaw, now in his thirties, twisted his knee and wound up in the hospital. It was a poignant moment. Renshaw sang at the show's after-party. Howard Spector listened, hanging on every word of "Wonderful Tonight"—Renshaw's big solo from years ago—backed by the Hullabahoos. "It's a crime that you're not still singing!" Howard said.

The Bubs refer to their alums as Dead Guys, and it's not so far off. Graduation is the death of one's a cappella career. For guys like Morgan Sword—talented in a karaoke sense—it's tough enough to move on. But for guys like Renshaw—the truly talented musicians—graduation can be a heartbreaking sucker punch. It's like being torn out of the womb. One day you are in the Philippines with your best friends, being interviewed live on television about your music. The next day you are playing open mic nights to half-empty coffeehouses. Or worse, sitting in a cubicle. Seeing Renshaw on crutches that night—it was like seeing a fallen Superman. Renshaw's not the only one. John DeTriquet, a former Hullabahoo, was at the show too. He's living in Nashville, hosting karaoke nights at the Wildhorse Saloon (under his stage name, John Deech), hoping to make it big on the country music circuit with his band, Mack Cadillac. A few months before the Big Spring Sing Thing XIX, Renshaw finally hung up his guitar and enrolled in grad school. "Music just became about business," he says. "It wasn't fun anymore."

The thing about college a cappella is that it exists in this incredible space: college. It's the one time in life where everything is momentum. With a cappella—a great tradition on these campuses—one can both step out and blend in entirely. For the same reason one joins a fraternity, or an athletic team, one joins an a cappella group. The problem arises when you take a cappella out of the context of college—then what is it, really? A cover band. With no instruments.

Which is why some a cappella fans believe that, for the sake of legitimacy, groups like the Bubs need to write their own material. But even Alexander Koutzoukis of the Bubs admits, for all their musicality, "our fans don't want to hear original tunes." James Van Der Beek remembers his college days with Drew University's 36 Madison Avenue. "I had some friends who played in actual bands," he says. "And ten people would show up to their gigs. Meanwhile, we were singing for hundreds of fans." There's a reason. When you've got the entire canon of popular music to choose from, what's the chance some kid is going to write something better? And then arrange it for fifteen voices?

But what if it didn't have to end? In the summer of 2007, Deke Sharon started a new program with CASA. He called it the Contemporary A Cappella League. "There are approximately five thousand experienced college a cappella singers graduating each year, and most of these folks have little or no opportunity to continue singing in a similar ensemble," the Web site reads. "CASA intends to change that through the formation of this league....This is not your grandmother's community chorus. For lack of a better term, imagine a postcollegiate group modeled after and comprised of members from the best college groups." Deke was bullish on the league's success. Twenty-three collegiate a cappella alums across the country signed up to organize groups. But there was something sad about it maybe: It was sort of like Will Ferrell starting a fraternity for adults in *Old School*.

And what memories they are. Over the summer of 2007— like countless coeds before him—Joe Cassara, having just graduated from the University of Virginia, went to Europe to celebrate. He was at a hostel in Nice, France, when a girl looked at him funny. She'd just graduated from Virginia Tech. "Um, are you in the Hullabahoos?" she said. "I just downloaded 'Wonderful Tonight.'"

APPENDIX

A note to readers:

Pitch Perfect is, in many ways, a love letter to collegiate a cappella. The idea was born from my very fond memories of singing with Cayuga's Waiters, Cornell's oldest all-male a cappella group. In fact, I am still making memories.

Every year, on the first Friday in April, I drive up to Ithaca, New York, where a handful of my old college buddies meet in the basement of Ruloff's—a local bar named after a mass murderer. This was our regular drinking spot. And for years, members of our group would carve their nicknames into a table in the corner. Now we run our hands along that same table looking for our mark, reminded of stories about guys we called Meatball, Pork Chop, and Skippy. We cannot stay away.

The occasion is Spring Fever. And this is how it goes.

We alumni leave Ruloff's drunk and happy, making our way up to Bailey Hall, an imposing 2,000-seat arena on the Cornell University campus, where a pair of blinding-white searchlights crisscross in the air like this is all some misplaced Hollywood premiere. Inside, the rows closest to the stage have been roped off for us and we take our seats, shamelessly drinking Olde English amidst freshman girls and their moms. When the lights go down, one of us will inevitably call out *Bay-gooooooo*. And the rest will echo, in perfect harmony and for reasons I can't explain, *Baygo de la nocheeeeeee*. On a campus with no discernible school spirit, Cornell's Bailey Hall will sell out—all because sixteen men, most with marginal talent, decided to put on a concert. It's been this way for nearly sixty years. Just ask the old timers, the original members of our esteemed group, who still make it back every now and again to check in.

Why do they come back? Why do I come back? For many reasons. But mostly for the last five minutes of the concert, when the undergrads invite us alums up on stage to sing with them. Because for those five minutes we feel like heroes again.

When I am standing on that stage, for that brief moment, I let myself wonder what it would have been like if I'd become a big time musician, if we'd somehow gone pro. Well, in late 2008, an a cappella group from Indiana University got that very chance.

That story, which I reported for *The New York Times*, is reprinted here.

A CAPPELLA DREAMING:
10 VOICES, ONE SHOT

Ten years ago, the founding members of Straight No Chaser— an undergraduate a cappella group from Indiana University— performed at Carnegie Hall. They sang the national anthem at a Chicago Cubs game. They took road trips, ensnared female fans and created a lasting tradition on campus. And then they graduated.

Save for the odd wedding or college reunion, these men had not sung together with any regularity since. Until 2008, when Craig Kallman, the chairman and chief executive of Atlantic Records, offered the ten-man group a five-album record deal.

This may be the year's most unlikely major label story.

David Roberts, thirty-one, a project manager for a Midtown bank, was sitting in his cubicle in January when he got the call. Michael Itkoff, also thirty-one, a sales rep for a medical device company, was at home in Atlanta. Jerome Collins, thirty-two, was in Hong Kong starring as Simba in a theme park production of *The Lion King*.

"We thought it was a joke," Mr. Itkoff said. "But Atlantic flew us to New York and put us up at the Dream Hotel. There was a fruit plate in my hotel room. They were talking about a tour with Josh Groban or Michael Bublé. I thought, 'Are you kidding me?' "

Mr. Kallman—like nearly eight million others—discovered Straight No Chaser on YouTube in December, through a 1998 video of the group performing an unlikely riff on "The Twelve Days of Christmas" (a riff that incorporated snippets of everything from "I Have a Little Dreidel" to Toto's "Africa"). Randy Stine, an original member, had uploaded the clip strictly for the group's own amusement, but it quickly went viral.

"We thought the attention would die down after the New Year," said the group's founder, Dan Ponce, thrity-one, now a reporter for ABC News in Chicago.

But Mr. Kallman smelled a potential holiday crossover hit in the vein of the Trans-Siberian Orchestra, a metal band famous for playing Christmas music in large, sold-out arenas. That band has sold more than five million albums, and last year it played a ninety-city tour that grossed more than $45 million.

"We're at a time when we're entertained by air-guitar video games and reality competitions about hairstyling, dressmaking, and grocery bagging," Mr. Kallman said in a telephone interview. "Straight No Chaser was this organic YouTube sensation. The idea is to develop an act with real resonance for the holiday season and build a brand in the a cappella arena."

Major labels have flirted with a cappella groups before. R&B acts like the Persuasions had been signed to the majors in the 1970s before moving to smaller labels in recent years. In 2005, Tonic Sol-fa, an a cappella quartet out of Minneapolis, was briefly signed to Vivaton Records (a division of Sony), but the label folded a week before the group's album hit shelves. At the height of the 1990s boy-band boom, an a cappella group called 4:2:Five (featuring a young Scott Porter of NBC's *Friday Night Lights*) met with Sony, but when the executives suggested adding backing tracks and choreography, the members walked.

That kind of tinkering is perhaps understandable. While there are more than 1,200 collegiate a cappella groups in the United States, according to estimates from the Contemporary A Cappella Society of America, mainstream attitudes toward the genre are not kind. A cappella is regularly mocked on screen, notably on the NBC comedy *The Office* and recently in the Will Ferrell film *Step Brothers*. Still, Mr. Kallman was not deterred. He did not want to hide that these men were an a cappella group. Rather, he hoped to embrace it.

"Group harmony is in the air," he said. "*Jersey Boys* is a worldwide phenomenon. The *Mamma Mia!* sound track is number one." With Straight No Chaser, Atlantic is aiming for the mass audience that made Mr. Groban's *Noël* the top-selling album of 2007.

Perhaps the idea of a major-label a cappella Christmas hit isn't so far-fetched. "Once in a while a fresh Christmas album breaks through and has a chance of becoming a perennial seller," said Jay Landers, senior vice president of A&R at Columbia Records, an Atlantic competitor. "Josh Groban and Mannheim Steamroller will continue to sell for years. A cappella might be considered a niche signing, but if the repertoire is fresh and accessible, then it could work."

And so a Straight No Chaser album, *Holiday Spirits*, is due out October 28 on Atlantic's Atco imprint. The album is a collection of twelve Christmas classics (and two original holiday tunes), including a live version of "The Twelve Days of Christmas." (Richard Gregory, seventy-six, now a retired music teacher in Massachusetts, wrote the original comic arrangement of the traditional carol while serving in the Navy in the 1950s. It became a staple of the Princeton Nassoons, and Straight No Chaser added its own funny flavor.)

There may even be a reality show on the horizon. Mark Burnett of the *Survivor* franchise, Jesse Ignjatovic, the executive producer of this year's MTV Video Music Awards, and Atlantic are shopping a competition show featuring Straight No Chaser that is tentatively titled *A Cappella Nation*.

"Look at what's working in the reality space—family-friendly entertainment," Mr. Burnett said. "There's no way this is not a big hit. It's great music. It's fun for the whole family."

The Straight No Chaser "Twelve Days of Christmas" video had a certain kitsch appeal, what with ten men harmonizing to "I Have a Little Dreidel." But the eight million people who clicked on it were also likely responding to the genuine, unironic enjoyment plastered across the members' faces; the video begged to be forwarded.

But the trick was capturing that energy on disc. Straight No Chaser—the name was inspired by the Thelonious Monk composition—began album rehearsals in March, and the first day was surreal. "It was like we were right back in the senior year of college and we were going over music for a show at a sorority house," Mr. Itkoff said. "It was like no time had passed."

Except time had passed—nearly a decade. Mr. Itkoff, the medical device salesman, was married now and had to convince his wife that frequent trips to New York (and whatever might come next) would not upend their life in Atlanta. They'd recently had a baby, and his wife had stopped working. "Her biggest worry was that I'd leave her for months at a time, with no income and a child."

For a similar reason, one original member, Patrick Hachey—a high school music teacher in New Jersey with three kids and a wife—declined to join the reunion. (Another original member, who had fallen out with others in the group, was not asked to join, and the slots were filled with two younger alumni. The group has had several lineups at Indiana University.)

Most of the album was recorded over two weeks in July in Bloomington, Indiana. Steve Lunt of Atlantic, an industry A&R veteran who has worked with Britney Spears and 'N Sync, was brought on to produce.

Though they were recording for a major label, the budget was conservative. Not counting travel and other expenses, they spent roughly $20,000 on recording.

Mr. Lunt flew to Bloomington twice to put his stamp on the project. "Collegiate a cappella is intentionally goofy and tongue-in-cheek and ironic," he said. "But there's a thin line between goofy and stupid, and goofy and funny."

The members of Straight No Chaser understand Mr. Lunt's concern, and they are in on the joke—to a point. "It's great to see a cappella lampooned on shows like 30 Rock," Mr. Stine said. "We laugh at a cappella along with everyone else. Clearly it doesn't have the coolest reputation. Maybe we can change that."

Still, Mr. Lunt refers to the finished project as "Beach Boyz II Men," a comment that highlights the inherent marketing challenge. "This is a ten-piece, slightly overgrown college vocal band," he said. "We're trying to catch lightning in a bottle. We're swimming upstream. There are a lot of mixed metaphors here. But the genuine enthusiasm you feel from these guys is infectious."

Despite the excitement of a major-label deal, most of the group members have kept quiet about it until now. "We had to protect our jobs," Mr. Itkoff said. "We're not nineteen anymore. But it was like leading a double life."

With the album's release approaching, it is hard for the members not to daydream. To that end, Mr. Stine recently quit his day job, in part because he couldn't get two weeks off to record the album but also because he hopes the project will have legs. Mr. Roberts, the Manhattan finance guy, is more conservative. "The economics in the group are tough," he said. "There are ten mouths to feed here, and any money will be split ten ways."

Mr. Kallman of Atlantic described the project as "low risk." He signed Straight No Chaser to what is called a 360-degree deal, meaning Atlantic will share in potential revenue from merchandise, concert tours, even ring tones. The group was given a very small advance (basically just enough money to cover recording costs), and it will take a "standard cut of net sales," according to Mr. Ponce. "We're happy with the deal."

There's a distinct possibility, all involved agree, that this excitement could disappear as suddenly as it arrived. "We're talking about a cappella," Mr. Roberts said. "Let's be honest."

But if the scene in Bloomington is any indication, perhaps there is hope for an a cappella Christmas hit. On one of the last nights of recording, the boys were out celebrating, playing a drinking game called Sink the Bismarck at an old haunt. There was a bachelorette party a few tables over. A member of Straight No Chaser was making small talk when one of the women—an Indiana University alumnus—interrupted him.

"Are you the original members of Straight No Chaser?" she asked. And then she screamed.

When it came time to promote *Pitch Perfect: The Quest for Collegiate A Cappella Glory*, some friends suggested I start a blog, which I did. (See the unfortunately named PitchPerfect-TheBook

.blogspot.com). While updating the thing was sometimes a burden, it was also damn good fun, allowing me to share a funny story that didn't make it into the book, or celebrate a pop culture moment in real time. (Thank you to Ed Helms and *The Office* for your continued mocking of a cappella!)

A few of your favorite blog entries are reprinted below, including a Q&A inspired by the *Times* piece above. As they said on *Carmen Sandiego*, Do it, a cappella!

Who Is Dick Gregory?
(posted on October 4, 2008)

Ten years after graduation, the men of Indiana University's Straight No Chaser suddenly scored a major label record deal when one of their videos became a surprise hit on—where else?—YouTube. The song was a comedic take on "The Twelve Days of Christmas" (incorporating Toto's "Africa"!) and it was viewed nearly eight million times. Atlantic Records is talking about sending these boys (or rather, these men) out on the road with the likes of Josh Groban.

But what about this arrangement of "The Twelve Days of Christmas"? Where did it come from? As I reported in the *Times*, though the arrangement has evolved over the years, it began as the handiwork of one Richard Gregory, now seventy-six, an alum of the Yale Whiffenpoofs and a retired music educator from the Williston Northampton School. I tracked down Mr. Gregory to get the story behind the music. He speaks:

What inspired you to write this arrangement of "The Twelve Days of Christmas"?
I was in the Navy in the 1950s, stationed on the Island of Guam. I had a singing group of Naval officers, and we needed something

fun for Christmas. I was diddling around one night writing music. These Christmas songs—a lot of these songs have the same chord structure. They're easy to play together in counterpoint, and I'm fascinated by counterpoint. I wrote a primitive version of the arrangement. It wasn't as long and it wasn't as good. I came to the Williston Northampton School in the sixties and began an a cappella group of students, the Caterwaulers. I polished up the arrangement and taught it to the boys. We sang it and people liked it.

Why the Caterwaulers?
Caterwaul is what cats do on the back of the fence when there is a female cat in heat. That's the name we adopted.

Nice.
One of the Caterwaulers—the person who was the so-called music leader, the one who blew the pitch pipe—went to Princeton and joined the Nassoons. And he took that song with him. And the Nassoons have been calling it their arrangement ever since. They put it on a phonograph as their arrangement. It was strange for them to learn that I had written it.

How did they come to find out that you'd written the arrangement?
One of the graduates of the Nassoons was auditioning at Williston Northampton for a teaching job. Someone at the school knew I'd written that song and made a point of us meeting. I said to him, *Do you know who wrote the arrangement? I did.* That's how they got the news. By that time, the song had been given from hand-to-hand to groups around the country.

I heard from one of the Nassoons. He tells me they credited you on their 1976 recording of "Twelve Days..." He points out that your name wasn't taken off, really. Rather, the song was subsequently taught by ear. That's where the disassociation happened. Anyway, now the song's going to be on a major label.
So it's not dead yet....

When did you get a sense that "The Twelve Days of Christmas" was such a phenomenon?
It was after Christmas last year. I hadn't heard of YouTube. I don't have a computer. In fact, today I'm writing a letter on a manual typewriter. But my friends began to talk about it. And some people would call me—including a father whose son sings in the Indiana University a cappella group. He tracked me down.

Where did you see the video?
I went to a friend's house. And it was good fun listening to it. Then that other song came on.

Yes, that's Toto's "Africa."
It's a good song, but one I've never heard of. The Indiana group cut off the last—and best!—third of my arrangement and stuck on this other thing. They lost "I'll Be Home for Christmas" and "Chestnuts Roasting."

Is there money to be made here?
I've been glad to have anyone sing it who wants to. The University of Michigan glee club put it on a CD. It's beautifully sung. The choir director called and asked me and I said it was fine. But really, no one cares very much about rights and so on. A publisher called me after the YouTube success and showed some

interest in selling the arrangement, but I think they realized that they won't make much money off of it. Everyone who wants the arrangement already has it.

As an undergrad at Yale, you sang with the Whiffenpoofs. What do you remember about those days?
I graduated from Yale in 1954. But I was pitch pipe of the '56 Whiffenpoofs as a graduate student. We went around the country. I sang solo on the stage of the San Francisco Opera House. It was a song called "Slow Motion." It's in the Yale Songbook, I think. It was something I wouldn't have the nerve to do now, but being young and fearless I did it and I got through it. As part of the glee club, we sang with the Boston Symphony at Tanglewood. Back then, the Whiffs traveled with the glee club. The Whiffs of '56 still sing together—all twelve of us.

Really? Where?
Different parts of the country—California, Wisconsin. Only four of us are on the East Coast. And yet we all get together, along with our wives. We still sing pretty well for guys in our seventies. But by now the fun is more important than the singing.

Did the Whiffs perform at Williston while you were teaching?
Yes. It was an ego trip. They'd call upon me to join them for the "Whiffenpoof Song." It was good for two or three days. Then everyone would forget about it.

How has a cappella changed?
During the seventies, it was not cool that kind of music. And now there has been a big revival of it. Things have changed.

Did you ever think you'd be talking about "The Twelve Days of Christmas" fifty years after leaving Guam?

I'm grateful for some notoriety. But I would have preferred other works of mine to become notorious. I've written three operas and a lot of choral music and chamber music—which is not fashionable.

Ben Folds: High Five!
(posted on June 9, 2008)

Collegiate a cappella groups cover Ben Folds's music about as often as they do John Mayer's tunes. Which is to say, early and often! Guess what? Indie rock God Ben Folds has noticed. And he's pleased! Here, in an interview with the *Pitch Perfect* blog, he addresses the a cappella-ification of his catalog.

When did you become aware that so many collegiate groups were covering your music?

Years ago on the road, people would hand us CDs with a cappella versions. But I didn't know that the culture existed or that it had ballooned—until I saw loads and loads of a cappella groups on YouTube. That was about a year ago. My bassist sent me the first link, I think.

Were you flattered? Confused?

First of all I was impressed. And then I was moved. Some are better than others. But some of the interpretations are just so—I don't know—just so genuine. We're so inundated with music made by certified platinum-selling rock stars, which is fine, that's cool, too. But there's really something to be said for smart music. Some of the a cappella interpretations of my songs—on a lot of levels, they're better than the way I did them. They're better than the originals.

Really?
I think so. They couldn't come first. Or maybe they could. I don't know. But it highlights something pure about the songs. These groups have to be inventive. They have to figure out a way to arrange these songs and these harmonies. In an age where music education is just going to down the shitter, on college campuses maybe you expect karaoke or a wet-shirt contest night. You don't expect kids to get together, break down the arrangements, rearrange, reinterpret, and then practice.

Or record them in professional studios. The Beelzebubs recorded *Code Red* at Long View Farms—where the Rolling Stones rehearsed for the *Tattoo You* tour.
As music is eroding popular music, the record industry is in depression, and what's being spoon-fed isn't necessarily working. It's interesting that people have to make music. They don't just accept that music is dead. They make it themselves.

Why do you think your music works so well a cappella? College groups also do a lot of Guster, too. Any comparisons?
I think the music is built well. My music has worked really well with symphony orchestras. Guster's and my music are pretty dorky. It's also put together. It's got some integrity. It seems to work a cappella. It might be hard to put a lot of bands to that. Sufjan Stevens's music would work well.

Is there one a cappella version you remember that really moved you?
There were a few versions of "Brick." And one of "Still Fighting." And then there was this one—and it's not up anymore—of a little high school kid singing the song "Gone." This little redhead kid with braces on. And he was singing the shit out of it.

The Baudboys of Pro A Cappella
(posted on May 6, 2008)

The other day, I blogged about an a cappella group made up of Microsoft employees. They call themselves the Baudboys, and for a bunch of self-described geeks, they talk a lot of smack! Herein, a *Pitch Perfect* exclusive interview with Baudboy bass Dave McEwen.

So, what do you do at Microsoft?
I'm a marketing guy. I work for the Developer & Platform Evangelism group.

Uh, what's that?
The group that thinks far out into the future and tries to secure the future of the platforms. So, when Vista came out, there were programs ready to run on Vista. That's Evangelism.

When did you start singing?
I grew up in Alaska in the middle of nowhere. The first time I heard something that moved me was Glad, and their album the *A Cappella Project*. Then I found Take 6. I've been an a cappella freak since then. I was a teenager. And once I found Take 6 I thought, I've got to do this. For a guy with pedestrian music talent like myself, I couldn't lead a group. I was a tuba player at the

time. I'm a band geek. You see all these glee clubs on TV. I couldn't wait to go to college to join one. And then I went to a college without an a cappella scene, Northwest Nazarene College in Nampa, Idaho. So I created a couple. One was called Noise. None of them lasted longer than one performance. We had fun. I figured that was the end. Until I came to Microsoft in 2000. There were a bunch of guys from Yale and Princeton still singing. I thought, I've got another chance. Take two! I said, I don't care if you let me in or not, but I'm going to be a Baudboy.

What were the auditions like?
Grueling. But not as bad as some of the auditions could have been. One of our members was the former pitch of the Whiffenpoofs. We have a guy who was with the Harvard Krokodiloes. Another guy was the Princeton Nassoons's director. They know what hardcore auditions are like. These guys could reduce you to nothing if they chose to. But the talent out here in Redmond is harder to come by than at Yale.

What do you remember about your Baudboys audition?
I think I had two rounds of call backs. There were maybe eight people trying out for bass that year. It went from eight to four to two. I'll be honest: When it got down to two, I realized the other guy had more talent. So I focused on making them laugh by quoting *The Matrix*.

Nice.
We're all Microsoft employees. We're geeks first and singers second.

How often are auditions held?
We only bring people into the group when someone cashes out their stock options and leaves Microsoft. That's when we put the word out to the other singing groups.

Wait. There are other a cappella groups at Microsoft?
Yes. The Microtones have been around since the late eighties, at least. I don't want to speak ill of them, but they used to be the primary group at Microsoft. I don't want to toot my own horn but I am in marketing. When people at Microsoft think of music, they think of the theater troupe and the Baudboys.

There's a theater troupe, too?
The Microsoft Theater Troupe. They do a Christmas show. They did *Grease.*

Please tell me there are on-campus rivalries. . . .
Not really. We have a rule: If you're in the Baudboys, you can't be in the Microtones. We encourage a cappella here. But in return, when we have an opening we occasionally take their best singers.

Where does the name Baudboys come from?
All of the original members are gone, and nobody kept records back then. But it was something like this. Around the fall of 1990, four guys from the Microtones (who wanted to sing their old collegiate barbershop music) split off. They'd sing as part of the Microtones concerts. Someone yelled, What's your name? In true geek fashion, they hadn't thought that far ahead. Someone said, let's call them the Bad Boys—because they left the Microtones. Then someone said, what about the Baudboys. Baud is the speed rating of an old-style modem. We've talked about changing the name, but we have just enough brand recognition now.

So you have a sense of humor about yourselves.
We mock ourselves. We're geeks. We know it. We'd rather get a laugh than a tear.

The Baudboys won the Northwest region of the Harmony Sweepstakes this year. Why compete?
Up until 2003, we were a bunch of guys singing in conference rooms for fun. We'd hold on-campus concerts once a year. If there was an open mic, we'd polish up "Coney Island Baby" and that was pretty much it. Then we heard about the Harmony Sweepstakes and we thought, how hard could it be? So we went. And we got our asses kicked. We saw what people could do. We had our eyes opened. In true Microsoft fashion we said, we're going to remake ourselves. We're going to add vocal percussion. We're going to drop the four-part harmony and become a pop group. And we'll determine our success by how we do at the Sweepstakes. That's what we call Cyclical Iteration for Improvement. It's a planning phase. We modify, build, and then we perform at sweeps.

How did you do at the finals this year?
A group from Germany won. Vocaldente. They were insane. I don't have bitter feelings. The right team won. We practice one day a week. In a conference room. From five to six on Tuesdays. And we're going up against groups that practice eight hours every day. It was all pro groups—and then one group of geeks with day jobs. We're not gonna harmonize these guys to death. Our whole thing was, let's go after audience favorite vote. We came close. I will say, we had the longest standing ovation of the night.

What was the set list?
We sang Red Hot Chili Pepper's "Aeroplane." We sang "Gonna Make You Happy Tonight," a comedy song from an Australian a

cappella group, Tripod. It's about a guy telling his wife he's going to make her happy, and do all the things she wants him to do—just as soon as he's done with the video game he's playing. The crowd got it. The applause was deafening.

Hilarious. Are the Baudboys celebrities on the Microsoft campus?
Good heavens, no. Though I have been recognized as a Baudboy before. In the cafeteria, someone said, "Dude, you're a Baudboy!" I got up to do a presentation on Application Lifestyle Management. There were 100 people in the room. Someone said, "Go, Baudboys!" from the back.

Any paying gigs?
There are now! Because people know who we are. The word is out.

What's the word?
Microsoft has this geeky singing group. And they're good now.

Do you perform on campus?
We've always been big on campus. We'll sing in Building 16 at lunchtime. It's an office building with this real nice atrium. We routinely have crowds of 200 or 300 people. And if you're walking by, it's hard to ignore us. If there's a group holiday party, we'll show up at that.

Any chance there's an a cappella group at Google? Yahoo!?
We sang the national anthem for the Microsoft Hockey Challenge—where they play the teams from Sun Microsystems or Google. Someone from Sun said, "We have an a cappella group that would kick your ass!" But then they disbanded. Groups come and go at Google. We think they're running from us

[laughing]. I'd love for someone from Google to hear that and challenge us.

When is the Baudboys album dropping?
We hope to have one for the fall. That's our goal. Making a CD costs money. We've been a non-profit group. We'd rather sing at a nursing home and spread the love. But I want to get us more paying gigs. It's not greed. We just want to give fans a CD. We have a demo CD. We recorded it in a small studio down in Renton. I'm a Seahawks fan. I've missed one game in the last decade. That was the day we were recording our demo. We could self-record, but we want to do it right.

Who decided on the group's jeans-and-blazers look?
Funny story. We kept getting asked for pictures. Being a PR guy myself, I said, we gotta spend some money here. So we went to Sears.

Like, the Sears Portrait Studio? At the mall?
Yeah. I gave Sears eighty bucks and said, take as many photos as you can. We didn't have matching clothes. So we ran down to the clothing depart and grabbed jackets off the rack. The guy in the back, with his hands in the air? You can see the tags on his jacket. After the photos, we went and put the jackets back on the racks. That photo has been in the *San Francisco Chronicle*, the *Seattle Post-Intelligencer*, some London paper. . . . That was the best eighty bucks we ever spent.

ACKNOWLEDGMENTS

Thank you to Brett Valley, Patrick Mulligan, Rachel Ekstrom, Farley Chase, Howard Sanders, Jim Nelson, Fred Woodward, Michael Hainey, Jason Gay, Mark Kirby, the staff of *GQ*, Joshua Jacobson, Ben Berentson, Andrea Oliveri, Alanna Zahn, Robert Alarcon, Deke Sharon, Bill Hare, Tim Vaill, Keith Bachmann, James Gammon, Danny Lichtenfeld, Joseph Campagna, and Cayuga's Waiters. A special thanks to my parents, Jane and Lenny Rapkin, Jon Rapkin and Erin Rapkin, and Julio Gambuto.

I'd like to thank the Beelzebubs, the Hullabahoos, and Divisi—both the current members and their alumni—for sharing their stories with me.

THE 2006-2007 UNIVERSITY OF VIRGINIA HULLABAHOOS

Dane Blackburn
Christopher Brown
Joseph Cassara
Brian Duhon
Myles Glancy

Bobby Grasberger
Patrick Lundquist
Brendon Mason
Kyle Mihalcoe
Matt Mooney
Chad Moses
Blake Segal
Pete Seibert
Morgan Sword
Brian Tucker
Alan Webb
Joe Whitney

THE 2006-2007 UNIVERSITY OF OREGON DIVISI

Emmalee Almroth
Meghan Bell
Michaela Cordova
Sarah Klein
Andrea Lucia
CharliRae McConnell
Keeley McCowan
Marissa Neitling
Megan Schimmer
Haley Steinberger
Jenna Tooley
Andrea Welsh
Rachelle Wofford
Betsy Yates

THE 2006-2007 TUFTS BEELZEBUBS

Paul Alvarez
Benjamin Appel
Tim Conrad
Adrian Dahlin
Arkady Ho
Ben Kelsey
Alexander Koutzoukis
Matt Kraft
Nick Lamm
Matt McCormick
Matt Michelson
Andrew Savini
Doug Terry
Matt Thomas
Chris Van Lenten
Lucas Walker